AMERICAN
POLITICS
REAPPRAISED

AMERICAN POLITICS REAPPRAISED

THE ENCHANTMENT OF CAMELOT DISPELLED

Charles R. Adrian
*University of California
Riverside*

Charles Press
Michigan State University

McGraw-Hill Book Company
*New York   St. Louis   San Francisco   Düsseldorf
Johannesburg   Kuala Lumpur   London   Mexico
Montreal   New Delhi   Panama   Rio de Janeiro
Singapore   Sydney   Toronto*

AMERICAN POLITICS REAPPRAISED
The Enchantment of Camelot Dispelled

1234567890BPBP79876543

This book was set in Times Roman by Black Dot, Inc. The editors were Stephen D. Dragin, Ronald Kissack, and John M. Morriss; the designer was Joseph Gillians; the cover illustration was done by Newton Meyers; and the production supervisor was Thomas J. LoPinto.
The printer and binder was The Book Press, Inc.

Part Opening: Music and lyrics from *Camelot* copyright © 1960 by Alan Jay Lerner and Frederick Loewe. Used by permission of Chappell & Co., Inc.

Library of Congress Cataloging in Publication Data

Adrian, Charles R
  American politics reappraised.

  Published in 1965 and 1969 under title: The American political process.
  1. United States—Politics and government.
I. Press, Charles, joint author. II. Title.
JK274.A5295   320.9'73   73-11205
ISBN 0-07-000441-2

CONTENTS

PREFACE

Sacred cows should be poked, kicked, or painted purple—anything but treated with reverence or deference. We had this thought in mind in writing this book and we hope that the reader as citizen, and as a student of democracy, keeps it in mind now and then. An important difference between an educated and an uneducated person is that the former has some glimmering of what he does not know, the latter often has great difficulty distinguishing between his knowledge and his ignorance. We hope to add just a bit to the stature of the reader by helping him to better understand what is known and what is not known about American democracy and its public policies. This book therefore raises more questions than it answers, because most public policy is adopted in ignorance of its probable results and is not importantly shaped by empirical data.

The problem we face initially is that of defining sacred cows. Most readers probably think we are talking about the Catholic Church, the National Guard, the seniority system in Congress, or the Reverend Norman Vincent Peale. Sometimes we are. But these are really only semisacred cows. They, in fact, get laced into by someone almost every week. The true sacred cows are those honored by the mass media—the kind of people and organizations no one dares challenge lest Tom Wicker and the entire *New York Times* editorial staff frown and drum the challengers out of the nation's cultured elite. We take our chances and refuse to treat as taboo such free spirits as Garry Trudeau, Henry David Thoreau, Ralph Nader, the Sierra Club, Consumers Union, or even William F. Buckley, Jr.

We will ask the reader to take a frank look at the real political world, not a romantic look at a make-believe world. After the decade of the 1960s, during which many students of American politics darted about on the fringes of quixotism, it is not easy (almost not fair!) for us to ask the reader to take a close look at what is actually crawling around in the political woodwork, but that is what we have attempted to do. As a result, in this volume we emphasize that governmental decisions are based far more on assumptions than on data; that TANSTAAFL* or "opportunity costs" are always involved—that is, that you must always give up something in order to gain something you want even more; that public policies affect not only those who are intended to be affected, but others as well and often in unpredictable ways; that the good intentions of decision makers do not necessarily equal good results; that something is not necessarily true simply because we wish it to be true; and that the time is long since past when the sacred cows of the New Deal era of the 1930s should have been put out to pasture.

In a dull world, including that antiseptic one dreamed of by anarchists, everything would be done without cost to one's self or anyone else. That is not the way God or nature put this one together. Yet the politically naive often believe that such a world is possible. Some (fortunately only some) upper-middle-class young people think that we could "end poverty" without damaging their parents' take-home pay—or their own generous spending-money allowances. Some civil libertarians believe that justice is served if only the rights of the defendant are protected, that the rights of society will take care of themselves—and they often seem totally unconcerned with the rights of the innocent bystander (e.g., the bank teller who is callously gunned down by a bandit). In other words they refuse to see that while the defendant's rights are a necessity in a society seeking justice, they are not free—they come at the cost of the rights of other individuals within society, such as the innocent bystander.

We ask the reader to recognize that ours is a dangerous and risky world, that neither he, nor the authors, nor anyone else knows much about what the future will bring or which set of

---

*TANSTAAFL: "There Ain't No Such Thing as a Free Lunch"; the first law of economics and politics, one which apparently only a few anthropologists, sociologists, or newspaper columnists have as yet discovered. Some would-be rebuilders of the world claim that when they come to power, this law will be instantly repealed. If they do reach power, they will find, however, that doing so is right in there with repeal of the law of gravitation as among formidable-projects-not-likely-to-succeed.

policies would best prepare us for future developments. The future is, indeed, seen only through a glass darkly, or as the New English Bible puts it, "Now we see only puzzling reflections in a mirror. . . ." (Doubting Thomasses might look for verification to a little game that a national news magazine's editors play. In a December issue at the end of each decade, they carry one or more stories on what the next decade "will be like." If so much of what later actually happens were not tragic, these predictions would make for very good comic reading ten or more years later. Fortunately, some of their most alarming predictions are also as far from the mark as are some of their movie reviews.)

Most of all, we have attempted to gear this book to the purpose of developing critical thinking in the reader, along with a healthy skepticism concerning "conventional wisdom"—those beliefs that are popularly thought to be true irrespective of what the evidence indicates or even whether any meaningful evidence exists at all. And we advocate questioning conventional wisdom whether it be that of the political left, center, or right.

This book is normatively oriented—it expresses a point of view—but it is not the purpose of the authors to indoctrinate readers with any particular political position. Rather, we hope to increase the reader's capacity to analyze American politics. In seeking to do so, we have often enthusiastically (no doubt in the view of some, outrageously) attacked many assumptions that have been uncritically worshiped as truths by many politically active persons. Instead of genuflecting whenever conventional wisdom is mentioned, we have occasionally made rude noises.

Some readers may consider our approach cynical or flippant, but we do not. We believe it can effectively be combined with an agnostic, religious, stoic, or existentialist view of life. Indeed, some may even astonish us by combining it with utopianism. We do not expect to escape having readers carve us up with the scalpel we have encouraged them to use in analyzing others. We anticipate that a few readers may find us less than nearly perfect! (We have even entertained such doubts about each other.) But we suggest in real seriousness that it is dangerous to take politics or any other important aspect of life too seriously. We suspect that the overly serious political activist is often irresponsibly frivolous, acting out his own psychic needs at the expense of society. And as Lincoln is said to have asked when criticized for telling jokes while the nation bled: "How else can I retain my sanity?"

The ideas of many persons have been incorporated into our synthesis of the contemporary American polity. We have tried to credit by appropriate references those whose writings have most impressed us. But our referencing is deliberately light in order to make for more readability and we have no doubt slighted many who are deserving of mention. For a fuller listing of those who have influenced our thinking over the years, see the footnotes and bibliography in our *American Political Process*, second edition, published by McGraw-Hill in 1969. That book is, incidentally, also an appropriate source for descriptions of ideas, institutions, and processes that are necessarily given brief treatment here. The person needing more background information should read it.

A selective glossary appears in the back of the book. It should prove useful to those readers who seek a clearer understanding of various terms used in the course of our discussion.

Although we assume full responsibility for the contents of this volume, we wish to express our thanks to many persons, both known and unknown to us, from whose criticisms we have profited. In particular, we wish to thank Professors Paul C. Bartholomew of the University of Notre Dame, Jose M. Angueira of Miami-Dade Junior College, and Edwin Strong of the University of Tulsa for their constructive suggestions.

Finally, if we were to have followed the quaint Victorian custom of offering a dedication for this book, we might well have used the thoughtful words that introduced the popular radio soap opera of a generation ago, "One Man's Family": "Dedicated to the mothers and fathers of the younger generation and to their bewildering offspring." Or in order to emphasize a point we implicitly attempt to make many times over, we might have dedicated it to the Frenchman who first said (in French, of course): "The more things change, the more they stay the same." And so, read on. Cheers!

Charles R. Adrian
Charles Press

1

INTRODUCTION:
ASSUMPTIONS AND
UNCERTAINTIES

Camelot

Ask ev' - ry per - son if he's heard the sto - ry;—

—— And tell it strong and clear if he has not:

That once there was a fleet-ing wisp of glo - ry—

—— called Cam-e-lot. Don't let it be for-

got That once there was a spot For one brief shin-ing

mo-ment that was known As Cam - e - lot.

Chapter 1

Let Us Make
This Perfectly Clear

We begin where high school civics left off. We all know that the public policy-making process in the United States, as in every nation, is encrusted with an elaborate set of myths, symbols, rituals, and no small amount of irrational behavior. Citizens, elected officials, and bureaucrats commonly act as if policies are rational, predictable as to outcome, based on the careful study of data, and designed to carry out the "will of the people" or "the public interest." In fact, however—and this is the central theme of this book—public policy is made in the face of pervasive uncertainty as to causes or results and it flows from the *assumptions* that are made concerning the nature of a social or economic problem far more than from the available data.

We will pay some attention to the decision-making process in the face of uncertainty (including uncertainty about the validity of assumptions). We will also look at the fact that nearly all policies are costly and many extremely costly, so that not everything can be done at once. We live in a world of limited resources. Public policy decisions often must involve the problem of deciding what to give up in order to get something else—a problem often ignored by both the typical citizen and the idealistic zealot. We will also look at the decision makers—the leadership groups, as well as the counterelites—those who would like to take over the decision function—and the nonelites or masses of ordinary people.

Finally, we intend to argue that we are biased in favor of the American political system. We do not consider it to be anything even approximating perfection and we do not even assume that it is moving toward perfection. Instead, it is our belief that the system is probably about as good a one as is feasible under existing conditions, that the realistic alternatives to it are all less desirable, and that although the system is a conservative decision process, it does allow for considerable flexibility and for various groups of persons with differing political goals to move simultaneously toward those goals. Indeed, it would be our position that the essentially conservative nature of the system is a desirable thing and we present arguments in defense of this conclusion.

UNCERTAINTY: THE CONDITION FOR PUBLIC DECISIONS

The outstanding characteristic of any proposed change in public policy—any minor change and much more so in the case of a major change—is that we usually cannot know what the results of that change will be. Indeed, the problem is broader than that. We do not know, in most cases, the cause of any particular situation, whether we are talking about the causes of war, crime, or many other things. Sometimes, it is true, research has given us at least the hazy outlines of causes. This is the case, for example, of economic recessions and of inflation. We also have some understanding of the causes of environmental pollution. But often we simply do not know what causes a particular situation that society regards as a problem. And the lack of knowledge of a cause is often a severe handicap in trying to determine which of a number of approaches should be used to ameliorate the problem.

Policy Making: Whistling past the Graveyard   The mystery of cause is not nearly as important as are the mysteries of the likely results of policy changes or that of the possible side effects of such changes. What, for example, will be the final result of the policy of accumulating nuclear weapons as a protection against an attack by another nation? How much safer, if at all, would we be by doubling the number of nuclear weapons in our arsenal? What would be the result of a policy of developing only defensive weapons or of nuclear disarmament, unilaterally, or multilaterally? The fact is, that we do not know. Indeed, we have only the haziest guesses and they are based primarily on conventional wisdom and personal ideology. Their validity can be tested only in what may prove to be the hard way.

In the eighteenth century, British pickpockets were hanged in public, partly for the entertainment value, but also as an "object lesson" to others who might be tempted to turn to a life of crime. As Jeremy Bentham pointed out, however, the highest incidence of picking pockets occurred at such spectacles because the crowds were large and off guard. The lesson may have been learned by some, but not by the hard-core professionals.

In similar fashion, we do not know the causes of poverty (see the following section). We are also ignorant of the possible cures for poverty. Knowing neither cause nor cure, any attempted remedies introduce grave uncertainties and a high risk of failure. The use of logic may be of no help. For example, some people believe that one of the continuing causes of poverty is the fact that jobs that poor people might occupy are located in industries beyond the reach of their mobility. Being unable to own a car and confronted with inadequate or nonexistent public transportation systems, the argument runs, poor people cannot reach the site of potential jobs. Logically, then, the jobs should be brought to the poor. Businesses and industries could be established in the ghetto areas, and this would result in a drop of unemployment in the slums, right? Wrong! In cases where this has been tried, the result has been exactly the opposite of that intended. Unemployment in the particular ghetto where the new jobs have been established has increased rather than decreased.[1] Why should this be so? The reason lies in the fact that the planners did not take into account all the possible variables that might affect the outcome. Indeed, this is classically the case in all social policy planning.

Unlike the circumstances facing the chemist or physicist in attempting to solve a problem, the social scientist is always confronted with a bewildering, unmanageable number of variables, and, in addition to other problems connected with them, he is not able to identify in advance, if ever, their order of importance. In the above case, the error resulted from a failure to consider the effectiveness of a communications network among the poor. Instead of reducing unemployment in a particular ghetto by bringing into it x number of new jobs, the end result worked something along the following lines: Let us suppose that a new factory was established in a particular slum area, a factory that provided for, say, 150 new jobs. We can suppose, in the first place, that some of those jobs would go to nonpoor persons living outside of that ghetto. But that was not the most important problem that resulted. What actually happened was that the word went out by means of radio, television, letters, and every other possible communications medium that a new factory was located in the Zilchville ghetto and that the factory manager had announced that company policy was to hire people from among the poor of the adjacent ghetto. After we think about the problem for a short time, it becomes obvious to us as to why the unintended result was to *increase* rather than *decrease* unemployment in the ghetto: The news of the available jobs attracted many more people from the nationwide job market than the number of new jobs that had been created.

Blind-siding the Quarterbacks   Not uncommonly, a new public policy introduces unexpected side effects or complications. In some cases these developments may be unfortunate. For example, social workers have long pointed out that current welfare policies encourage fathers to leave home rather than to become self-sufficient through holding a modest job. The discouragement of initiative and the disintegration of families were not the goals of the program, but they have often been the result. Vigorous enforcement of the narcotics laws was intended to reduce the use of drugs. Instead it drove up the prices, pushing addicts into a life of crime in order to satisfy their craving needs. Again, driver education in high schools was expected by many to result in a lower accident rate. This did not happen. The assumption was that accidents happen because young people lacked knowledge about how properly to use the vehicle. Actually, they result from personality factors that affect driver attitudes. Because driver training does not significantly affect personality, the accident rate is unaffected.

In other cases, the end result has been a much happier one. For example, the United States grimly entered World War II as a direct result of the Japanese attack upon our military installations in Hawaii. Secondarily, we entered the war in order to help defeat the Nazis and Fascists of Germany and Italy. At the time, little if any attention was paid to the side effects of the massive social changes that would result from such a decision. For example, the benefits that were provided for veterans after the war allowed many persons of the working class and lower middle class to move up to higher status and class positions as the result of securing educations that many most likely would not have had without the governmental subsidies provided for veterans. Similarly, large numbers of veterans and their families became eligible for government-guaranteed home loans that enabled them to become homeowners. The unintended result was one of contributing to the opportunities and problems that resulted from the postwar development of suburbia.

DATA FOR DECISIONS: WHO NEEDS THEM?

"If we can land men on the moon, we can end poverty," is a statement one sees in occasional letters to the editor. But one does not follow from the other. It is vastly easier to land on the moon. Doing so involves only technological problems. Dealing with poverty involves often conflicting individual and group values. More importantly, it involves lack of data and the difficulty of interpreting data.

Uncertainty often stems from the existence of inadequate data, contradictory data, or unconvincing analyses of data. Often the research needed for basing public policy upon data simply has not yet taken place. In other cases—and, unfortunately, very possibly in the vast bulk of the important cases—the means for carrying out the research and analyses are simply unknown and possibly unknowable. Once again, there are too many variables for us to determine cause-and-effect relationships or, sometimes, even the rank order of importance of the variables or what variables are, indeed, important. Even in cases where appropriate scientific information is known or knowable, the findings will remain unconvincing to the great mass of the public. This being the case, seekers of elective office will handle recommendations from so-called experts in a gingerly fashion.

Probabilities Have to Be Good Enough   The data from experts are of restricted value in making public policy for yet another reason: Most social science knowledge is based upon probability rather than certainty. Given certain assumptions, a mathematician can calculate precisely when a space vehicle and the moon or any planet will come together. Rarely is such precision possible in the social sciences. For example, let us suppose that a committee of the nation's most distinguished psychologists were to devise a plan to bring assured peace to the world. Let us suppose that after careful study, rechecking their data, and consulting with every possible outside expert, they sagely conclude that the surest way to bring peace in the world on a permanent basis would be for the United States to disarm unilaterally. They conclude that if the United States were to do this, China, the Soviet Union, and every other power would do the same.

We can clearly picture the scene when the distinguished committee files into the Oval Room of the White House: After the opening formalities and perhaps a harmless joke or two about the most recent activities of Henry Kissinger, the President would ask the committee members what they had to offer. Let us suppose that the committee—and this is a very big assumption—could convince the President that its conclusions were very probably correct. The President would then proceed to the most critical question of the meeting. He would ask them, "How certain are you?" If the scientists responded that they were 100 percent certain, he would hasten them to the door, muttering to himself about the need for a better appointments secretary. Absolute certainty would not be believable. But suppose that instead, the psychologists said that they were 95 percent sure. That might be believable to the President, but the result would be that he would thank them politely and excuse them. Another great plan would gurgle down the drain. Why? Because their response indicated that there was one chance in twenty that they could be wrong. The President, like every other public official, acts in a *fiduciary* capacity in relation to his constituents. That is, he acts on their interests and in their behalf, at least in theory. Because of this special role, the greater the cost of being wrong, the fewer the chances the decision maker is willing to take. Because the psychologists were talking about putting us, temporarily, at the mercy of other nations' nuclear weapons, the risk of utter disaster for the nation, no matter how small it may be, would be too great for any person in the White House to be willing to take. And, of course, the President is not likely to be anxious to go down in history as having presided over the demolition of the nation.

The Art of Minimizing Risks   Decision makers do not refuse to make decisions because of uncertainty, but there are several ways they try to play it safe. The typical pattern is to make cautious, incremental changes, rather than to experiment with the dramatically different. This is done by probing a little bit here and a little tinkering there and testing to see what happens as a result. Thus, public policy in the area of welfare is constantly being adjusted in this fashion because something must be done about the problems of welfare and welfare recipients, but no obviously "correct" policy is known to exist.

Governments conduct experiments which, if successful, can be applied to an entire program. Thus, in 1971, the United States Army experimented with a new form of basic training which would eliminate much of its Spartan character. Among other things, the experimental barracks—which through the magic of public relations had now become "dormitories"—contained private rooms, chintz curtains, and a beer dispenser. After some study, it was decided that this approach was an idea whose time had not yet come, at least not in the United States Army. The plan was abandoned at much less cost than would have been the case had the entire Army converted to the approach.

Another technique for reducing risk in the face of the unknown is to pursue a number of different, even contradictory, policies simultaneously, hoping that one or more of them will prove to be successful, or that the weaknesses in one will be offset by the strengths in the other. For example, the U.S. Department of Agriculture has, for about forty years, followed a policy of having separate sets of programs, one to show farmers how to raise more crops and the other to pay them to produce less.

How Do You Picture Poverty in *Your* Head? Whether proceeding in a marginal or a multidimensional fashion, the decision maker in the executive, legislative, judicial, and bureaucratic branches of government alike does not choose his approach at random. His assumptions tend to fit into a more general pattern called an *ideology*. This is a network of loosely interrelated normative values that we cling to on faith. Data may be useful, but they are not really necessary. Each of us has a set of values that defines what we mean by "the good life" or "justice." Ideology serves a double role by helping us to direct action toward the satisfaction of existing wants and to establish new goals for ourselves. Ideologies are based on faith or belief.

An example of how ideologies affect assumptions, which in

turn become the basis for one's public policy position, may be borrowed from issues centering around the conditions of poverty in America. The causes of poverty are not known. Therefore it is difficult to know whether any particular set of public policies can do anything to reduce the level of poverty in the nation. (We assume that by "poverty" is meant the legally defined concept of it. The actual concept of poverty is, of course, a cultural one. In an absolute sense, poverty will always be with us simply because as a nation becomes more affluent the definition of poverty is revised upward.) Serendipity is always possible. One may stumble upon a cure for poverty or anything else by accident, but that is unlikely.

Jane Jacobs has argued that poverty has no cause, that only prosperity has causes. To her, the existence of poverty results from inefficiency in the economic system.[2] Her argument, although powerfully presented, has no great political appeal because it does not point a finger at either the good guys or the bad guys. In looking for causes, scholars have presented at least four popular explanations of poverty.[3] One, a moralistic view, says the poor are simply lazy, that they could improve their condition if they had the moral stamina and motivation to do so. This is a favorite argument of right-wingers, although not restricted to them. The Salvation Army and Alcoholics Anonymous both are strongly moralistic. A second is a romantic or ethnocentric view. It holds that the poor are really just like everybody else, they just happen to lack education or training, or good health perhaps, or are the victims of discrimination. This is the common view of the upper-middle-class liberal who projects his image of himself upon others, and particularly upon those with whom he has had little or no direct experience. To him, the solution to poverty will be found in large governmental programs that provide jobs, education, housing, and information about "rights" and benefits available to the poor. He believes we can buy our way out of the problem.

A third view is a conspiratorial or paranoiac view which holds that the poor are victims of an "oppressive" economic and social system. Proponents argue that poverty can be ended only through a drastic change in the social and political system and that this can take place only by giving political power to the poor and to those who would lead them. This is, of course, the general picture of the problem from the New Left.[4] Finally, there is the sociological view that the poor are members of a separate subculture that is devoted to immediate personal satisfaction. The poor are trapped because of their own ideology or outlook on life, and particularly by their lack of future orientation. Because they do not save part of what they receive, do not defer gratification in order to secure an education and a good job, they are doomed to remain poor. The only ones who can escape are those relatively few who reject the culture of poverty and develop an orientation toward the future.[5]

As we have noted, we do not know which of these is correct. It is sensible to suppose that most complex social phenomena have no one cause and it is very possible that all these theories are correct, but we do not know if they are the only ones or which one accounts for what proportion of the total poor. But does the fact that we do not know the causes of poverty keep us from acting as if we did? Of course not. We proceed as if we knew what we were doing, even though each of the theories implies a different set of public policies. (The authors are inclined to think that the fourth theory explains more about those in the grip of the hard core of poverty in our nation than do the other three. We think it unlikely, however, that it will ever become the basis of public policy because the theory implies that such poverty is a chronic problem about which not much can be done short of brainwashing a substantial proportion of the population. Most Americans expect public policy to be based upon some kind of cheerful optimism and the anticipation that the solution to the problem is just beyond the next election.)

SHALL WE GIVE UP RUTABAGAS IN ORDER TO GAIN CAULIFLOWER?

One of the most useful concepts in dealing with policy making in the United States is that of *opportunity costs*, an idea borrowed from economics. Opportunity costs represent what we pay in the way of giving up one desirable thing in order to gain the opportunity to choose an even more desirable thing. Almost all goods and services in the world are economic in character, that is, they are not free. Political systems, like economic systems, distribute scarce goods and services. Few people can have all that they would like because of this scarcity. Much of politics involves not only who is going to get what, when, and how, but also what is to get done within the political system and what is to be left undone.

Unfortunately, most people are ignorant of economics, including political economics. There is a tendency to think that if we want to have something we will simply decide to have it. Indeed, naïve people sometimes believe that if we are lacking in adequate housing for some, if the environment is polluted, or if not everyone is employed, it must be because "the Establishment" or "they" do not want to permit some people to have life's good things.

One of the authors was once attending a conference on "urban problems" and at one point there was considerable discussion of air pollution. The talk centered on causes and corrections and the urgent need to do something about cleaning up the air. There was seeming unanimity on this point when suddenly a black participant said: "In my order of priorities, air pollution is light years behind black slums as an urban problem. After we clean up the buildings, I'll be ready to talk about the air." He recognized that both problems were costly in their solution, and he was willing to let the one go—at least for the time being—in order to concentrate upon his higher-priority item. He was thinking in terms of opportunity costs.

Recent lobbying to repeal or reduce the punishment for "victimless" crimes reflects the tendency to be unaware of opportunity costs. A truly victimless crime is a rarity. What has happened to New York's Times Square in recent years is a case in point. The area abounds with heterosexual and homosexual prostitution, pornography shops, and places that show what were once called "obscene" movies—all "victimless" behavior. But there are victims: the owners of a multimillion dollar investment in the entertainment industry and a drastic loss of real estate investments, not to mention the rude shock and disappointment for thousands of tourists for whom Times Square has symbolized a romantic, glamorous mecca for generations.

The typical citizen is not concerned with opportunity costs but primarily with achieving those things he thinks most important. As a result, politicians also try to avoid the problem by giving a little bit of monetary support to a large variety of problems. This can, of course, result in too little help being given to any of the programs, so that they all become ineffective. In the real world, large numbers of problems tend to be interdependent. What happens in the case of one may affect what happens in the case of many others. And how much is spent on one program affects how much will be spent on a number of others. The phenomenon of opportunity costs is another reason why there are so few instant solutions to social problems.

The High Cost of Stopping the Slaughter One further illustration of opportunity costs should suffice. Americans believe that human life is precious and should be preserved at all costs. Right? Perhaps, but only if the statement is sharply modified will it be even approximately correct. Let us look at this in terms of the automobile. Approximately 55,000 persons have been killed in automobile accidents on American highways in each year since 1968 and more than 35,000 have been killed in every year since 1949. Tens of thousands are permanently crippled each year. (The 55,000 figure is nearly 7,000 higher than that for all American battle deaths in Southeast Asia through all the years of that conflict. And who is to say that killing by motor vehicles is less immoral than killing by making war? We rationalize the deaths with the euphemism "accident," as if they "just happened.")

In this particular case, there is little uncertainty as to how this figure could be reduced. Specialists on the subject know of policies that would quite certainly reduce this figure by about 90 percent. What would have to be done to achieve this goal? The first thing would be to prohibit automobile driving by all males under the age of twenty-five. Statistics show that these persons are by far the poorest drivers on the highway, measured in terms of persons responsible for crashes and deaths. Men in this age group are involved in about four times as many accidents and are culpable in about four times as many deaths as is their proportion of the driving population. A second policy would probably involve a requirement for annual eyesight and driving examinations for all persons over the age of sixty-five. A third would provide for the permanent revocation of the driver's license for alcoholics, drug addicts, and all persons whose records indicate that they are incompetent drivers, and would, furthermore, provide for drastic penalties (such as confiscation of the automobile being driven plus a mandatory prison sentence) in all cases of conviction after arrest for driving on a revoked license.

Is such a set of policies feasible? Of course not. It is very difficult to get convictions before a jury for drunk or reckless driving or, for that matter, for any moving violation, simply because one or more of the jurors can always picture himself or herself in the position of the defendant. (Remember that the prosecutor must usually convince twelve jurors; the defense only one to get a hung jury and possible dismissal.) Furthermore, young men would riot in the streets at the suggestion that they should be separated from their true love, the automobile. Old men would bridle at the suggestion they should no longer drive. The opportunity costs involved in greatly reducing the slaughter on the highways is more than most Americans are willing to pay. We are vain about our presumed (and usually highly imaginary) driving skills. Surveys have shown that about 90 percent of licensed drivers consider themselves to be of average ability or above.

Of course, the draconian measures suggested above need not be adopted in order to make a substantial reduction in automobile deaths. The National Highway Traffic Safety Administration has estimated that the toll could be reduced by 20,000 a year if every driver and rider did no more than to wear seat belts. But other administration studies indicate that many drivers do not wear belts because they prefer to pretend that automobile driving is not a potentially deadly business. (If the driver does not "buckle up," riders are not likely to do so.)

Another rational policy would be to remove the habitual offender from behind the wheel. More than one-half of the annual 55,000 deaths are caused by these incompetent drivers. Habitual offenders are commonly heavy users of alcohol and other drugs, reckless drivers, and speeders. Some states have passed laws against the habitual offender, but they are generously in favor of the bad driver. Typically they provide that a person convicted of three major, or ten to twenty minor, traffic offenses over a certain number of years loses his driver's license. If the person drives after being certified, a mandatory prison term is provided for convicted offenders. But conviction is not easy and juries are reluctant to apply the law. According to the *New York Times*, the Virginia law of 1968 resulted, in the first three years, in the certification of 2,700 habitual offenders. Only 36, or 1 in 75, had been sent to prison, a figure that must be a small fraction of those who continue to drive illegally. Even so, during the period involved, state highway deaths dropped by 20 percent.

Rather than dealing with the known root cause of the problem, Americans tend to seek to place the blame—to find the bad guy—outside of themselves. Instead of advocating taking the incompetent driver off the road, instead of lobbying for sensible speed limits within which the average driver can operate competently, the easy out is to blame the automobile manufacturer.

Ralph Nader made millions of Americans happy when he wrote *Unsafe at Any Speed.*[6] Of course, we know that the annual carnage is very little a result of decisions made in Detroit and very much of those made on the highways. It may well be true that automobile builders are more concerned with selling automobiles than they are with the safety of the driver and passengers. Certainly additional safety features would help avoid some deaths. So might better highway design. But neither of these is likely to have much effect upon the overall total of deaths. Better designed highways encourage faster driving. The majority of automobile owners will not voluntarily wear their seat belts. (The president of the Chrysler Corporation once testified that a woman had written him complaining about the seat belts—she said the fastenings were uncomfortable to sit on.) Among young people—the highest accident-risk group—wearing the seat belt is considered by many to be a sign of the "chicken." And the safety belt and harness—the greatest protector in the case of accidents, according to studies—is worn by only about 4 percent of the people riding in vehicles equipped with them.[7] Obviously, most Americans consider the opportunity costs involved if we were to seek to keep highway deaths at a minimum to be much too great and unattractive to pay. The costs, in terms of deaths, are worth less than the benefits. Besides, in an optimistic society, the assumption is that the penalty will have to be paid by someone else. That is the American way.

There Is No Such Thing as a Free Lunch Decisions about opportunity costs face us on almost every hand. Are we really willing to accept a lower standard of living in order to reduce environmental pollution? Are we willing to accept highly restrictive policies concerning the recreational use of public lands, as advocated by such upper-middle-class groups as the Sierra Club, in order to maintain undisturbed various areas in their natural beauty if this may also mean depriving lower-middle-class and working-class persons of an opportunity to have the only kind of vacation—inexpensive—that they can afford? Are we willing to provide equal per-pupil dollar support for educational programs at the primary and secondary levels if the result may be mediocrity in all educational districts rather than excellent programs in some?

Are we willing to abandon an obviously irrational and defective prison system in an attempt to better protect society and give the truly reformed criminal another chance if this must be done at the at least temporary—and possibly permanent—cost of allowing a larger proportion of criminals to escape any accounting for their acts? Are we willing to accept the possibility of greater unemployment, at least temporarily, in exchange for the closing down of factories and oil well drilling sites in return for a cleaner environment? These are the kind of questions that the existence of opportunity costs require us to confront.

EVERYONE WANTS TO GET INTO THE ACT

The impact of policy on human beings is not only direct and involves opportunity costs, but it is also indirect. The economists call the secondary or indirect effects "spillover" or "externalities." For example, when the city fathers move to close one of those storefronts that advertises itself as an "Adult Porno Bookstore" and the ordinance is challenged, this small businessman and his customers feel the direct impact. Under one decision, the customers get to buy what they want; under another they do not. But others also feel the effects of whichever policy is adopted finally, however in a more indirect way. The presence of a shop with the windows painted white on the inside and the garishly lighted sign over the door, "$1.00 Admission, Refunded to Purchasers," affects the quality of life in the community in which it is located. According to whether the shop flourishes or is closed, the hamburger stand around the corner may experience a decrease or an increase of business, or a change in its type of clientele. Parents, even far distant, will argue that the store's presence is a bad influence on the neighborhood. "Women's Lib" groups will regard it as a monument to the continuing male exploitation of their sex. Newspaper columnists, discussing the latest find of the body of a raped and murdered girl in a lonely forest preserve, will wonder aloud whether the presence of this friendly little bookstore encourages or discourages such acts. All will claim some indirect harm or benefit depending on the public policy which is adopted in regard to adult porno bookstores.

Economists traditionally handle the problem of externalities by arguing that the producer of the costs should pay for them. If he can do so and still make a profit he is permitted by the free market to continue production. If not, he must stop production. Economists find difficulties in measuring such external economic costs. The measuring of social cost spillovers is even more difficult. As we have noted, no one really knows what they are. Nevertheless some system has to be devised to reach a decision about what will be permitted. The American hit-and-miss system has many imperfections, but it does permit some feedback to the policy makers from those affected by the policy, first in anguished cries and second in votes. These aid in testing the reality of the assumptions of decision makers.

WILL WISHING MAKE IT SO?

A characteristic of public attitudes toward policy making is that people have a tendency to avoid facing up to conclusions that are unpleasant or unwanted. We all tend to rationalize our positions and it is not difficult to develop a defense for any policy an individual happens to prefer. Similarly, the individual is likely to insist that a policy *will* work simply because he *wants* it to work.

The law concerning abortion is a good case in point. Scientists do not know exactly how life begins, but the only point that reason would bring us to is that it begins at the moment of conception. Thus, despite a 1973 Supreme Court ruling that the unborn are not yet persons in the "whole sense," an abortion involves the taking of a human life. Yet there are increasing numbers of persons who argue for flexible laws on abortion and many even hold that the question should be decided unilaterally by the pregnant woman. This carefree attitude toward human life is probably made easier by the fact that a fetus lacks a personality. (Probably many advocates of abortion do not know that fetal brain waves have been monitored as early as the forty-third day, that by the sixty-third day the baby moves his mouth, turns his head, and may suck his thumb, that by the fifth month the baby feels pain the same as does a postpartum child, and that he or she sleeps and awakens, and can be awakened by loud noises.) The authors do not argue against easier abortion laws, only that individuals favoring them should recognize what they imply. Public policy, after all, often calls for the taking of human life, and this is considered legitimate, at least by large numbers of persons. Most people (judging from the 1972 California referendum) still favor capital punishment for murder. A policeman is excused if he kills a criminal when his own life or that of an innocent person is threatened. A soldier who kills in combat is thought to be justified under most circumstances. Laws permitting abortion are a part of this legacy.

Life beside the Wishing Well   In other cases, we act as if wishing would make it so. This is true, not just of the garden-variety citizen, but also of major decision makers. For example, there is impressive evidence to indicate that educational failure is the result, not of the teachers or of the quality of the school equipment, but of attitudes the child learns early and from peers or in the home.[8] Despite this, many decision makers continue to insist that changing the educational system will change the learning rate of youngsters. A favorite theory is that students who do badly in school do so because their teachers *expect* them to fail. The argument is that the children are stereotyped and the result is a self-fulfilling prophecy. The children of upper-middle-class persons do well in school; the children of the poor, especially poor blacks, fail.

Testing these essentially erroneous assumptions, the Office of Economic Opportunity in 1970 and 1971 conducted an experimental program of "performance contracting." Private firms were hired and encouraged to use all kinds of experimental teaching materials and electronic gadgets in an attempt to raise the level of student achievement among the poor. The private firms would, in return for a fee, take over the teaching in the school. If the students did not reach a test-score level agreed upon with the local school board, a portion of the fee would have to be refunded. The private firms had every possible incentive for having the children succeed. Not only did they make more money for teaching if they did, but the program would open the door for the sale of huge amounts of new kinds of teaching materials. Yet, after a one-year study in eighteen school districts involving 13,000 children, the performance scores were no different from those in the control group, an equal number of children with similar backgrounds, but taught in a conventional way by regular teachers. It cost the taxpayers $5.6 million to find out what was already known, but what the decision makers were reluctant to believe. And even after the results were in, some educators still refused to face reality. They argued that the experiment must somehow have been faulty.

Similarly, when confronted with evidence we do not like, we often choose to attack the evidence and to impugn the reliability of the witness rather than to reexamine our concept of the problem. For example, in the late 1960s, there were a number of oil spills in the Santa Barbara channel off the California coast resulting from accidents during undersea oil drilling. Persons concerned with pollution of the environment—certainly a legitimate and real concern—raised a great hue and cry, demanding an

end to oil drilling off the coast and painting terrifying pictures of
the damage done to sea animals and birds, as well as to the plants
on the floor of the ocean. Then Gale Straughan, a marine biologist
at the University of Southern California and a young woman
deeply committed to scientific research, if perhaps not very
understanding of politics, decided to find out exactly what
damage had occurred as a result of the largest of these spills.
What she found was that, in fact, virtually no permanent damage
had been done to the ecosystem as a result. When she published
her findings, to what was apparently her absolute amazement,
calumny rained down on her head from almost every direction.
Sundry attacks were made upon her, even though her findings had
been carefully documented. Even if she was not completely
correct it is clear that her critics simply *wanted* to believe what
they wanted to believe, not what scientific investigation revealed.
So is it always in politics.[9]

HUMAN NATURE AND POLITICS

In the immensely popular *South Pacific*, Oscar Hammerstein II
inserted a song about racial prejudice in Polynesia. Its message
was that a person must be carefully taught to hate and fear other
races and ethnic groups.

Almost the exact opposite seems to be the case. Hammerstein's view was that the noble savage is corrupted by institutions
or by the social environment. He assumed people are naturally
good and will love each other if no one tells them otherwise. In
fact, people have to be taught to be friendly to strangers and to
accept those with different skins, religions, languages, or even
hair and dress styles. Any child who moves into a new neighborhood and enters a new school knows what the natural reaction of
his new acquaintances will be: It is one of suspicion of those
different from or merely outside the group. Civility comes only
after much patient teaching by example, reward, and punishment.
But no child has to learn how to be angry or cross, to be
self-centered and egotistical, or even to tell lies or to appropriate
other peoples' toys (property).

Thus the beginning of realism in politics is to recognize that
human beings are not innately inclined to altruism. The tendency
toward self-interest concerns is accentuated by what economists
call the *collective-goods problem*. They note that often when a
good is for the benefit of all, it is in the interest of every individual

to avoid paying his fair share of its cost. Thus Stuart Mott, Jr., one of the millionaire supporters of Senator George McGovern, a man who did not earn but inherited his money, was found to be one of 122 millionaires who paid no taxes at all in 1971. At the same time he advocated higher taxes on the wealthy. When asked if this were not a contradiction, he replied that he thought it right that his taxes should be increased, but that as long as the system's rules permitted tax writeoffs, he would take advantage of them. In the same way it is assumed that grades in a college course are defensible if no students are permitted the extra advantage they would gain by cheating. Yet it is tempting at times for any individual student to crib while others do not. Thus the rules of the game often encourage the antisocial tendencies of individuals—in the collective-goods case by providing them with an additional payoff if they do not contribute voluntarily, if they are not caught breaking the rules, or if the rules have loopholes.

Self-Discipline and the Sense of Legitimacy The common way of counteracting the collective-goods problem is through coercion, or by rewarding special benefits. We have taxes because no one would otherwise pay the government's bills voluntarily, and we are today trying to recruit a volunteer army by increasing pay scales.

But these alone are insufficient to counteract the antisocial tendencies that all of us have from time to time. One other trait of human beings comes to the aid of those who govern—the desire of people to identify themselves with a larger purpose outside of themselves. In the case of individuals experiencing extreme psychological or social maladjustment, this need becomes quite pathological and often leads to the behavior of the "true believer" who, as the writer Eric Hoffer argued,[10] attempts to submerge himself in a larger cause and forget his own, often ruined, life. More commonly this commitment is less dramatic or zealous and is expressed in moderation. The man washing his car in the driveway on a sunny Saturday or the grandmother chatting with the supermarket clerk in the produce section both play by the rules. They want to live in comfortable decency with their neighbors. They want to preserve what they have found to be a comfortable way of life. The beneficiaries of such identification are such entities of the political and social system as the church, the work organization, the family, or the nation.

This moderate commitment is, nevertheless, in essence an acceptance of the legitimacy of the system—its social and political rules. Such commitment is enough to lead individuals to accept the moderate self-discipline and sometimes self-sacrifice associated with living in a civilized society. A loss of this kind of commitment such as followed World War I or occurred during the Vietnam war may be associated with periods in which self-indulgence is given priority by many individuals. *When the individual loses faith in his commitment to the system's legitimacy, most forms of self-discipline are seen as unnatural and often as repressive.*

In a speech at Oxford at the height of his political career, the British Prime Minister Benjamin Disraeli noted that "youth must seek a form of government that can be loved and not merely supported. It must understand that men are led only by the power of the imagination. It must possess heroic ambition, the sentiment without which no state is stable, lacking which the political life is a dish without salt, the Crown a bauble, the Church an administration, the Constitution a dream."[11]

The imagination Disraeli refers to is what modern social scientists call an "ideology" or "loose belief system" which gives meaning and direction to political action. It is based on a set of assumptions about reality and what is desirable. Marx and others have argued it is little more than a rationalization of selfish interest—a dressing up of egotistic motives in the costume of idealism. But while this is often true, we also assume such ideology does draw men beyond their own immediate self-centeredness to larger and hopefully more desirable goals.

We thus build into the set of assumptions on which this book is based two somewhat contradictory tenets: (1) Man is naturally prone to be self-serving; (2) but to complete his own nature he also needs to feel some association with a belief system that gives a larger meaning to what he does. The human being is but an animal, yet in contrast to other mammals, he knows that he, the individual, will soon die. He feels that his life must surely have some meaning beyond the short three score and ten. He fights shy of accepting the sober view of life as expressed in Shakespeare's *Macbeth*: "Tis a tale told by an idiot, full of sound and fury, signifying nothing."

ELITE AND MASS

Another assumption made by the authors is that participation in the making of political decisions is not equal among all persons under any system of government whether or not it is one considered to be a democracy. This has always been the case and, in the absence of any indication that there is a trend toward broader effective participation, we assume that this situation will continue into the indefinite future. Society is invariably divided into elites, or leadership groups, and the masses that constitute the remainder. Elites offer leadership to the masses, members of which consider the elitists to be legitimate leaders. However, in an imperfect society, no group can satisfy everyone as to its competence or appropriateness in leadership positions, or adequacy of goals.

Dominant elites, not being able to achieve the expectations of all who depend upon them, generate counterelites, leadership groups that appeal to the discontented within the regime. The dominant elite, together with its mass supporters, constitutes "the Establishment"—in the United States, the vast bulk of the population. In a passive manner, the dominant elite and its supporters also benefit from the apathy of the large number of persons who are apolitical, or nonparticipants in the political process. The counterelites are left only with a constituency of the discontented, a group of varying size through time, but one that historically has usually been quite easily contained and directed by the prevailing elite. Part Two of this book will be concerned with the relationship between elite and mass.

Every elite must be thought of as providing leadership in at least two ways. First, it possesses power through its various resources and leads through the selective use of this power. Secondly, its activities are based upon certain ideas about the uses to which power should be put. It thus provides leadership in the shaping and reshaping of societal goals; it provides an ideology for itself and the masses.

COOKS AND PUDDING EATERS

In times when the institutions of society are under frontal attack, social critics face a special temptation. Because the role of public scold is fashionable, he or she is tempted to parade good intentions for the admiration of the rest of us. Like the Pharisee of biblical times, social critics are inclined to beat their breasts and posture for applause; they demand to be judged by what they proclaim is the purity of their motives. They shout to all who will listen, "the proof of the pudding is in us, the cooks." But it isn't.

The proof of the pudding is in the eating and for this one must consult the person who faces the risk of indigestion.

Throughout this book we will rather perversely call attention to this fact by insisting that *social policy must be judged by the way it affects individuals, and not by the good intentions of those who pronounce it.* This means policy is judged by the way it ricochets off of persons, such as members of the family that lives in the house halfway up the next block, as well as the way it shapes the lives of those one sees walking through the K-Mart or on TV at the Macy Thanksgiving Day parade. Thus through their own experience or from experiences of others these people have some notion about how the draft really worked, or what the police response is when a home in the neighborhood is plundered. They appreciate what it means to collect social security and try to live on it, or how laborious it is to work their way through the long form 1040. The final judgment about the desirability of a particular policy has to be how it looks to them; not what the policy makers claimed were their intentions.

Because this process of feedback is difficult and haphazard, it is tempting to try to dodge it by judging policy by the self-proclaimed goodwill or good intentions of the policy maker or the shining loftiness of his assumptions. To reject this temptation means facing a fact that may be shocking and hard to swallow: *Social evils may result from people acting from the best of motives; social good may result from people acting from base motives.*

Good intentions do not necessarily lead to utopia, but may lead to hellish results. For example, by cupping and bleeding patients, physicians of the enlightened eighteenth century no doubt killed a good many of those they were trying to help and who had put trust in their judgment; George Washington, among them. The idealism of Neville Chamberlain, who so desperately and selflessly wanted to give his generation "peace in our time," led to the capitulation to Hitler at Munich in 1938 and set the stage for the armies of World War II. Selfish motives, by accident or if properly channeled by the laws and customs of society, may lead to socially desirable results. Such self-serving inclinations inspire farmers, shippers, packers, grocers, and others to all the trouble of moving a coffee bean from the cool mountain slopes of Colombia to the pot on our dining room table. Similarly, the selfishness of New England merchants and ship builders had at least as much to do with the founding of our nation as did the beautifully expressed sentiments of Patrick Henry.

Assumptions take the place of knowledge about what the results of social policy may be. But assumptions cannot be judged by their altruistic content. The social impact of policy is found in the way it warps, bends, and shapes the lives of individuals.

IMPERFECT MAN IN AN IMPERFECT SYSTEM

The late political scientist George Belknap was the discoverer of Belknap's second law, destined to take its place with the laws of Parkinson and Gumperson, as well as with Peter's principle. He noted that everyone knew how disorderly and uncoordinated he himself was and how much so his own home and office were. Still he imagined others, with whom he was unfamiliar, were different. He imposed order on them, particularly if they seemed to operate with machinelike efficiency. Whatever they did, they did because they planned to do it.

Belknap's second law applies especially to institutions. Some people imagine they do exactly what their leaders intend them to. Institutions are probably more fallible than individuals, however. They cannot help but be inefficient because they include inefficient human beings. Our officials are not all-seeing. The best we can expect is that they concentrate on real problems and not buy simple-minded and ineffective proposals for "solutions."

The authors of this book afford this reasonable break: We admit to a bias in favor of American democracy. We do not argue that the American system is perfect or even that it is moving toward perfection.

The Watergate scandal makes clear that our system is not foolproof or corruption proof. The ambitions of our politicians can sometimes lead to an astonishing and frightening arrogance just as in more authoritarian systems. Yet we put our faith in that system of rules, and the ideology that inspires it, to carry us into the future. In the chapters that follow we will argue that this system, now the oldest government in the world, as logically and demonstrably imperfect as it is, has and will continue to have a great amount of desirable flexibility, that it builds in self-correcting feedback to ambition, and encourages the leadership of counterelites, but that it never has or ever will provide instant solutions to social and economic problems. We argue, further, that alternatives do not offer any reasonable assurance of being an improvement upon the present system and that the goal of the American or any other political system is not one of solving problems on a permanent basis and achieving complete justice and harmony for all. Rather, the political process is one of continuous marginal adjustments which are intended to reduce as much as is practicable the sense of dissatisfaction, unhappiness, and fear that exists in a society. We doubt if any political system can realistically strive for any higher objective.

NOTES

1 See, for example, U.S. Department of Labor, *Manpower Report of the President*, April 1967; Clair Wilcox, *Toward Social Welfare*, Irwin, Homewood, Ill., 1969; Walter Galenson, *A Primer on Employment and Wages*, Random House, Inc., New York, 1966.

2 Jane Jacobs, *The Economy of Cities*, Vintage Books, New York, 1969.

3 Charles R. Adrian, "Urban America: Social Science as Catharsis," *Polity*, 4:385–393, Spring 1972.

4 The literature is vast. As rather typical, see James Boggs, *Racism and the Class Struggle*, Monthly Review Press, New York, 1970; Tom Hayden, *A View of the Poverty Program*, Center for the Study of Unemployed Youth, New York University, New York, 1966; William Ryan, *Blaming the Victim*, Pantheon Books, Inc., New York, 1971.

5 On the culture of poverty, see Oscar Lewis, "The Culture of Poverty," *Scientific American*, 215:19–25, October 1966; and Edward C. Banfield, *The Unheavenly City*, Little, Brown and Company, Boston, 1970.

6 Ralph Nader, *Unsafe at Any Speed*, Grossman Publishers, New York, 1965.

7 Data from the National Highway Traffic Safety Administration.

8 See Christopher Jencks et al., *Inequality: A Reassessment of the Effect of Family and Schooling in America*, Basic Books, New York, 1972; Daniel P. Moynihan and Frederick Mosteller (eds.), *On Equality of Educational Opportunity*, Random House, Inc., New York, 1972; and other publications that rework the data of the Coleman Report of 1966.

9 *West* magazine, *Los Angeles Times*, June 6, 1971.

10 Eric Hoffer, *The True Believer*, Harper & Row, New York, 1951.

11 Andre Maurois, *Disraeli, A Picture of the Victorian Age*, Random House, Inc., New York, 1942, p. 174.

2

LEADERS, FOLLOWERS,
AND DISSENTERS:
THE MOBILIZATION OF BIAS

Camelot

Chapter 2

Elites and Masses: The Distribution of Social, Economic, and Political Power

In every political system there are leaders and followers. The leadership class or group is called the *elite*, while the followers are referred to as *mass*. The dominant elite makes most of the important decisions in a political-economic-social system. But the elite—the current vogue term is "Establishment"—does not dictate policy, at least not in countries with some form of democracy. Instead, the elite has but a tenuous hold on policy direction. It is necessary for this group to make concessions to the beliefs and resulting wants of the masses or common people. Even where leaders get their own way, they often can do so only by putting an enormous amount of effort into bargaining and persuasion. Furthermore, in contrast to the simplistic or conspiratorial notion of the elite that is held by some critics of democracy, the elite itself is often badly divided on ideology and hence upon policy goals.

For one thing, there is competition among those who agree on general values and goals for the most part, but desire to hold office. We refer to both groups in this type of competition as the elite establishment. Seekers of major offices among both Democrats and Republicans are thus included in the Establishment.

There may, however, also be a sharper division based on whether the particular leaders are accepted as legitimate. Usually, this question has not been very important in the United States, but since the early 1960s the nation has been in a relatively unstable situation which might be described as a crisis of legitimacy within the elite itself. This opposition elite, we will call a *counterelite.* Together with its mass followers, we have the anti-Establishment.

The dominant elite and the counterelite differ in two important ways. The elite controls the most significant of the decision-making positions in both public and private life, but not necessarily all of them. In addition, the elite is committed to an ideology that defends, for the most part, the current distribution of statuses, monetary resources, and political power in the society. The counterelite disagrees with the existing distribution (see Figure 2-1) and the present means for gaining rewards and benefits.

The concept of elite is, in any case, a fuzzy one and not very useful or meaningful as a basis for analysis. Indeed, the whole idea is very much a tautology. Who makes the decisions in a society? The leaders. Who are the leaders? The elite—that is, the persons who make the decisions in society. This does not tell us very much except that we cannot all be generals, even if we might think that is what we prefer—which may be the case for those of us who are not generals.

THOSE WHO LEAD

In any complex social structure, leadership is essential and every social system has some process by which to recruit its elite. The

Division of Ideology

	Establishment	Anti-Establishment	
Elites	Leaders	Leaders	
Masses	Followers	Followers	Division of power

Figure 2-1 The distribution of power and ideas.

elite may be determined by inheritance, as in feudal societies, by intellectual ability, as in Plato's Republic, or by co-optation of nonelite persons who meet certain criteria, as in the United States and the Soviet Union.

The principal difference between the elite in a democracy and in an autocratic political system is one of degree, not of kind. In a democracy the elite tends to be a larger proportion of the total population, it is more diversified with a broader spectrum of ideology, and the activities of counterelites are more tolerated. In both systems, office-holding roles are crucial, whether public or private. That is to say, whether a person is viewed as having a *legitimate* right to make decisions that affect the rest of society depends in large part upon the formal office that he holds and whether he is viewed as having achieved that office in a proper fashion.

Harry Truman may not have been more intelligent or wiser than many another Missouri farmer, but as President of the United States, his opinions and decisions took on a new meaning. John F. Kennedy may have had an undistinguished career in Congress, but when he became President his pronouncements took on a profundity that had not been previously noticed. Richard M. Nixon may have used many kinds of tactics that a number of Americans would consider suspect, while advancing his political career, but when he became President many a citizen concluded that he must be more deserving of the position than they had realized. We tend to conclude that the person in the particular role does, in fact, fit the expectations that we have of proper behavior in that role. And this is true of all offices, high or low, public or private.

The elite must be divided between the dominant elite that leads the supporters of the regime and the counterelites that lead the discontented and are willing to make radical changes in the system. It requires a revolution to remove a dominant elite and replace it by a counterelite. This rarely happens, simply because a well-functioning elite tends to absorb into itself outside persons who have demonstrated leadership ability. In England, the old landed aristocracy maintained itself as the effective elite by accepting the leaders of business and industry—previously despised persons who were said to be "in trade"—during and after the Industrial Revolution, giving them the titles and honors that symbolized membership in the elite. This process of co-optation has been so widespread in England that there are only a few families of the nobility today that can trace their titles and possessions back to the period prior to the Industrial Revolution that began in the eighteenth century.

The same pattern has been followed in the United States, even though the symbols of acceptance are not quite so obvious as they are in the United Kingdom. Thus the founder of the Ford Motor Company was the son of an undistinguished farmer. He became highly successful by the standards of his day, however, and he and his family were accepted into the elite. His wealth and the fact that he was a white, Anglo-Saxon Protestant aided him, of course. By the 1970s, however, the flexible elite was willing to accept a person who a generation earlier might have been snubbed—an American with an Italian surname who became president of the company. In 1968, a person of Greek descent could be elected Vice President of the United States. As early as 1928, a Roman Catholic could be nominated (though not elected) by a major party for the Presidency and, in 1960, one could be elected President. By 1972 it was widely agreed that one's religion (except possibly for Jews) was no longer important as a consideration for presidential nomination (probably because religion itself was no longer central to the lives of most people) and Senator Edmund Muskie, a Roman Catholic of Polish descent, found that his background and religion were not important considerations as he sought the Democratic nomination. Society's leaders, preaching tolerance, had succeeded in teaching the common man to set aside some of his prejudices and the elite, as usual, was quite willing to accept men of talent and ability if they could be made acceptable to the common man.

COUNTERELITES FOR THE COUNTERCULTURE

In any society that will permit their existence, there will be counterelites. Indeed, they may exist even where thoroughly illegal, as in the case of Fidel Castro's guerrilla army in the Sierra Maestra mountains in the years before he came to power in Cuba. One example of a counterelite—that is, a leadership group of the discontented—is that of the New Left in the United States. This group has made it possible for many young idealists to project their hopes and images of the good society upon this "movement." It has lacked any kind of specific set of policy goals. This has been attractive to many recruits because it allows individuals to imagine that their personal ideals are the goals of the New Left. On the other hand, the lack of specifics after a time leads to a lack of confidence in the ability and meaningfulness of the leadership. The New Left has little commitment to traditional American politics with its incremental change and its emphasis on electoral rather than "participatory" democracy. But it does have a connecting link to traditional American politics in its chronic optimism.

Attempts at Thunder on the Left Some of the characteristics of the New Left as an anti-Establishment counterelite include the following:

First, there is the assumption that a solution exists for every human social problem. There is no logical reason for assuming that such is the case. Mathematicians, working with fewer variables, long ago learned that not all their problems have answers. We have already indicated that poverty cannot, in any realistic sense, ever be eradicated simply because the definition of it changes as affluence expands. There is no reason to assume that there must necessarily be a solution to every, or even to any, problem. One of the authors was once discussing the matter of a cure for cancer with a research scientist. He wondered how long it would likely be before a cure might be found. He was quickly brought back to reality by the response, which was something as follows: "We are likely to find the answer within the next ten or twenty years—that is, if there is a cure."

Secondly, there is a tendency in the New Left to adopt a conspiracy theory about the use of political power. In general, this sees political decisions being made by a small elite acting entirely in its self-interest, in constant and highly efficient communication with one another and sharing a common set of values and goals. The authors are convinced, however, that this view of how policy is made is essentially paranoiac in character. It greatly exaggerates the rationality, purposefulness, and levels of information possessed by the decision makers.

Thirdly, the New Left retains the ancient belief in the perfectability of man. The tendency is to ignore the biological fact that man is an evolutionary animal and, as such, is no more perfect than he needs to be in order to survive in a hostile world. The old belief that somehow man's intelligence and reasoning ability can carry him far beyond what is biologically required survives despite the lack of any evidence of marked advancement during the period of man's recorded history. The New Left also generally supports a romantic idea, borrowed from Herbert Marcuse,[1] that the next step in man's development requires a quantum jump to a new level of knowledge, one that transcends the scientific method and positive (that is, demonstrable) knowledge.

This type of counterelite is seeking popularity and support through denying the knowledge that man has accumulated throughout history. It offers wishful thinking in lieu of an honest evaluation of man's actual condition.

The New Left, furthermore, shares another American political tradition by its heavy commitment to populism, the notion that the American people are·not merely qualified to select their rulers, but are, in fact, able to rule themselves, a notion that goes back to the populism of Jacksonian democracy.[2] Although the rhetoric of the New Left would indicate an equalitarian system of government in which all people are considered to be equal, even intellectually equal, and that there should be no elite, they do not actually believe this. As Leo Rosten has suggested, "All power to the people" actually means "All power to the people who shout 'all power to the people.'" The leaders of the New Left would not abolish elite leadership; indeed, there is no observable reason to believe that such an abolition is possible, without even considering the question of its desirability.

Finally, the dominant elite controls not simply because of its own power alone. In fact, the masses have resources that can be used by the ruling elite, by a counterelite, or by the masses directly. As we shall demonstrate later, the total resources of the masses are potentially greater than are those of any elite. Great power can be exercised if a way can be found to organize and use it. The strength of the elite is to be found in its leadership ability and experience, that is, its ability to retain the support of most of the masses. So long as persons showing leadership ability are co-opted into the elite, the potentially greater power of the masses remains unorganized and hence not an effective political force by itself. The common people can, in theory, exert their enormous power whenever they wish to do so. As followers, they can simply refuse to follow. But they rarely see sufficient reason or have the incentive to do so. Ever since preman left the forests and moved into the plains where he became a carnivore and had to organize hunting parties, he has recognized and generally accepted the necessity and legitimacy of leadership.

ELITE: POWER AND IDEOLOGY

One of the common mistakes concerning the dominant elite is that it is interested only in power. It does have such a concern, of course, but its goal generally is one of seeking to preserve its own position of control. At the same time it justifies its position by claiming to help improve the lot of all citizens. Being the "do-gooder" and seeing itself as idealistic are part of the traditional function of the elite.

Holding the image of itself as the transmitter of society's

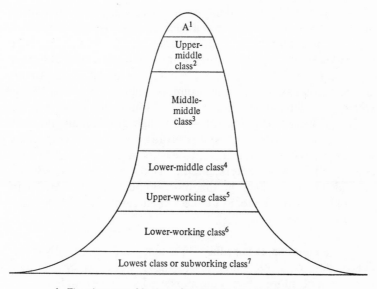

1. The aristocracy. Members of wealthy, famous, "old" families.

2. E.g., top corporation executives, the most successful professional people, the highest-status public officials.

3. E.g., middle-management people, the less successful professional people, and government bureaucrats.

4. E.g., white-collar clerks, small businessmen.

5. Skilled and semiskilled blue-collar workers.

6. Low-skilled or unskilled workers.

7. Persons who are chronically welfare recipients.

Note: Class, education levels, and income are closely related. When one rises or declines, the other two tend to follow.

Figure 2-2 The American class system.

ideals is a most powerful force in shaping the behavior of the elite. Its ideologies, whether conservative, liberal, or even radical in character (it is ordinarily, in part, all of these), tend to shape the agenda of the social system and its governmental institutions. In this chapter, we will note how the elite uses its power and how it relates to ordinary citizens. In the two chapters that follow, we will emphasize the function of the elite as, through its divergent ideologies, it serves both to preserve and to criticize and challenge the basic value systems of a society.

The American aristocracy or upper class—the Cabots, Roosevelts, du Ponts, Tafts, Rockefellers, and the like—is far too small a group to serve alone as the leadership elite. But these have been society's traditional leaders and almost any member of this class is automatically eligible for an elite leadership role if he or she wants it. The aristocracy is important, of course, because of its status, wealth, education, talents, and other qualifications. But it needs assistance. The group available to aid it and upon which it is dependent is the upper-middle class, those who fill society's decision-making roles—the high government officials, corporate executives, high-status professional people (especially judges, attorneys, physicians, professors in higher-status universities, widely read writers, major artistic performers, editors, journalists, and others in the more important mass media of communication), members of the armed forces who wear stars, and a few others.

The Function of the Elite   In a democracy, especially in our democracy with its small aristocracy, status is based upon achievement more than inheritance. The upper-middle class consists of persons who earn their positions—through talent, work, and often a little luck. It serves as the custodian of the society's ideals, as the furnisher of job holders in government at the decision-making levels, as the innovators and creators of change, as the nation's conscience. Members of the upper-middle class have the resources in terms of wealth, education, talent, a cushion against direct threat to their own statuses through social change, and the energy to perform this function. Members of the lower-middle class and the working classes (the middle masses) cannot do so, for they are too much concerned with the everyday problems of earning a living, preserving their own status positions, and keeping open the channels for their children to advance to higher social levels to be able or willing to spend scarce resources upon "reforming" or "improving" society. And the middle of the middle class is only slightly more likely to do so. The task of preserving our democracy and of "improving" it—however that may be defined—therefore falls to the critical group at the top of the middle class.

One of the grave difficulties that complicated the 1960s, the authors believe, is that a very considerable proportion of the upper-middle class did not clearly understand its duty to lead the nation responsibly and effectively. Persons of the class, more often their children, began to wonder if radical changes were not necessary. As a result of guilt feelings over race relations and the war in Vietnam, they played their role as critics, while at the same time failing to come up with workable proposals and also holding on to all their power resources. Lacking a sense of the attitudes and concerns of the common man, with an idealism unrelated to the practical possibilities of achievement in social change, and an ignorance of the high costs of seeming to promise more than could possibly be delivered (hence ignoring the serious social problems of discontent in the face of rising expectations by those who stood to gain by their proposed new approaches to public policy), upper-middle-class persons abetted a level of social discontent that encouraged riots, civil disobedience, bitterness, pompous nonsense, and general confusion.

Although the task of the elite is to keep a social system focused upon its ideal goals, it also has a responsibility to keep the society from seeking to achieve a level nearer to the ideal than is realistically possible. Social progress, in all but the rare case of successful revolution, is dependent upon social stability. A reasonable amount of social discomfort or dissatisfaction is necessary if change ("progress") is to be achieved; but beyond a certain point, the encouragement of agitation for change becomes dysfunctional, throwing the system into turmoil and often resulting in a slowing down of the movement toward the desired goals. Thus a substantial proportion of the upper-middle class and especially its younger members, did not understand that the result of turmoil is to create a great desire for order, even at the risk of possible loss of some liberty. The "hard-hat" response to the upper-middle class and its favored candidate, George McGovern, is the result.

In other nations, past and present, members of the elite have always made a point of seeking to inform the next generation of the character of their role within the social system. The failure of many upper-middle-class persons to do so in contemporary America has raised important problems as to whether the leadership elite had, through its commitment to the ideal of the essential equality of men, allowed itself to be confused concerning the historic responsibility of its class, a responsibility that has existed ever since the upper-middle class of Great Britain took over control of that nation at the time of the Glorious Revolution of 1688–1689.

THE MIDDLE MASSES

Up until now we have been principally concerned with members of the elites, those who take an intense interest in political, economic, and social decisions. We must also consider the typical citizens, who are effective enough politically to count. It is for these people, we will argue, that the American system really operates. We have called them the middle masses because they include the middle-middle and lower-middle classes and the upper-working class (skilled and semiskilled blue-collar workers—the "hard hats"). They are people who live decent but often undramatic lives and are often the subject of ridicule by intellectuals, who dismiss them as philistines because they are the ones who provide the applause for TV comedians, watch mediocre movies, and follow soap operas or professional sports.

We make some assumptions about them, following generally the ideas expressed by Walter Lippmann about fifty years ago in such books as *Public Opinion* and *The Phantom Public*. These assumptions have been borne out by analyses of election results and public opinion polling data collected over many years by social scientists.

The main facts about the middle masses are that they make up a large proportion of the citizens and have many interests more important to their lives than politics. Most such people are almost totally uninvolved in politics, except perhaps to vote. When they do express political opinions or vote, it generally has been in terms of traditional identifications with groups they have come rightly or wrongly to associate with their own self-interests. The middle masses do not feel they can afford the luxury of broader concerns.

Occasionally, but with nonlasting effects, some of the middle masses may be drawn from traditional predispositions. Generally, this is when they are acting out some kind of good-citizen role in response to appeals with moral overtones. Less frequently they may be moved with lasting effects to new opinions or political action. This occurs only as the result of what they consider a major reevaluation of what their self-interest really is.

Such deviations from predispositions, whether long-term or transitory, occur because events have caused some of the middle masses to look at politics in a different way. These events may be felt personally and directly, but more frequently they are experienced through the secondary influences of the mass media or of a political campaign. In these ways, the middle masses may, from time to time, be jolted into reconsidering the need for political action outside of the well-worn ruts of traditional response.

TORKELSON AND KOWALSKI PICK UP THE TAB

A typical citizen of the middle masses is not easily politicized. Let us assume we are talking about Oswald Torkelson, the mailman. Getting information about politics or participating in politics always requires that Torkelson pay some opportunity costs in terms of the limited monetary, time, or energy resources he possesses. If he chooses one option, he reduces or eliminates his opportunity to choose an alternative. Thus when Mrs. Torkelson tells him that the school-board candidates are coming to PTA the same night that the Miss Universe contest is on TV, he has to choose how he is going to spend his evening. Even Torkelson cannot easily be in two places at once.

These opportunity costs are of two types, absolute and differential, and it is well to distinguish between them. The absolute monetary price of running for the city council may be the same for Pete Kowalski, a General Motors production line worker who makes $150 a week take-home pay, as for William H. (Cold) Cash, the corporate executive who lives in posh, suburban Vertigo Heights. But the worker, Kowalski, and the executive, Cash, experience these absolute costs differently. For Kowalski, shelling out $500 for literature and lawn signs may mean giving up his summer vacation plans. To Cash, spending $500 is scarcely noticeable. We first examine the impact of these differential political costs and then discuss the ongoing significance of the other type of opportunity costs, absolute political costs.

Differential political costs are mainly the result of marked differences in personal income, status, occupational position, and education. Low income, for example, limits the opportunity to gain information. Relatively expensive out-of-town newspapers, such as the *New York Times*, are a luxury. Those with low incomes settle for radio or TV or the local paper where costs are less and the stories are shorter—the *Times* tells the typical reader more than he wants to know about most subjects, thus wasting his time, a precious asset. (The same is, of course, true for political participation for those at the poverty level. What is less commonly noted, however, is that the lower-middle and working classes may find the differential costs higher than those of the lowest class, those on welfare, who may be subsidized and often have time on their hands.)

Low income also limits political action. Running for Congress would mean foregoing actual wages for Pete Kowalski, because of the time missed from the job, or for Smiling Lucifer Luxton, the used-car man, time away from the lot. Any requirements that make political participation more costly affect this involvement. The costs of attending weekend party conventions in a city 100 miles away or even of having to make a special trip to city hall during working hours to register to vote or of standing in a long line at 7:30 P.M. to exercise this privilege, or of traveling through a rain or snow storm to get to the polls represent costs that discourage participation among the middle masses. (Upper-middle-class voters are also affected, but to a lesser extent for various reasons, and they, in any case, feel a greater obligation to vote, so the marginal sacrifice seems less.) The costs of making a living may also drain away energy. Torkelson, after a hard day with the dogs on his route, may decide to conserve his energy and rest his aching feet watching the lovely ladies on TV rather than going to that school-board meeting.

RAISING THE COSTS—A MEANS FOR EXCLUSION

Political costs of participation can be added to by design and elites have used this technique very effectively in discouraging participation by those of low status. This has frequently been the strategy of "racism," but it has also been directed at other lower-status groups such as immigrants or temporary residents. In an *apartheid* society political participation is made impossible for the discriminated-against groups by law. The methods formerly used in the United States after 1865, such as intimidation or making the process more complicated, as in the white primary, the poll tax, or overly detailed registration procedures, were more subtle. Another method, property qualifications to vote in bond-issue elections, was the rule in four states until recently. Even the voting machine may create such costs. All who are to some degree downgraded socially, whether women, blacks, the uneducated, the young, or the foreign-born, are differentially affected by such additions of participation costs, as studies by political scientists indicate.

The same factors work in respect to occupational position. Where one's occupation places one in a communications network that gives information about politics and encourages participation, involvement rises. Members of the elite, of course, are the most likely to be so placed. Thus the professional man or the Main Street merchant, but also the college student who is made to feel a duty to vote and who can visit the polls during the day at his convenience when voting is likely to be light, will pay lower involvement costs.

Education reduces political costs because the educated have more political information to start with, can better judge the value to themselves of getting more information, are more likely to know how to go about collecting and analyzing more information, and will be able to fit what they learn into some realistic conceptual scheme. Thus when Senator Herman B. Schurtz outlines his proposal for reducing poverty, the educated would likely know who he is, what kinds of political assumptions he holds, how realistic these assumptions may be, and how to get more information about him and his proposal if they want it.

These are the major sources of differential costs and it is important to recognize that they are built into the social structure of *every* society. It is also important to emphasize that reducing the differential impact of political information and participation costs is what much of the struggle that has characterized American politics since Jefferson's election in 1800 has been about. The legal right to vote has been steadily broadened and some of the most blatant discriminatory procedures have been eliminated. Some inhibitions still remain and will continue as long as there are even minor differentiations of wealth, status, and power; which means that we will never reach political perfection.

If we could at a stroke eliminate or even sharply reduce all these differential costs to an acceptable minimal level, the absolute political costs in themselves would, however, be enough to cause significant differences in political involvement. The

structures and rules of society set absolute costs and not everyone has the same inclination to pay them. Thus the monetary cost
of effectively running for U.S. senator against an incumbent in a
competitive state such as Ohio may approach one million dollars
no matter who the candidate is. The cost in time of registering to
vote may be a twenty-minute trip to city hall. The cost in energy
for distributing literature for a candidate door to door around
one's block is a fixed amount for everyone on the block. Whoever
decides to participate politically in such ways can at a minimum
expect to pay at least these same absolute costs. Even if the
low-income, low-status, and uneducated people would no longer
be discriminated against, the large middle mass would continue to
choose to remain uninvolved politically most of the time. Everyone's time and energy are limited and the middle mass of citizens
can be expected to choose different ways by which to invest their
efforts, with politics probably not rated high on the list of most
persons.

POLITICS—LOW PRIORITY FOR MOST

It is perhaps comforting for the reader to imagine that the kind of
person we have been describing as middle mass is a confused and
misguided Archie Bunker in need of help from his betters. Yet if
the reader looks around himself carefully, he will find most
people he knows and respects fit into this group and so probably
does he himself. Most informed people conclude that the middle
masses are right—there are usually (or certainly *seem* to be) more
important things in life than politics.

  The major thrust of most people's lives will always be in
other than political directions—deep involvement with a job,
particularly if one is just establishing him or herself in a career
such as selling real estate, starting a law practice (even one as a
Nader raider), being a dentist, or even being a preacher; court-
ship, marriage, and raising a family, or some other creative effort,
as well as enjoyment of the good things of life as they define them
for themselves—reading historical biography, camping out, attending X-rated movies, travel, social climbing, gardening, bowl-
ing or golf, collecting antiques, spectator sports, symphony
concerts, flying kites, activities described on women's pages,
birdwatching, cooking, watching TV, or living in and taking care
of a nice home in a nice neighborhood, or amusing oneself with

any one of the million other activities that can be enjoyed within a modern and affluent society.

This does not mean that the middle masses will take no interest in, or will not on occasion devote some effort to, political matters. Torkelson cannot enjoy the Miss Universe contest quite as much knowing that perhaps he should be with his wife at PTA. Even the major investments of effort into a few activities that all of us make leave some free time for occasional investment in whatever interests us at the moment. Many citizens, even of the middle masses, regard it as their civic duty to vote occasionally and maintain some superficial interest in candidates and elections. Usually this is for the big event such as the presidential election. Less frequently, it is in state or local elections. Even when major bond issues or state constitutional amendments are being voted upon, the average citizen may elect to pass. In such elections information costs often seem to be too high for the potential payoff that is expected, so the typical middle-mass citizen lets those who seem to know something about it turn out and decide the outcome.

Of course the interests of the middle masses are not wholly disregarded in the political arena. Candidates continue to bid for their support or scheme to keep them from getting riled up, and occasional middle-mass interest and activity—or threat of it—is sufficient to gain them some political payoffs.

NOTES

1 Herbert Marcuse, *One-dimensional Man,* Beacon Press, Boston, 1964.
2 See Arthur M. Schlesinger, Jr., *The Age of Jackson,* Little, Brown and Company, Boston, 1945; Glyndon Van Deusen, *The Jacksonian Era: 1828–1848,* Harper & Row, New York, 1959; Marvin Meyers, *The Jacksonian Persuasion, Politics and Belief,* Random House, Inc., New York, 1960.

Chapter 3

Establishment Viewpoints: Supporters of the Regime

We have already noted that every social and political system has an elite or leadership group. Some people have more influence than do others over the direction society and its politics take. These are the people who hold important positions (or play significant roles) in the major segments of society: in business, industry, government, the high-status professions, and organized labor. Because some roles are more important to a society than are others, an elite always exists, not just in America, but in the most socialistic of nations. That is what Robert Michels, a famous political scientist of two generations ago, called the "iron law of oligarchy." ("Oligarchy" means government by the few.)

For purposes of stereotyping, the elite usually has a nickname, a term that often carries with it implications concerning the ordinary citizen's and the dissenting citizen's attitudes toward the elite. One segment of turn-of-the-century society called itself "the 400" after Ward McAlester put only that many names in his "blue book" of people "worth knowing." Others, less reverent, designated the same group as the "upper crust." The elite of England was once known as "the aristocracy," which carried connotations of respect. On the other hand, the current American vogue term, "the Establishment," which includes elite as well as the followers who accept their assumptions, carries overtones of suspicion, conspiracy, unconscious envy, and lack of a sense of community.

Every member of an elite has the ability to share in decision making, which is one definition of "power." The sources of power are many. Role is significant; sometimes it is earned—the "self-made man"—sometimes it results from power someone else has earlier accumulated. One doubts that Henry Ford II would be chairman of the board of the Ford Motor Company if he were not—well, Henry Ford II. Power results from such things as role, wealth, high status, or fame (for whatever reason—some congressmen first rose above the undifferentiated mass as Olympic stars, or actors, for example), the ability to deliver votes (a professional politician or a labor leader), leisure time, or specialized knowledge. Motivation, when accompanied by other traits, may be an important source of power. Richard M. Nixon, for example, came from a lower-middle-class family, his father was poor and a nobody, but the son almost literally willed himself into the White House.

A dominant elite has its base in power, then, but the way that power is used depends upon the ideology of its membership. Power need not be used, of course. It may lie fallow for long periods of time, for a member of the elite may be more interested in playing polo or chasing women, say, than he is in influencing public policy. And he will not likely use his power unless he *believes* that something needs doing. But when he speaks, he is listened to.

There is a tendency among those outside of the elite, and particularly those who are resentful or suspicious of its leadership position, to think of the leadership as a homogeneous group, with shared values, goals, and political commitment. The elite is, however, vastly more complex than that, particularly in the United States, but probably in nearly all modern nations. This chapter will concern itself with the matter of identifying the American Establishment, how its members behave, particularly in relation to political matters, the assumptions they make about politics, and what they want from life in general and government in particular.

IDEOLOGICAL VARIETIES

When things go wrong, many people think it was planned that way—someone else brought it about. The reaction is paranoiac:

"They" are to blame. A basic question of political analysis is who the "they" are, how much influence over events "they" have, and under what conditions "they" can exert this influence.

Both members of the elite and ordinary citizens may be located along a curvilinear continuum on the basis of their assumptions about how the system should or could operate, about the kinds of social arrangements that are desirable and the part that government should play in bringing them about. Commonly we assign people to classifications from the reactionary on the far right to the radical on the far left. (See Figure 3-1.) This suggests the degree to which they would want to change the distribution of powers in society and the rules of the game for gaining power. If we could picture this continuum in three dimensions, we could also add to it a time factor, with emerging new versions of these ideologies entering their appropriate points in the continuum and older points of view becoming less meaningful to the contemporary political scene and therefore fading into the background. Hence, we have the New Left after the Old Left of the 1930s and 1940s, nineteenth-century liberalism, and the liberalism of the 1930s through the 1960s.

The Right   On the far right within the complex group that is the governing elite is a small collection of reactionaries. These are people who would like to turn the clock back to their version of a better earlier day, one which they have usually romanticized.

The Political Continuum

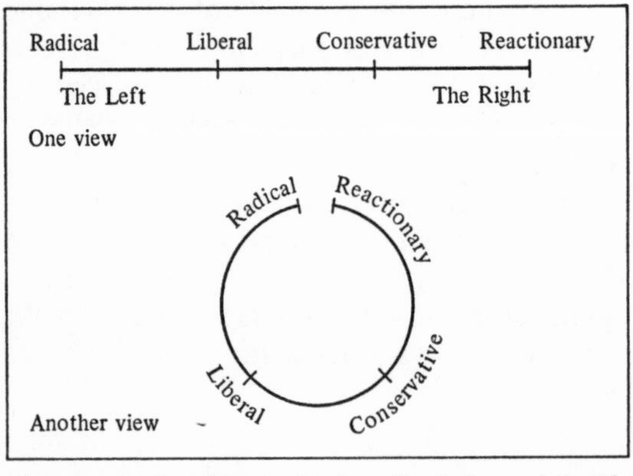

The extremists in politics tend to be authoritarians and sometimes jump from the far left to the far right or vice versa.

Figure 3-1 Political views may be tolerant or intolerant.

They are populists of a special kind. That is, they believe that the ordinary people are good and really quite sensible if left to themselves. Right-wingers are suspicious of elites, seeing America as being dominated by one that is made up of the "Eastern Establishment, controlled by Wall Street." To the reactionary, the country has gone past its ideal civilization, which was to be found in rural and small-town America, with its God-fearing people dedicated to law, order, and love of country. True, they say, people are basically good, but they are, unfortunately, easily misled.

The small but noisy reactionary groups want minimal government in the style of the nineteenth century, but they also see it as a useful and usable instrument by which to restore the conditions of "the good old days." A relatively few members of the leadership elite are reactionaries. They are particularly to be found among those persons who have gone from poverty to great riches. But these are only a comparative handful in number. Unlike the reactionaries, most members of any leadership group are hard-headed realists who have little time for romantic views of a better world as it presumably might exist under some other conditions.

The wealthy reactionaries do supply generous funds to various right-wing groups, but the great bulk of the support for reactionary candidates, for persons like Barry Goldwater who ran for the Presidency in 1964, comes from middle-mass America, not from the Establishment. (Goldwater referred to himself as a conservative, and still does, but by the terms used in this book and by most political analysts, he was a reactionary, looking backward to what his imagination described as the best kind of America.)

The Conservatives Probably most members of the American Establishment are conservatives and consider themselves to be such. Like all conservatives, they accept the world as it is, as a "given," and see it as being not at all bad—because they have reached the top or somewhere where they want to be, under the existing rules. They want only to get on with their individual activities. Conservatives are not opposed to all change, as is the image of them that is encouraged by their opponents. Instead, they believe that the burden of proof should be upon those who would make changes in the prevailing system. In contrast to liberals and radicals, they believe the odds are that change is likely to worsen rather than improve a situation if it is undertaken at too great a speed or with too few precautions. And they seem to be much more aware than are persons in other parts of the political spectrum of the great uncertainties that accompany the adoption of new public policies.

Unlike reactionaries, or for that matter liberals and radicals, conservatives reject a romantic view of life and emphasize the need to be "realistic" and "practical." (Most of them can afford to take such an attitude.) Unlike their other political brethren, they oppose all forms of populism and accept the need for a leadership elite. (Even conservatives who are not members of the elite do so.) In rejecting a romantic view of life, conservatives express real doubts about any possible "perfectability" of man and see the typical human being as a person of modest capabilities. Conservatives find democracy not the best system of government, but rather about the best we can hope for. And as for the people ruling themselves, the conservative might ask this question: "Would you trust your life to people who believe television advertising?"

Conservatives can be divided along a time dimension. The *traditional conservatives* emphasize individual freedom and advocate a laissez faire economic policy to the greatest extent possible. Along with Thomas Carlyle, they see government as being "anarchy plus the constable." They prefer government to perform only the traditional functions of preserving law and order and enforcing contracts and other business arrangements.

In the nineteenth century, these conservatives were known as "liberals." About a century ago, Thomas Hill Green, lecturing at Oxford University, emphasized that government could do more than preserve and protect individual freedoms, that it could become a positive aid to the individual.[1] Green's ideas, which strongly influenced the future governing elite in both Great Britain and the United States, laid the foundation for "welfare state" liberalism. The old or pre-Green liberalism then gradually came to be considered a conservative ideology and is almost universally so viewed in the United States today. Few Americans know that historically traditional conservatism arose along with the Industrial Revolution in the late eighteenth century as a liberal ideology. Indeed, with its emphasis upon the individual rather than the collective good of the community and society, traditional conservatism is still correctly categorized as a form of liberalism.

A *new conservatism* has gradually been emerging in response to welfare-state liberalism and, particularly, to its costly failures. This new conservatism tends to emphasize the notion that the needs of community and society are sometimes greater than those of the individual, while at the same time accepting the basic idea of democracy as the most acceptable form of government because government is a necessary institution for the maintenance of social stability and the achievement of justice. These new conservatives, like the older ones, reject populism and emphasize the need for a ruling elite in both government and the economy, an elite based upon incentive, foresight, education, knowledge, and intelligence. Although accepting the need for and indeed the desirability of a class system in society, the modern American conservatives accept a basically open-class system in which anyone has a chance to reach high status irrespective of background. In other words, they accept a system of status by achievement rather than by ascription.

The sense of social obligation is strong among the new conservatives and they often accept governmental positions at considerable sacrifice in time or money or both. Unlike the old conservatives, the modern ones are not opposed to all-but-minimal governmental services and activities. As with all conservatives, however, they believe that the burden of proof is upon those who would make changes in social policy and they recognize the difficulty—because of bureaucratic inertia and vested interests—involved in abolishing a policy once it is adopted, no matter how ineffective it may be.

They give strong support, however, to policies that do achieve or approximate their goals. For example, the old conservatives opposed the establishment in the 1930s of the Federal Deposit Insurance Corporation (FDIC) as being socialistic (which it was) and governmental interference in an area of business (which it was). But the FDIC has been immensely successful; indeed no depositor has ever taken a loss on an insured account since the corporation became active. Modern conservatives give their full support to this type of successful governmental activity.

On the other hand, they are highly suspect of such things as the antipoverty program, which was undertaken with little or no knowledge as to whether it would be of any enduring help to poor people. (Over its first several years, the program appears to have had little or no impact upon the condition of poor people and the hundreds of millions of dollars spent have benefited primarily middle-class employees of the Office of Economic Opportunity and the local organizations it has spawned, as well as middle-class businessmen. For example, an antipoverty program for the "eradication" of rats in the Los Angeles ghettos paid the salaries of many bureaucrats and put a great deal of money into exterminator firms. It did not, of course, eliminate the slum rats or even reduce their number except for a few months.)

The Liberals   Today's *conventional liberals* are advocates of the welfare state, as mentioned above. They had beginnings in America at least as far back as the time of Theodore Roosevelt at the beginning of the twentieth century, but most of the ideas of Establishment liberalism date from the New Deal period of the 1930s or later. They tend toward the romantic view that human beings are inherently "good" and potentially "wise." The leadership elite tends to be populistic with a strong sense of *noblesse oblige*. The members believe that government can furnish programs that will make life better for all and that government can be structured so as to provide equal treatment for all individuals.

The number of old liberals among the elite is not great, but these people have provided the connecting link between business and government for at least forty years, particularly during liberal presidential administrations. These old liberals emphasize the achievement of social reform through the orderly and legal institutions of government and they often call for some degree, usually quite unspecified, of redistribution of the wealth within society. Having had little or no experience with the life-style or outlook of poor people, skilled workers, or members of the lower-middle class, they tend to create social reality in their own minds, probably often projecting wishful thinking rather than available concrete data.

A modification of the liberal ideology began to appear in the late 1960s and continued into the 1970s. In general, this *new liberalism* differed from the older form primarily in that instead of emphasizing government as an instrumentality for furthering the interests of all people, it came to concentrate more upon the use of government to alleviate the problems of the poor and particularly of racial minorities. This upper-middle-class liberalism has perhaps most definitely been colored by a sense of guilt, a feeling that people who have had the advantages of large incomes should seek to aid the most impoverished members of the society and to stop the squandering of natural resources. But their sense of *noblesse oblige*—the obligation of the nobility that has existed in Europe from feudal times—stems from different motivations from those of the conservative aristocrat, who feels no guilt.

These new upper-middle-class liberals have passed on this sense of guilt and concern to their children, some of whom have become anti-Establishment activists and radicals. That is, unlike their parents, the offspring have been less willing to work within the established polity.

Many organizations have been created or enlarged in membership by the new upper-middle-class liberals because their goals seem to be humanitarian or an improvement over existing conditions, but the do-gooders may not recognize the full implications of the programs of such groups. For example, the Sierra Club has fostered a well-meaning type of conservation program that would improve the natural environment of the nation, but if the club's policies were adopted as national policy, the result would be to deprive many moderate- to low-income families of vacations in natural settings. The economic implications of policies advocated by upper-middle-class environmentalists have been scarcely noticed by their advocates. Indeed, this is a common characteristic of the new liberals: They are unaware of or ignore the implications of the opportunity costs discussed in Chapter 1.

Another organization strongly supported by the upper-middle-class new liberals is the American Civil Liberties Union, an organization founded in 1920. Except for some criminal lawyers and judges, most of its 170,000 members have had no direct experience with the problems of law enforcement or with the consequences that arise when a dangerous criminal is freed to move about in society. Civil liberties tend to be treated as an end in themselves rather than as a means by which to achieve a more individually satisfying society.

The new liberalism is thus not based upon a cautious and careful analysis of the problems of society and the known ways of coping with those problems, but is rather dominated by feelings of guilt, by idealism, and by a highly incomplete analysis of the costs involved in making major changes in the allocation of social benefits.

The Left A very small proportion of the leadership elite is to be found on the far left politically. These people are followers of what Tom Wolfe has called "radical chic."[2] Persons in this category are usually leaders in areas well removed from politics; particularly they are well known in the fine arts as actors, musical conductors, or painters, or they are the children of the wealthy with no careers of their own. They know little about politics or the problems of the poor or about their life-styles and ideology.

To these dilettante radicals, the support of offbeat causes is simply a fashionable activity, or an unusual and attention-getting hobby. They enjoy such unlikely activities as raising funds for the defense of Black Panthers who have been charged with felonies. They may make contributions to such funds or to the campaign coffers of radical political parties or candidates. But, typically, such persons, although perhaps well known and highly skilled or talented in particular areas of activity, are not politically influential except to the extent that their financial contributions may be helpful.

LESSER LEADERS

It would be difficult to say just where the highest echelons of the elite end. There is no need to be precise. Somewhere below the top decision makers are the less important, less powerful, but still significant leaders of government and the economy. This group includes the middle-class bureaucrats and the middle-range administrators and technicians who handle the complex but routine operations of both government and private industry and business. Technicians and professional persons, including engineers, scientists, ministers, physicians, all are overwhelmingly supportive of the Establishment. And we would have to add to this list the journalists and other members of the mass media who determine not only what it is that the ordinary citizen is to know, but also the manner in which he is to be told. (A generation ago most journalists were conservatives. Typically, they did not have college educations and they often came from modest backgrounds, but their profession permitted them to rub elbows with the wealthy and the famous, and they tended to absorb the conservative values of these people. Today, however, most journalists are college graduates in the social sciences and many have master's degrees. The former conservative bias has now been replaced by a liberal bias in the case of most reporters and even many editors.)

To all the above support groups we would have to add persons who are leaders in areas that many people do not ordinarily think of as being part of the Establishment: leaders in organized labor and leaders of most racial and ethnic groups. These people are establishmentarians because (1) they are leaders, and (2) they wish to work "within the system." In other words, they are not attempting to destroy the existing political organizations, but wish only to modify the distribution of its rewards and benefits.

WHAT THEY WANT

For years a debate has raged, both in the popular press and among political scientists, as to what it is that the dominant elite wants from the system. For what purpose does the leadership rule? How narrowly selfish or how public-oriented is it? There is no simple answer to these questions, it is safe to say, even though some liberals and virtually all radicals believe to the contrary. We have described the elite as being diverse in their ideological views. They are also logically to be assumed to be diverse in their personal goals in life. Some seek wealth, others power, others acceptance by high-status individuals, others to be known and given credit as do-gooders. The number of motivations may well run into the hundreds and the problem of analysis is complicated further by the fact that any individual may be motivated by several perhaps partly contradictory motives. Furthermore, he may have only the vaguest notion of why he does what he does. No wonder that little hard empirical research has been conducted in an attempt to answer the above questions and hence no wonder that we invent our own interpretations of elite motivation.

In political science, the answer to elite motivation is often given in one of two asserted explanations. One is known as "elitist" theory. It holds that the economic-social-political elite shares a common self-interest. These persons rule society for their own profit and advantage. They "exploit" members of the "mass" of society, and give up economic benefits, social status symbols, and political power only to the extent that this is necessary in order for the elite to remain dominant and to keep the *hoi polloi* from becoming unduly restless.

In contrast to this, the "pluralist" theorists hold that there are many motivations within the elite, not all of them compatible with one another. They argue that the "elitist" explanation is too simplistic, that it ignores the complexities of real life, that it assumes more rationality and purpose in the activities of members of the elite than is actually the case, and that it accepts a paranoiac "conspiracy" theory that cannot be justified by observable events. The authors of this book, while not dismissing some partial truths in the "elitist" theory, believe the "pluralists" have the better of the argument and that some "elitists" have been

misled into a conclusion that the "pluralists" deny the existence
of an elite, which surely no sophisticated "pluralist" does.
Furthermore, we conclude that the controversy between the two
theories is often more a matter of rhetoric than of difference in
kind and that much of the controversy has been polemical rather
than analytical in character.[3]

The "elitist-pluralist" debate has, in any case, been characterized mostly by differences concerning what the individual
elitist wants from the system. This approach reflects the liberal
concern for the individual and a conceptualization of him as the
unit of analysis in politics. It is probably much more fruitful to
take a collective approach and ask what it is that the elite as a
whole wants from the political system. After all, very few
members of the elite, whether they are to be found on the far
right, the far left, or somewhere in between, are truly revolutionaries who would destroy the basic system and replace it with
something utterly different. A person within the elite but on the
far right may have romantic dreams of a better system based
upon fancied conditions of years gone by, but still one basically
the same as we have today, in need, merely, of some corrections.
An elitist on the left may believe, perhaps naïvely, that social
equality and economic security can be extended to all citizens,
but he does not view himself or his life-style as being doomed to
destruction in the process of achieving these changes. Individual
goals may differ widely, but collective elitist goals are largely
homogeneous and can be described with a reasonable degree of
accuracy.

What most of the American elite wants in a well-functioning
system is social stability and economic growth. The former is
largely a prerequisite for the latter. Any nation that is badly
divided internally by riots or rebellions or the threat of these is
certain to have difficulty in producing goods and services which in
turn will exacerbate the conflict. Social stability—law, order, and
a sense of prevailing justice—are hence the first order of business
of any elite. Even Establishment liberals prefer to effect change
at a rate slow enough so as not to cause much dysfunctional
social unrest.

Economic growth is generally preferred by both liberals and
conservatives over a steady-state economy for the simple reason
that it is through this method that it is easier to respond to
demands that are made upon the system for a higher standard of
living.

Recent calls by some liberals for a halt to economic growth
in the interest of preservation of the environment are strong

enough that they cannot be ignored, but they are not likely to change the emphasis by much, for a steady or declining level of economic production would result in a lower standard of living among some or all segments of the nonelite. The resulting social dissatisfaction would be too great for the system to bear easily. The opportunity costs for a really clean environment—given existing technology—are too high to pay.

The American elite has generally been able to maintain social stability, although this is always difficult to accomplish in a society devoted to rapid change and there have been some rough moments when the stableness of the system has been seriously challenged. The summer ghetto riot has occurred from time to time in American cities since the 1830s and so have other kinds of disorders going back to the Whiskey Rebellion of 1794, when Pennsylvania farmers reacted violently against a federal tax on the whiskey they were making. And on the occasion of the Civil War, a condition of instability arose because of the inability of the system to find an area of agreement within itself concerning the issue of slavery. More recently, the Watergate scandal raised doubts about system stability.

The mature American economy no longer expands at a very great rate, but the productivity of the system is so enormous that it has been possible to avoid populistic pressures to redistribute the wealth. Indeed, there is some evidence to indicate that a disproportionate share of economic expansion is being absorbed by the nation's economic elite so that wealth is actually still slowly being concentrated into fewer and fewer hands.[4] This does not mean that no redistribution is taking place, of course. The black middle class, for example, has greatly increased in size in the last generation, a fact that is often not noticed simply because the proportion of blacks in the middle class is much smaller in relation to the total black population than is the case with whites. Within the working class, there has been a considerable redistribution of income. As a result of the efforts of organized labor, the share going to union members has increased while that for nonunion labor has decreased. However, the total share of the gross national product going to members of the working class has remained virtually unchanged throughout the twentieth century.[5]

HOW THEY BEHAVE

Members of the elite in any society are the pace-setters and pattern setters. They are the high-status, successful people and they will therefore be emulated. As a result, whatever may be their private ideas or personal behavior patterns, they are aware of the need to project a particular type of image, one that they would want to have respected and widely imitated. Most of the members of the leadership elite consider themselves to be practical and realistic in their outlook on life and its problems. They realize that their decisions will have important results and will affect the lives of many people. That is, they recognize that they cannot engage in grand theorizing and that they are not dealing with hypothetical situations. The recognition that they are dealing with real-life problems and that their decisions will have real-life results tends to make most establishmentarians conservative and unwilling to take chances with the unknown and untried policy.

Characteristically, persons who have been members of the leadership elite for more than one generation develop a sense of *noblesse oblige*. The size of the true aristocracy in America is very small but with the exception of only a few families, this sense of obligation to use one's wealth and status for the benefit of society in general is very strong. It is perhaps best exemplified by such families as the Roosevelts and Rockefellers. However, even in the case of the first-generation self-made man, the sense of an obligation for public service is strong. At the same time, this conventional behavior is highly functional for the purposes of maintaining elite control, for there is a good deal of exchange of executive-level persons between business and industry on the one hand and government on the other. To a large extent, the persons who go into temporary governmental service will vary according to whether the presidential administration is liberal or conservative, but every administration uses some persons from the economic elite who are of various ideological persuasions. All kinds of persons from business and industry are brought into government service from time to time, but bankers and lawyers tend to predominate.

Many members of the elite spend a good deal of their time on what is often called "do-gooder" activities. These involve various kinds of charitable efforts and the volunteering of time for various purposes. This kind of activity is important for purposes of encouraging social stability, for it indicates that the elite is concerned about the common man and even the poor and destitute. Such activities are, of course, simply one aspect of the sense of *noblesse oblige*.

Another important activity of the members of the elite is to make contributions to political campaigns. Such persons provide both the major proportion of the large amount of money that is required in order to mount a modern campaign as well as special skills that are useful in the campaign. In addition, the candidates for the major political offices—those for President, senator, congressman, governor—are members of the elite, though not necessarily at the highest level.

Finally, the American elite, like that in many other nations, permits and encourages the important process of co-optation. That is, members of the elite are constantly on the watch for persons from lower strata who show potential for leadership at the highest levels. Persons of such ability present a threat if they are not brought into the dominant elite, for they are likely otherwise to form a counterelite that could then seek to take control by either legal or illegal means. Because the elite has many resources, including wealth and high-status positions, that it can bestow upon the newcomer of ability, it can usually convince such persons that they are best off to "work within the system." It is through this process of co-optation that the leadership elite finds an important means of maintaining itself in power.

The Establishment is thus made up of the most successful people in any social system as measured by the values of that system. This elite has, typically, the necessary resources to govern for long periods of time, often for centuries, because of its control of wealth, talent, the symbols of success, and perhaps above all, of the means by which to co-opt potential members of counterelites. It controls not only the most prestigeful positions in a social system, but also the routes by which one advances toward those positions.

NOTES

1 T. H. Green, *Lectures on the Principles of Political Obligation,* reprinted by Longmans, Green & Co., Ltd., London, 1950, and "Liberal Legislation and Freedom of Contract," in *Works,* vol. 3 (1888). Reprinted by Longmans, Green, & Co., Ltd., London, 1906–1918. For a sophisticated, if unconvincing, criticism of the new conservatism, see Joseph Epstein, "The New Conservatives," *Dissent,* Spring 1973, pp. 151–162.

2　Tom Wolfe, *Radical Chic and Mau-Mauing the Flak Catchers,* Farrar, Straus & Giroux, New York, 1970.

3　The elitist position is given in Peter Bachrach, *The Theory of Democratic Elitism, A Critique,* Little, Brown and Company, Boston, 1967; the pluralist in Nelson W. Polsby, *Community Power and Political Theory,* Yale University Press, New Haven, 1963, as well as in the works of Robert A. Dahl and David Truman.

4　Frank Ackerman et al., "Income Distribution in the United States," *Review of Radical Political Economics,* 3:20–43, Summer 1971. Reprinted in K. M. Dolbeare and M. J. Edelman (eds.), *Institutions, Policies, and Goals,* D. C. Heath and Company, Lexington, Mass., 1973, pp. 227–247.

5　*Ibid.*

Chapter 4

Anti-Establishment Viewpoints: Critics of the Regime

Within every political system there is opposition to the entrenched power holders. There are always discontented people in any system. They may express their attitudes through strikes and demonstrations, but more commonly through various forms of criminal activity. It is striking that in our own age, when the system's legitimacy has been severely questioned, crime has increased sharply. Bus drivers no longer feel it safe to make change, the danger of being mugged seems to increase steadily in large cities, while drug addiction and alcoholism appear to be at an all-time high.

Persons who seek their own goals outside the system through a life of crime are not of central interest to us here. Instead, we will be concerned with the organized opponents of the dominant elite. These people have their leaders in *the counterelite.* Opposition may come only from politicians who wish to be elected to office through democratic means and who propose to make only mild or no policy changes at all; these we have already included within the elite itself. However, there are others, persons who wish to destroy the entire existing system through revolutionary action and to establish a different kind of regime. In between are those who move back and forth, sometimes taking a revolutionary line, but not acting on it—in fact, holding on to their current resources and seeking to gain even more under the current rules while verbally condemning the system.

In Cuba, there is opposition to the Fidel Castro establishment, just as Castro had previously led the opposition to the government of Fulgencio Batista. Those who opposed the established power of both Batista and Castro have always been confronted by the possibility of drastic and probably fatal punishment if apprehended. The same was true of the Nazi regime in Germany. In contrast, in the United States and many other democracies, a wide range of dissent is tolerated and sometimes actually encouraged. Behavior that could lead to a death sentence in Cuba, China, or many other nations is tolerated with a reasonable degree of cheerfulness by the Establishment.

However, neither in the United States nor in any other country is there complete toleration of dissent. Fundamentally, the first law of the state—any state—is its own survival. Behavior or threatened behavior that is seen as potentially destructive of the fundamental belief and behavior systems of the Establishment may be prevented or punished. The Establishment within a given political system may be tolerant and survive, but only an elite that has no concern for its own future can afford the luxury of being foolish or naïve.

The most extreme antiestablishmentarians are revolutionaries. A revolution is any change in the basic rules by which the rules are made, if this is accomplished by illegal means. A revolution need not involve the shedding of blood, although it often does. By the very nature of government and social organization, the odds are almost always against the success of any rebellion that is designed to bring about a revolution. Usually, the odds are very long indeed. Revolutionaries, however, either believe that life under the current regime is so unsatisfactory that the odds are worth risking, or they simply believe so firmly that what they are doing is right that they fail to recognize the nature of the long chances they are taking.

Punishment for attempted revolution has historically been very severe. It is somewhat less so in the United States than in many other nations, past and present, in which any identified revolutionary often suffers summary execution. Even so, the actions of judges, juries, and parole boards in the United States are probably affected by the traditional and logical hostility that is shown toward those who would destroy the prevailing system.

Thus apologists for such revolutionary groups as the Black Panthers and the Weathermen are probably right in suggesting that their punishment for crimes is more severe than it would be if those crimes were not of a political character.

Most leaders of the anti-Establishment are only play-actor revolutionaries, who may think they wish to make extensive changes in the social system, usually in relation to the allocation system for economic goods. But typically they have no plans to pay the costs of this action. Such dissenters generally believe that the present system does not provide for an adequate degree of economic or social justice, but typically they are not quite certain they want to destroy American democracy; they only want to redefine it. The same is true for civil rights and liberties and for the system of economic production. (It should be kept in mind that antiestablishmentarians are to be found both on the left and on the right, but not anywhere very near the center.)

The Extremist Syndrome   The extremists who oppose the ruling elite tend to share certain characteristics whether they are radicals or reactionaries, that is, on the far left or the far right. All such extremists tend to believe that they have the correct answers to cure the ills of society. They tend to be rather paranoiac in their view of the world, that is, to see the ruling elite as operating a conscious conspiracy against those persons and things that the extremist views as being particularly important. They feel persecuted, threatened, and fearful. (The 1972 finance chairman of the right-wing American Party—actor Walter Brennan—said that his party was "not committed to the big money establishment that dominates both of the old political parties.")

Because they have, in their own minds, answers to social questions, they do not need data and are impatient with those who wish to study problems before acting. In particular, they are contemptuous of data that are not supportive of their strategies and goals. People who have "answers" do not need data. Again, because they have "answers" which they consider to be principles, the extremists are generally incapable of much compromise. Their organizations typically encompass a very small segment of the political continuum and divisions within the organization are notoriously common, as is also the tendency for groups to splinter off and form their own organizations. For example, within a half-dozen years after it was organized, many of the members of Students for a Democratic Society (SDS) had left the organization in disillusionment. Those remaining had split up into at least three factions: the Weathermen, advocates of the necessity for violence in order to disrupt and terrorize the Establishment; a Maoist faction; and a third, more conventional group. These and others all claim to be the true SDS organization, although in fact, internal differences had caused the organization to fall apart and cease to exist early in the 1970s.

Another characteristic of extremists, more particularly those on the left, is an inability either to lead or to follow. In contrast to successful revolutionary leaders like Washington, Lenin, Mao, and Castro, the typical left-wing American is not accustomed either to making difficult decisions or to disciplining himself in order to follow the instructions of competent leaders. This is probably so because such persons in the United States typically come from upper-middle-class families where they have not experienced deprivation or discipline and have been accustomed to receiving whatever they want at the asking. The notions of adversity, sacrifice, hard work, and discipline were not a part of their training. As a result, many (not all) of the young, self-fancied revolutionaries on college campuses in the late 1960s lacked the rigid discipline that is necessary to bring about successful major social change, whether revolutionary or not. And, with a few exceptions such as Mark Rudd, who led one of the last major student protests at Columbia University and who effectively outgeneraled the president of Columbia,[1] the typical campus anti-Establishment leader of the period was someone who lacked the skills to organize a paper route, much less a revolution.[2]

THE NEW LEFT

The New Left was formed in the mid-1960s, primarily by college students who had been born after World War II and who had experienced only the prosperity enjoyed by their indulging upper-middle-class parents. The name, as is so often the case, was bestowed by the press and was designed to distinguish its members from the left that had existed from the 1920s and was now, of course, promptly designated the Old Left. The Old Left, which continues to exist with a small membership, can be distinguished from the newer variety by its much greater intellectualism and, consequently, its emphasis upon theoretical ideas. The Old Left generally followed the line of Soviet Communism or of the Trotskyites. Differences and organizational fragmentation stemmed largely from disagreements over ideas. In contrast, the

New Left was not ideologically rigid. It tended to be antiintellectual, and differences among its membership centered on differences as to tactics and goals for achieving a new social system.

SDS Forever... Well, for Six Years Probably the best known New Left organization was that of the Students for a Democratic Society (SDS). Members of this loosely organized group got together in the summer of 1965 at Port Huron, Michigan, and drew up a statement concerning the beliefs of the group. (It has been reprinted in many anthologies.) The Port Huron "statement" is an expression of what these young people believed to be wrong with American society, dwelling particularly upon racial discrimination, militarism, and the unequal distribution of wealth. It is, of course, easy for any group to express dissatisfaction with existing conditions. It does not require much thought or effort to do that. It is quite another thing, however, to propose alternative programs and the process by which they can be achieved. In the half-dozen years of its lifetime, SDS never was able to come up with a constructive, positive program. It was quick to suggest what it did not like about contemporary society, but was never able to move beyond that point. Its youthful members were always impatient with practical problems. Members were fond of saying something like: "After the revolution, we will worry about who is going to pick up the garbage."

Persons of the New Left never favored that term, no doubt because it implied that they were a dissident group on the periphery of the American pattern of development. Instead, they tended to use the term "the Movement," which carries implications of self-importance and dedication. By the early 1970s, this ill-conceived, ill-led, ill-planned movement seemed to be dead. What had it accomplished? One critic made the following observation:

> It has justified massive budget cuts for American education. It has made "student" a term of opprobrium in many parts of the society. It has messed up some lives with narcotics and embittered, if not a whole generation, at least a part of a generation by raising the hope that complex questions could be answered by quick and simple solutions.
>
> In fact, about all it really accomplished in a positive way was to influence the fashions of an era. And while long hair, beards, rock music, marijuana, bell-bottom trousers, and nudity are something of a change, they are scarcely a revolution in any sense that the word has ever previously conveyed.[3]

Has Anyone Seen the Third Consciousness? Perhaps the most popular work dealing with the ideas of the New Left was published by Charles A. Reich, a man trained in the law rather than in the social sciences.[4] He wrote after the first flush of hope and belief that there would be a widespread and spontaneous response to the revolutionary call of the New Left. He gave new heart to "the Movement" by suggesting that the new politics or new America would come not from reform or violent revolution, but through a new life-style of young adults which he labeled "Consciousness III." In keeping with the views of the New Left, he saw this new consciousness as coming from the grass roots— as if the typical dissenting college student represented the American grass roots. The book is either naïve or hypocritical, for what Reich describes and advocates is a simplistically op- timistic view of what the human being could be like if he were not confronted by the evil, self-seeking Establishment, the people who have achieved only Consciousness II. He argues that the affluent society is one in which we can "believe in the goodness of man." Like the old-time anarchists, he concludes that "the politics of controlling man become unimportant" under current circumstances. He sees antagonism as being "derived from scarcity." Surely, he must know that the tendency toward antagonism, hostility, aggressiveness, and violence is not a result of scarcity, but of uncertainty. The human being is insecure, filled with doubt and dread, and in constant need for reassurance; or as Thomas Hobbes (1651) said: He yearns for "safety, income, deference."

Reich was only one of those who flattered (and profited from) those involved in the "Movement" and their sympathizers. His romantic and nonsensical message that these were the people who had the solution to the human riddle and were to be the leaders of the future was irresponsible and misleading. But he was not the only one. Young people were only too happy to believe Kenneth Keniston when he told the same generation of college students that they were morally superior to their prede- cessors. Who would not be pleased by such a message? Even those who realized that it could not be true must have been impressed by it. The same was so of the word sent by Herbert Marcuse, who told this same group of dissenters that they could lead man on to higher and better things if they were to make a quantum jump beyond the knowledge of science to new insights. Similarly, Theodore Roszak told them what they wanted to hear—that their irrational behavior represented a new creativity.[5]

Free Advertising for the Left The New Left has always received a disproportionate amount of attention in the news media. This is in part because newsmen are constantly looking for the dramatic, the unusual, the controversial. Newspapers, despite ever higher levels of education in the United States, still find it more profitable to entertain than to educate their readers. Exactly the same is true of television. Television has the additional advantage of the cameraman's ability to control the width of his lens' angle. The relatively rare person who taunts and stones the police can be isolated from the more typical person, creating in the mind's eye of the six o'clock news watcher the notion that the nation must be close to total revolution. In 1968, it was more dramatic for the mass media to report the campaign as if it were Eugene McCarthy's "children's crusade" that had derailed the Johnson Establishment than it was to report the rather drab fact that most Americans were fed up with the war in Indochina, the endless promises to win it, and the endless failures to perform on those promises because political circumstances would not permit a winning strategy. They created folk heroes out of zany, offbeat publicity seekers, such as Abbie Hoffman and Jerry Rubin and their virtually nonexistent Youth International Party (Yippies).

The mass media were also guilty of distortion concerning the New Left in part because so many newsmen, although not themselves sympathetic to or believers in the New Left, had personal liberal inclinations which they could present incidental to reporting the activities of leftist groups or events that such groups would approve of. The antiestablishmentarianism as well as the antipatriotism and the bias toward nations other than the United States and against American institutions have often been sympathetically reported. As Arnold Beichman has said, "Unlike the other 143 countries in the world, only America is to be judged by the exacting and unattainable standards of a Utopia."[6] For example, in March 1972, the People's Republic of China exploded a very powerful thermonuclear device. (The event was reported not by the Chinese government, but by the U.S. Atomic Energy Commission.) The effect of the explosion was to raise the radiation level over much of the world, including most of the United States. Although the press reported the event, it did not give it extensive coverage, and this threat to the pollution of the environment and the poisoning of human beings went scarcely noticed. Had the United States, however, discharged such a device, it would be safe to predict that peace and environmental groups would have protested vigorously all over the world.

Demonstrations would have taken place in front of the White House, and American embassies in nations large and small would have been stoned. There would have been demands for a special session of the United Nations to condemn the American action and our newspapers would have played up the story for days. But there were no protests, no demonstrations, no demands for UN action. The explosion did not symbolize the world's most powerful nation sharpening up yet another tool, but only a second-class power playing catch-up in the dangerous game of human annihilation.

A few months later, a California jury found the avowed Communist and political activist Angela Davis, a black woman, innocent of charges of conspiracy to commit murder. It had been proved that she had purchased a veritable arsenal of guns, some of which had, a few days later, been used in the murder of a judge and several other persons, but the jury decided that she did not know that the guns were to be used for this purpose and that she had purchased them for legitimate reasons. In the evening following the not guilty verdict, the jurors were invited to attend a "victory" celebration. Ten of them did so. The judge did not remonstrate with them or even comment on the fact that while this may have been a victory for Miss Davis, it was not a victory for the jurors, who presumably were only doing their duty of weighing the evidence as available and presented and reaching a verdict. This story received relatively little coverage in the news media and only a very few editorials raised the question of the propriety of the invitation or its acceptance. Yet one can readily picture the denunciations that would be brought down upon "the system" and the jurors if there had been a guilty verdict and ten of the jurors had accepted an invitation from the district attorney to attend a "victory" celebration. What is the meaning of these examples? Certainly one meaning must be that most people, in this case radical activists and liberal newsmen, are much more interested in putting forth their own particular ideas and values than they are in seeking equal justice or equal treatment for all.

Cocoon or Coffin?   By the early 1970s, if the New Left was not dead, it had at least gone into a cocoon stage and, if such were the case, would shortly be emerging in a modified form. The most revolutionary groups had been contained or their members detained. It had been discovered that confrontation politics does not work except under those conditions where the opposition is either naïve or cowardly, as was sometimes the case in the early years of student violence during the 1960s. A recession during much of the first Nixon administration had also added a touch of reality to the upper-middle-class activists who formed the core of the New Left and who, prior to 1969, seemed to believe that personal income and economic conditions were not of any meaning to them. Radicalism as an amusing hobby or a simple shortcut to idealistic goals had been replaced in some instances by apathy and cynicism and in others by a more sober realization of the difficulties, the hard work, the discipline, and the patient effort that are required to achieve fundamental changes in a complex social system that is dominated by the powerful influence of inertia. During the heyday of student radical activism the slogan was "all power to the people." The upper-middle-class types shouting the slogan, having little notion of what "the people"—that is, the ordinary citizen—are like, made the comfortable and convenient assumption that the ordinary citizen was very much like himself, despite the popularity of the amiable bigot and ignoramus, Archie Bunker, of "All in the Family."

Populism Strikes (Once) Again What seemed to remain of the radicalism of the 1960s was, in the early 1970s, another in the periodic reappearances of populism. It had been popular during the triumphant emergence of Jacksonianism in the 1820s and 1830s, once again in the farmers' protests against the giant transportation and marketing corporations of the 1870s in the Granger movement, in the efforts of William Jennings Bryan in the 1890s to radicalize the Democratic party (with the only result that he destroyed a potential for that party to emerge as the majority coalition), and in the New Deal movement of the 1930s. As it has done every generation and one-half or two throughout American history, populism had reemerged in the late 1960s and early 1970s as a powerful force in American politics but, as in the past, it was not necessarily destined to become a majority influence in the electoral or policy arena.

In the 1972 presidential campaign, two old populist strains reemerged. Southern populism was represented by Governor George Wallace of Alabama and prairie populism by Senator George McGovern of South Dakota. Both types have traditions that go back at least a century and both are manifestations of the Jacksonian "cult of the common man." The favorite villain of both is the large corporation. Populists have traditionally favored full employment, fewer taxes on the "little man," higher taxes on big business, better social security systems, and the elimination of tax dodges and the government subsidy of big business or big agriculture. There have historically been undercurrents of isolationism and this appeared in modified forms in both the Wallace and McGovern approaches. Another longtime strain in populism has been that of anti-Semitism (Jews were pictured as nonproductive middle men), but as is the case generally in the United States, anti-Semitism is on the decline and is of importance to only a few far-right groups today. The chief factor dividing the Wallace and McGovern forces and the one that prevented them from joining together in 1972 was the matter of traditional prejudice against blacks on the part of Southern populists. Wallace gained a good deal of support in all parts of the country for his strong antiwelfare and antibussing positions. These were only partly, though significantly, racial matters and this prevented a united populistic front, even though the two groups of populists shared more viewpoints than they disagreed upon.

It is well known that the McGovern campaign, with its simplistic good-guys-versus-bad-guys approach, was highly attractive to young voters. What is perhaps less well known is that the also simplistic Wallace movement attracted large numbers of young persons, too. The main difference was that the young Wallace-ites had, for the most part, not gone to college, while the McGovern support came primarily from the college campuses.

It is somewhat difficult to categorize the prairie and Southern populists (now both primarily urbanized). Although McGovern, Wallace, and others claim to be antiestablishmentarian and that they want to return government to the "little man," both men hold important positions of power and influence in America and perhaps can best be classified as dissenting establishmentarians rather than antiestablishmentarians.[7]

THE WHITE KNIGHT SYNDROME

The rising concern in the late 1960s and onward about environmental pollution has led to another type of anti-Establishment protest. Of course, concern for quality of the environment is not, in itself, antiestablishmentarian in character, nor is it particularly new in American politics. Theodore Roosevelt and Gifford Pinchot made concern for the conservation of natural resources, as it was then termed, an upper-middle-class do-gooder activity early in this century. The Sierra Club carried on in this tradition. And concern for the environment is quite legitimate. There is no question but that pollution problems are increasingly becoming offensive to aesthetic tastes and even dangerous to human health and life, not to mention the lives of plants and animals of all kinds. In historical terms, this nation has only recently ceased to be a frontier society. On the frontier, the practice is to foul one's nest and then move on. Prophylactic measures simply do not seem to be worthwhile where land, air, and water are plentiful and clean. But in an urban-industrial society, pollution becomes increasingly serious and increasingly it is important to do something about it. The questions are: Who is to blame? And who is to pay the high costs of reducing pollution? And which pollution is to be reduced first and by how much? Polluting is a means of socializing—spreading around broadly among the people—some of the costs of both producer and consumer. The Establishment says, in effect, that the typical citizen does not care enough about pollution to be willing to face the high costs of reducing it. But another answer is offered by some of the anti-Establishment.

The Head Raider Perhaps the best known and the most popular advocate of environmental protection and consumerism is Ralph Nader, who, along with a large number of supporters, operates an elaborate set of organizations designed to conduct various investigations and to make public reports. Although his favorite enemy in relation to both consumer and environmental matters is the large corporations—which certainly need to have gadflys watching them and which do act selfishly and thoughtlessly at times—Nader is not a populist.[8] Instead, he comes out of another line of American dissenters, persons who seek to serve as protector of the ordinary citizen who is otherwise innocently taken advantage of by a heartless, profit-hungry system. Unlike the populist, who sees goodness and wisdom in the common man, Nader is a muckraking elitist who sees himself and his followers as the people who should lead. Again, this idea of a specialized elite different from the prevailing one is not new. In the past, priests in some countries have felt that they had a right to be the elite. In the 1920s, an American elitist group called the "technocrats" thought that salvation was to be found by turning control of society over to the engineers. Nader's group consists primarily neither of priests nor engineers, but of lawyers. The great bulk of the youthful "Nader's Raiders" are recent law school students or graduates. It is this group that he sees as being able to fight off the self-seeking large corporation as well as the lazy government bureaucrat (who is all too often in league with the corporate leadership). He seems to see these young people as capable of acting not for the sake of personal power or of glory (though Nader himself certainly appreciates the value of publicity), but for the sake of a Nader-defined "public good."

Although the Naderites are opposed to the prevailing elite, they do not have a counterculture orientation that is antimaterialistic and present-oriented like the "hippies" or the "street people" who refuse to compete in the present culture. They do not appear to be interested in wealth or status, but rather see themselves as morally more capable of providing honesty and integrity than has been demonstrated by corporate or governmental bureaucracy. The great appeal of Naderism to college students seems to center on two factors. First, Nader seems to be talking about a better life for all, but without disturbing the basic middle-class amenities with which the typical college student grew up. Thus it would seem that he would want to end air and water pollution but not put a stop to the luxury of the individual having his own private "wheels" or boat. He attacks the methods and policies of corporations without suggesting that these may bear a relationship to the cost of the products of those corporations.

Indeed, his second basis for popularity rests on the fact that while his research is done primarily by lawyers, the subject matter of that research often involves not their expertise, but that of economists. As with so many others, the Naderites tend to gloss over the problem of opportunity costs in making their reports. Thus a casual reading of the reports and the news stories based upon them might give the impression that the environment might be cleaned up, automobiles be built more safely, and closer governmental inspection of consumer goods carried out, all without having to give up anything in return. Obviously this kind of a promise of having your cake and eating it too is attractive to a great many people. The fact is, however, that if we are not going to build hydroelectric or nuclear electric plants, people are not going to be able to use all the electricity they would like. If various consumer safeguards are vigorously enforced through extensive inspection systems or any other manner, the result is going to be higher-priced items in the supermarket. If our wilderness areas are to be preserved, it will mean that many persons will be deprived of enjoying a family vacation in the wilds—not the upper-middle-class Raiders or members of the Sierra Club, who can afford to pay the extra cost involved, but the lower-middle-class and working-class person who socializes (spreads among other members of society) some of his costs by camping out, defacing the terrain, littering, polluting streams, and carelessly causing forest fires. The world of Nader is not the economist's world, nor is it the world of the common man.[8]

NONWHITE EXTREMISTS

Radicals and antielitists are far more common among white, upper-middle-class persons than they are among blacks, American Indians, Mexican-Americans, Puerto Ricans, or other nonwhites. The typical nonwhite activist is not seeking to destroy the system or even to take it over. He views himself realistically as a member of a permanent minority group and essentially he is asking for a bigger piece of the action for himself and his friends, much as did members of white ethnic groups in the past. He is pressuring for a fairer place in the American Dream. In this type of demand, liberals and conservatives alike can sympathize; the liberal because this would seem to be only justice, the conservative because it siphons off from potentially discontented groups through the process of co-optation an important collection of leaders and, by keeping the lines of recruitment of leadership open, provides a stabilizing influence for the system.

There are some radical groups among nonwhites, of course. Perhaps the best-known group is that of the Black Panthers, originally dedicated to revenge and revolution. In their early stages of organization, the Panthers believed (or claimed to) that the only defense of black people was to arm themselves and to take violent action, including terrorist tactics, where these seemed appropriate. Unfortunately for them, however, there were more police and more police guns than there were Panthers. Eventually, the group suffered the fate of most extremist groups —it was divided by internal dissension and broke into at least two groups in the early 1970s.[9] The one group, ostensibly being run from Algeria by Eldridge Cleaver, became Maoist in orientation. The other, under Bobby Seale, decided to abandon direct violent confrontation. These events took place after the deaths of a considerable number of group members made it clear to the most reluctant and unrealistic person that neither the police nor the courts were likely to be intimidated by their tactics. Among Chicanos (Mexican-Americans) the Panthers were imitated by the Brown Berets and a few other organizations. Less violence took place in connection with these groups, though there was some.

Street Gangs or Social Protest? Among ghetto juveniles, whether black, brown, yellow, or white, street gangs have long existed. In fact, they have been quite commonplace throughout the history of the American city. In the dull, unchanging, and perhaps apparently hopeless life of the ghetto, these gangs have provided excitement and, through crimes against person and property, occasional profit. In the 1960s, gang leaders began to discover—sometimes through the assistance of OEO personnel—that they just might be more than street hoodlums and troublemakers. Or so they could claim. They began to portray themselves as leaders of rebellions against the Establishment. The argument was that they were the helpless victims of prejudice, discrimination, and lack of opportunity. This served to cover their activities with a patina of respectability. In some cases, they were even able to secure federal funds under the antipoverty program.[10] But the fact that these groups were not actually addressing themselves honestly to questions of social injustice became increasingly clear after a few years and, by the early 1970s, they seemed to be returning to their traditional status as street gangs with no constructive social or political purpose.

WOMEN'S GROUPS

The movement by women who were not willing to accept the role of housewife and mother and wished to be able to compete more effectively with men for high-status occupational positions became evident in the nineteenth century. But it was not until well into the twentieth that women activists became a major political force in seeking to modify the existing views concerning the appropriate role for women in society. Women were not guaranteed the vote until 1920. Despite some sporadic activity during the next two generations, political and economic circumstances did not afford a major opportunity for the effective presentation of greater demands until the early 1960s when a book by Betty Friedan raised the major issues of complaint by women who sought business and professional careers.[11]

The "Women's Liberation" movement (obviously a propaganda term) was developed in the late 1960s. As in the case of the environmental control movement and many radical groups, the members of the Women's Lib movement were characteristically from the upper-middle class and were not concerned with ordinary, working-class, or lower-middle-class job positions. Instead, they were persons who wished to become executives in government and industry or to achieve higher status within the professions. Significantly, a large number of them seem to have been graduates of high-status, private women's colleges who had moved into positions in broadcasting, journalism, and related fields. Without doubt, they had legitimate complaints about their lack of advancement opportunities in such positions and about differential pay scales. But the effective complaint was not against social policy in general, but rather one that concerned the personal interests of a particular segment of upper-middle-class society.

As is the case of many other groups dissatisfied with contemporary society, members of Women's Lib for the most part are not revolutionaries in any technical sense (as described earlier), but are essentially a dramatic and often strident interest group pressuring for changes that would be of benefit to themselves and only incidentally to society at large. Although many of their activities seemed bizarre, often neurotic, and only semirational, their goal has been only one of modifying the Establishment in order to make sex a less significant factor in determining who should hold positions of status and power. In the early 1970s, the Women's Lib movement could no longer be ignored, even though it still readily lent itself to ridicule. After being a part of the political scene for a bit longer and after achieving a greater degree of sophistication and a lower level of hysteria, it seems destined to become an important factor in the continuing movement away from male dominance toward a society in which the family becomes a changed institution and in which women maintain most of their traditional prerogatives while they gain something approximating equality in those areas that have traditionally belonged to the male.[12] The implications for changes in the law to fit the emerging pattern are many.

THE FAR RIGHT

The reactionaries of the far right live in a dream world, imagining that America has somehow bypassed the ideal society that might have been and is now bogged down in a morass of foreign and domestic policy which they see as being dysfunctional for the Republic, and as keeping us from returning to the point where we went astray and picking up once again the path toward the true American dream. Their politics is a politics of nostalgia. The reactionary shares many characteristics with the radical of the left, as we noted at the beginning of this chapter. Both tend to advocate politically unfeasible policies and procedures and in many cases their means are dysfunctional toward their ends even if they could be carried out. Furthermore, both are extremely impatient with those who disagree with them or who would resort to political compromise. This is because they are "true believers" who feel certain that they have proper solutions to the nation's ills.[13] Characteristically, they truly believe that there is a mammoth conspiracy by the Establishment to run the nation as it is being run and to keep their "truths" from becoming known or accepted. To them a wrongheaded world refuses to see and accept their (simplistic) answers to social problems.

The far right also differs in important ways from the far left, of course. The left is idealistic while the right is nostalgic. The left tends to be somewhat anarchistic or even completely so, believing that the innate goodness of man makes relatively few rules necessary and that many of the necessary rules should be designed to preserve equality among men and to control the behavior of that minority that is selfish, grasping, and repressive of the rights and benefits of others. The right tends to emphasize law and order and to give obedience precedence over conscience. The left is on the average much younger than the right and has more education. The left draws its membership primarily from persons whose parents were upper-middle class, the right comes from the lower-middle class and the working class. Most members of the left grew up in metropolitan area core cities or their suburbs, rightists have small-town backgrounds or wish that they did have. Both sets of extremists are usually well financed, but the "fat cats" of the left tend to prefer relatively little publicity and often to remain in the background while those of the right tend to be self-made men, newly rich, quite unsophisticated, but willing to become actively engaged, often in the center stage of rightist activities.[14]

Historically, many far right organizations have been antiblack, anti-Catholic, anti-Semitic, antiimmigrant, and generally opposed to those whose ancestors or who themselves came to this country fairly recently. In their minds, the true America is white, Anglo-Saxon, and Protestant (WASP). This was true of the Ku Klux Klan in the 1920s and immediately after World War II. It was also true of the White Citizens' Councils in the South, which sought to prevent the integration of schools and public facilities beginning in the 1950s. A few groups, such as the tiny American Nazi party, found too little to emulate in this country and turned to the Fascist groups abroad, just as many members of the Old Left became Stalinists and members of the New Left, Maoists.

In more recent years, broad-spectrum hating and the idolizing of foreign dictators have declined. The far right of the 1960s and 1970s has been characterized by one common fear and hatred, that of communism. Members of the right characteristically show fear and anxiety lest an inattentive America blindly fall into the hands of "atheistic communism" or that the Communists gradually infiltrate more and more American institutions and subvert them. Perhaps the most extreme and ludicrous expression of this phenomenon was that authored by Robert Welch, the founder of the John Birch Society, who once accused President Dwight D. Eisenhower of being an unwitting tool of the Communists.

And Here, on Your Right. . . . Probably the best-known far right organization is the John Birch Society.[15] This is a semisecret organization, largely authoritarian in structure and method, which sees virtually every member of the Establishment as either a fellow-traveler or a Communist "dupe." Its view as to the roots and causes of American foreign and domestic policy (in addition to its attack upon the conservative President Eisenhower, it sought to impeach the liberal Chief Justice Earl Warren and considered proposals for metropolitanwide governments to be a Communist effort to destroy American local government) is as irrational as is the New Left view that America entered the fighting in Vietnam in order to preserve natural resources (which are almost nonexistent) and a retail market (among people who have little purchasing power and, in any case, could buy more economically from the Japanese than from the Americans) for the large American corporations.

Paranoia is a haunting thing, difficult to shake off, and pathetic to the observer who fails to share it, but it can be a powerful political force. Extremists of both the left and the right possess two extremely important political assets: an ample supply of money and a fantastically high level of motivation. But even so, they are largely ignored by the huge middle masses and their impact upon political process and policy remains marginal.

CLOSING NOTE

Taking an anti-Establishment position is in many ways a highly frustrating business. There are few victories, and those that there are, are usually of little importance, although they may serve to inspire the group to further effort. If the goal of an anti-Establishment group is to displace the existing dominant elite and thus become the new (but "proper") elite, the odds against success are astronomical. Extremists almost always underestimate the staying power of the Establishment. They underestimate both the strength and the time required to overthrow it. Those of the anti-Establishment who merely wish to make modifications in the process or direction that the dominant elite is pursuing will, of course, have somewhat greater luck. Even in their case, however, the task is largely a story of frustration.

Perhaps the most important question about the anti-Establishment is not whether it offers a superior alternative to the existing elite, but rather as to what, if any, useful social function it performs. The answer to this seems to be that although its members do not see their activities in that way, the anti-Establishment serves to keep the dominant elite "honest." This is not true of all dissenters, of course. Some groups, such as the "hippies," with their hedonism, present orientation, and narcissism, probably make no social contribution other than by staying out of the way of those who wish to do so. But many of the others perform the useful function of forcing the effective decision makers to consider problems and alternatives that they might otherwise ignore, to reassess their own values and goals, and to recognize that their own points of view are not universally accepted and therefore may well not represent "truth." The antiestablishmentarian, without realizing it and perhaps often against his will if he does realize it, often aids and abets the causes and goals of the ruling elite. He serves a socially useful function even though it may be far removed from that which he thinks he is doing or would want to do if he could. Ironically, to some extent he is unconsciously doing about the last thing that he would want to do: He is being used by the Establishment to serve its own purposes and to preserve its position of power.

NOTES

1 Fact-finding Commission, *Crisis at Columbia,* Vintage Books, New York, 1968.
2 See Alan Adelston, *SDS,* Scribner, New York, 1972. For a later development, see Harold Jacobs (ed.), *Weatherman,* The Ramparts Press, Berkeley, Calif., 1971. For an expression of the unrealistic optimism of the 1960s radicals, see Richard Flacks, "Young Intelligentsia in Revolt," in Rod Aya and Norman Miller (eds.), *America: System and Revolution,* The Free Press, New York, 1971.
3 Andrew M. Greeley, "The End of the Movement," *Change,* April 1972, pp. 42–47. Quotation from p. 44.
4 Charles A. Reich, *The Greening of America,* Random House, Inc., New York, 1970.
5 See Herbert Marcuse, *Counterrevolution and Revolt,* Beacon Press, Boston, 1972; Theodore Roszak, *The Making of a Counter Culture,* Doubleday, Garden City, N.Y., 1969; Noam Chomsky, "The Student Movement," *The Humanist,* 30:19–25, September 1970; Kenneth Keniston, *Young Radicals,* Harcourt, Brace & World, New York, 1968.
6 Arnold Beichman, *Nine Lies about America,* Library Press, New York, 1972. On the appetite for power by the new class of intellectuals and their perversion of history, see David T. Bazelon, *Power in America,* New American Library, New York, 1972.
7 Books describing the Wallace and McGovern movements disinterestedly are yet to be written, but millions of column inches have been written by commentators of various political views.
8 Ralph Nader and Mark J. Green (eds.), *Corporate Power in America,* Grossman Publishers, New York, 1973, contains fourteen essays by critics of the corporation, its behavior, and its power. John C. Esposito, *Vanishing Air: The Ralph Nader Study Group Report on Air Pollution,* Grossman Publishers, New York, 1970, is a good example of a study that largely overlooks political and administrative realities, as well as opportunity costs. Richard J. Barber, *The American Corporation—Its Power, Its Money, Its Politics,* E. P. Dutton & Co., Inc., New York, 1970, offers a balanced account of the behavior of the contemporary corporation.
9 On the Black Panthers, see Tom Wolfe, *Radical Chic and Mau-Mauing the Flak Catchers,* Farrar, Straus & Giroux, New York, 1970; Philip S. Foner (ed.), *Black Panthers Speak,* J. B. Lippincott Company, New York, 1970; Earl Anthony, *Black Panthers,* The Dial Press, Inc., New York, 1970.
10 Wolfe, *op. cit.*
11 Betty Friedan, *The Feminine Mystique,* W. W. Norton & Company, Inc., New York, 1963.

12 See Elaine Showalter, *Women's Liberation and Literature,* Harcourt Brace Jovanovich, New York, 1971; Michael Adelstein and Jean C. Pival (eds.), *Women's Liberation,* St. Martin's Press, Inc., New York, 1972.

13 Eric Hoffer, *The True Believer,* Harper & Row, New York, 1951.

14 See George Thayer, *The Farther Shores of Politics: The American Political Fringe Today,* Simon and Schuster, New York, 1967, on extremists. Part II covers the far right, parts IV and V, the left, of the 1960s.

15 LaVerne Hutchins, *The John Birch Society and United States Foreign Policy,* Pageant-Poseidon, New York, 1968.

Camelot

Ask ev'-ry per-son if he's heard the sto-ry;—

—— And tell it strong and clear if he has not:

That once there was a fleet-ing wisp of glo-ry—

—— called Cam-e-lot. Don't let it be for-

got That once there was a spot For one brief shin-ing

mo-ment that was known As Cam - e - lot.

Chapter 5

Tradition! Tradition! And the Patent-Medicine Salesmen

The common man, although romanticized in American literature and the rhetoric of the political campaign, is a far more ordinary and predictable individual than is the scion of an elite family. He decides how to vote in a fairly predictable manner and, in particular, is conservative in his political attitudes. That is, although many who would seek his support at the polls believe him to be an advocate of quite radical change in the rules of the political game, he will accept a cautious movement in the direction that he believes will improve his personal position in preference to any proposal for dramatic reorganization of the rules of society that promise (but cannot demonstrate) a large, rather than only a minimal, improvement in his economic and social condition.

The ordinary voter is not highly informed about political events, does not know what the implications of change are likely to be, is not willing to spend much time in investigating the meaning of proposed changes in public policy, and yearns for simple explanations of the complex events that he experiences personally (as in unemployment), or notes casually as he glances at the daily newspaper or the evening news on television. He is far too cautious and too fearful to invest in the promise of utopia to be an idealist. What he seeks is security and a minimal prospect for an improved condition of life with the least possible risk of economic or social loss of position. This modest goal of the common man is what ultimately defines the direction of democracy, regardless of the twists and turns that may be taken by the elite leadership in the short run.

PARTISAN LOYALTIES AND DISLOYALTIES

When the middle masses are moved to express political opinion or take action, it usually will be with predictable regularity in terms of traditional predispositions formed as the result of earlier experiences. What we plan to outline first in this chapter is reference group theory in respect to politics.

All of us have invested an emotional commitment and identification with some formal and informal groupings to which we give loyalty and these in turn give cues for political behavior and so cut information costs for us. Often these groupings are directly tied to our occupation and economic interest, but they may also be with race, ethnic background, religion, locality, or social status or a mixture of these, e.g., the AFL-CIO, the retail clothing merchants' association, the Yale University alumni bulletin, the Catholic Church, the Polish American Community, the country club, Cass County, the Urban League, ACLU, etc. These specific groups are tied into broader class, racial, and ethnic groupings, and through them are generally associated with one or the other party or type of candidate. Supporting this traditional choice is generally to their own self-interest, which is probably on the whole correct. As V. O. Key observed in *The Responsible Electorate*,[1] after analyzing voting patterns in terms of reasonable assumptions about a citizen's perception of his self-interest: "Voters are not fools." Thus blacks identify with the black community and the Democratic party and so has labor and the rural South (although this association is weakening), while businessmen, through the Chamber of Commerce, and many large-scale farmers, through the American Farm Bureau Federation, will identify with the Republican party because these political groups seem to reenforce their own identities and their interests. Some college students can be expected for a while to identify with anyone in jail who claims charges against him are politically motivated, with youthful independents who say they are liberal candidates, or with whoever is the anti-Establishment fad along the campus lecture circuit.

Even a Ph.D. in political science, heir to millions, and with a year's sabbatical leave, will use cues from groups and individuals he trusts rather than pay the opportunity costs of learning for whom to vote for state legislator or even whether he should support a particular change in the electoral college system. This is because no one has the time or wants to pay the information costs needed to learn about everything political. All of us solve the problem of collecting political information by taking cues from others whom we believe we can trust and so shortcut the process. We also may take cues from those we distrust. When Professor H. Algerton Middlebush hears that Vice President Spiro T. Agnew and Senator George McGovern hold differing views on a tax proposal, he is assisted in the process of sorting out his own views on the issue. For some, in fact, such sorting out is almost instantaneous. For those who may hold jaundiced views about both men, the process is more complex.

Pigeonholing the Electorate   Involvement   through   such identifications are so predictable, and we should add reasonable, that a group of social scientists from M.I.T. once set up a corporation to prepare an election computer simulation based on such ties. In picking their categories, the social scientists recognized subcategories so that Catholics, for example, might be pigeonholed into two (or more) groupings on the basis of labor union vs. business ties, etc. Gallup and other polling agencies use a cruder form of such categories when they base their sampling on a composite number of citizens based on sex, race, region, and social class. If the pollsters or the social scientists could figure out all the politically relevant categories for every election and the number of persons in each and what they think politically, they could predict via computer simulation the outcome of every election from here on out.

A political scientist, Eugene Burdick, wrote a scary novel about this simulation project and called it *The 480*.[2] It suggested how scientists could predict and soon control political behavior using the 480 slots or voter types and then, by choosing the right appeals, manipulate the voters to their will. There is considerable truth in social identification analysis and we make it our first assumption about what the middle mass believes politically. We think it clear that a large part of the time the middle mass of citizens will become minimally involved and will thus respond primarily in terms of group ties and traditional partisan affiliations. These they themselves (rightly or wrongly from the view of the observer) regard as acting in their self interests.

Deviations from the Expected This procedure, however, does not work as consistently or as nicely as the social scientists in the novel supposed it would. Voters refused to remain in their assigned slots. The Simulmatics Corporation had to be abandoned. A number of reasons account for voter deviations from what should be their predispositions. Let us begin with the most trivial. There are always some who have idiosyncratic reasons for people not fitting neatly into the slots. Some such deviations are based on misunderstanding and confusion or on somewhat trivial or irrational prejudices such as that held by voters found to be against Thomas E. Dewey because of his toothbrush moustache. Finding out the causes of some of these deviations may not be worth the effort, since the reasons are so special, and the numbers of voters concerned is relatively small. Then too, some voters get cross-pressured between two commitments as when a labor union Catholic must vote either for a rich Catholic Republican or a labor union Protestant Democrat. If both ties are felt intensely, the citizen, social scientists have discovered, will try to avoid the whole issue by claiming the election is not important and he will most likely end up not voting at all, or will vote for whichever side drags him to the polls—Catholic or labor union friends. But the most important reason of all, why the simulation did not work out, is that in America these identifications are frequently not really very intense for a significant number of the middle masses and new experiences can change their opinion about their immediate or long-term self-interest.

Thus our second assumption about the middle masses is that the impact of new events can entice some from their traditional ties, especially as the time between the present and when they made them originally grows long. For even relatively trivial reasons, a significant number of citizens can be tempted for the moment to set their predispositions aside; and this number has been growing markedly since the 1960s.

What most often leads the voter momentarily from his traditional commitments is a characteristic in the makeup of the middle masses, who, the philosopher John Dewey said, "lust after absolutes." This is another way of saying that the average

American citizen is likely to feel he is a good citizen and will then behave in a moralistic fashion especially when his own interests are only partially involved or do not seem to him to be directly involved at all. He finds it difficult to tolerate uncertainties and minor frustrations and likes to indulge himself with the comfortable feeling that when he acts politically, he is acting decisively and disinterestedly to improve the world for the good of all. In an older age this was called being "carried away by one's passions."

Such deviations from traditional choices begin as temporary deviations and are a good deal like impulse buying. In politics, they are generally the result of candidate appeal or transitory events that may be momentarily irritating or emotionally attractive and touch the broad public interest rather than the voters' specific personal interests. Thus the great appeal of General Eisenhower in 1952 and 1956 did not signal the immediate breakup of the middle-mass Democratic party (as some Republicans hoped), but rather symbolized a moral response to an admired individual. In the same way, the rise in popularity reflected in the Gallup polls immediately after any President takes bold action in foreign affairs or a domestic crisis, is also generally of short-range duration. So too are local deviations that result from evidence of corruption or bungling by public officials. Though short-range, these and many other such events have defeated a good many incumbent governors, representatives, and senators. The American system of elections at many levels gives voters numerous opportunities to express short-run frustrations or moral enthusiasms. Governors particularly seem liable to such punishment.

Long-term Realignments   Deviation from normal patterns will have long-term effects only if the sense of morality can be combined with a direct appeal to the voter's own self-interest, including especially his hopes and fears about his own future. Events that touch him directly have the potential of becoming genuine issues. At this point the voter of the middle masses really becomes involved and may even become involved enough to care very much who wins. His response is closer to moral outrage than to relatively disinterested good citizenship. Such voters will shift from voting a traditional party identification to voting a genuine commitment. This act is likely to result in a partisan identification which for him sets a new traditional voting pattern. If widespread enough it results in what election observers describe as a realigning election and a new or reinvigorated partisan majority.

Such massive shifts appear to occur every thirty to thirty-five years or so (slightly more often than every other generation) in American politics. They may happen like a flash flood in a single election, but more commonly take two, three, or more national elections to complete. An example is given by the switch of voters and the activation of many nonvoters that resulted from the personal experience of the Great Depression and its probable effects on the hopes and fears of many citizens coupled with the genuine responses to the moral appeal of Franklin Roosevelt and his New Deal policies. The majority Republican coalitions which from the Civil War through 1928 had controlled the politics of most of the American states as well as at the national level, overnight became the minority. A sense of fear or moral outrage changed the Democratic minority to a majority and that majority continued to control most elections through the 1960s.

There are clear signs today that this Democratic party traditional coalition is in trouble. We are living through a period of erosion of political loyalties, where clearly the large middle mass of citizens are with increasing frequency straying away from traditional ties. Split ticket voting, partisan independence as reflected in opinion polling responses, and third-party candidacies have become endemic. Some, such as the astute political analyst Walter DeVries, argue we have entered the age of increased deviations because of television.[3] Its massive reduction of information costs to the middle masses have, it is claimed, politicized many more citizens than was ever possible before. He argues that a new partisan commitment of the old type may never occur again; that voters will continue as independents. Others feel more skeptical about the long-term enthusiasm of the middle masses. The trend toward independence from political party allegiance is clear, but we suspect that each period of heightened political interest will be followed by a declining politicalization of the middle masses.

The deviations from traditional commitments that we have described are the direct result of new events and of how these events are interpreted by the middle-mass citizen. When the event is direct and personal experiences are deeply felt, it in effect forces the citizen to pay some information costs because the payoffs seem to make it worthwhile. When college professors in California for two straight years learned they would receive no raises, even for cost of living, many were able to perceive a political reaction to campus events whose significance had not previously been fully appreciated. When the boy who used to deliver the daily newspaper grew up and was killed in Vietnam, as happened in the case of one of the authors, the same kind of involuntary shortcutting of the information-gathering process took place.

Secondary Influences on Change   Lesser impact on citizens can be expected from interpretations given events by the mass media and secondarily by candidates, particularly of the out-party, whose job it is to raise issues in the hope of gaining office. These probably have only short-term effects unless the citizen has already prepared himself for a change because of his own feelings about new events that affect him. We will argue that such secondary influences can affect the outcomes of particular elections and can continue to encourage the process of erosion of past loyalties. But until combined with a deeply felt direct personal experience, such deviations will not have long-term consequences.

Before examining the operation of short-run secondary influences, let us emphasize again that the recent situation of independent voting is unusual, though the percentage of persons who say they have no commitment to any political party has been growing since the late 1930s, especially among the young.[4] (This, of course, is the period of radio and television and declining party organizational structure.) Most of the time the middle masses retain their traditional commitments. Usually, they conclude that gathering information or participating is not worth the effort or the sacrifice and, most of the time, who is to say they are wrong?

TV JOURNALISM:
A BRANCH OF THE ENTERTAINMENT INDUSTRY

Studies by social scientists have yet to document the long-term impact of the mass media on individuals or groups of citizens. Propaganda studies in laboratory situations are relatively useless since their subjects are observed under controlled conditions that do not come close to simulating reality. It can be shown, for example, that a particular propaganda pitch will influence many subjects, but it is possible and indeed probable that many of the same subjects outside the laboratory situation would screen out such appeals if they go against their predispositions, just as the TV viewer forms the habit of screening out commercials.

For example, early on, observers noted that while President Franklin D. Roosevelt had most of the largest circulation newspapers vigorously opposing him, he consistently won elections, with many votes being supplied by the readers of those newspapers. This was even true in areas dominated by the Chicago *Tribune* and the Hearst chain, where editorial position directly dictated the way news stories about him would be handled. Thus on occasion in its portrayal of reality the *Tribune* substituted the words "Raw Deal" for "New Deal" in its news stories and found other ways it regarded as suitable for telling it as they believed it really was.

Perhaps a more awe-inspring indication of the limits of media impact is the studies of the heavily propagandized German citizens. After World War II and fifteen years of a steady media diet provided by Nazi propagandists, it was found that Germans had been able, to a remarkable degree, to resist the direct Nazi propaganda appeals if they were somewhat out of sympathy with the Nazis to begin with, or had become so as the result of personal experiences. Relatively few of the youth grew up to become the goose-stepping adults that Joseph Goebels, the propaganda minister, had planned for. It is likely that the Old Adam in man may be equally resistant to the propaganda efforts in China and the Soviet Union, and most certainly so in satellite nations such as Poland and Czechoslovakia, and East Germany with its wall, dividing citizens from traditional fellow countrymen. To summarize, despite the nightmare scares of a *1984*, propaganda and media distortion alone have a limited long-term effect, at least so far as present knowledge is concerned. Perhaps if combined with mind-bending drugs, true brainwashing could be achieved. Until then, it appears that personal experiences combined with one's own hopes and fears about the future will reduce the long-range impact of even the most carefully planned media propaganda campaigns.

But if the long-range effect of mass-media distortion is limited, this is not so in the short-run impact. It was the boast of the Hearst editors that they so whipped up popular passions in 1898 as to involve the United States in the Spanish American War. (Hearst's cable to the artist Frederic Remington in Cuba, who was complaining about the inactivity there and wanted to come home, was a chilling one: "You furnish the pictures and I'll furnish the war.") Clearly newspapers have had their greatest short-run impact in local political races, particularly in nonpartisan elections where the cues to voters from other sources are not as readily present and information costs from other sources are thus greater. Under such conditions newspaper slates may have a distinct advantage. The mass media can also be expected to have the greatest short-run impact among the less politically involved of the middle masses and among those whose traditional commitments have been shaken by new events. The relative ease by which radio and television cut down information costs suggests an influence similar to that of TV advertising—not overpowering when directed against personal interest or the strongly committed but influential when it can be harmonized with or will stimulate that interest and particularly effective in activating the unsophisticated.[5]

Thus on balance, we argue that the mass media are not all-powerful hidden persuaders and brainwashers, but, nevertheless, the way they handle the news may have considerable short-term influence. Thus in totalitarian countries, the media are immediately brought under government control and even in democracies, candidates as well as organized groups from the Black Panthers to the John Birch Society, strive for favorable treatment in the major news media and traditionally set up their own propaganda organs to keep their own actives committed. Because many such groups have limited financial resources, we can probably assume that experience tells them they know what they are doing.

It then becomes important to question how the news is in fact handled by the mass media and who decides how the media will present the news. Two groups are concerned: media owners and news reporters.

The matter of the predispositions of media owners is easily diagnosed. Fifty years ago William Allen White, editor of the Emporia (Kansas) *Gazette,* pointed out that most publishers of newspapers were political conservatives because a daily newspaper represents a major financial investment. In a small city, the daily is likely to be the second or third largest employer in town. The capital investment required to start competition to it grows greater each year despite the new technologies related to offset printing. The same may be said of radio and television stations or national magazines. The pressures exerted by capital investment will, through time, tend to make many owners take politically conservative viewpoints.

But the story does not end here. Whether to produce a quality product, or to compete with other parts of the mass media, or to secure the services of the most talented professionals, the publishers of the best newspapers, as well as TV station owners, must give to the news reporters, commentators, editors, or TV producers a great deal of freedom in the actual handling of the news that is printed or broadcast. These people are a good deal less conservative than the owners are. Their critical skepticism with the established order of things appears to make them romantically liberal. Nevertheless, in the past the canons of professional objectivity have resulted in some of the best newspapers printed anywhere in the world, as well, one might add, as some of the most flamboyant and worst. (Adlai Stevenson once remarked that an editor is a man who separates the news wheat from the chaff—and prints the chaff.)

Two facts of recent times have modified the way news is handled by the professionals. The first is television. Even more than in the tabloid newspaper or the national news magazine, professionals have concluded that television news "in living color" must be handled as entertainment. That means primarily melodrama. The kind of boy-loses-little-dog approach combined with shock produced by dramatic pictures and big red headlines that became the hallmark of yellow journalism when Hearst and Pulitzer brought the media to the masses at the turn of the century, has been transferred to the TV news in its frantic, hell-bent search for viewers. From there it has fed back to the more staid newspapers. William Randolph Hearst said he wanted the people who picked up his paper to say "Gee Whiz!" Charles MacArthur and Ben Hecht immortalized this approach to news handling in the highly entertaining play *Front Page.* That a similar kind of sensationalism ethic has for the moment captivated the most prestigeful parts of the news profession is suggested when Pulitzer prizes go to newspapers and reporters who earned their awards by becoming receivers of stolen government documents. Meanwhile, the exploration of space or the latest political assassination attempt is handled on the six o'clock news with all the depth of a Grade B movie trying to pass itself off as a documentary spectacular.

Pseudoevents This kind of dramatic newshandling is stimulated by the public's insatiable demand for round-the-clock momentous "news." The middle masses still see such programs as forms of entertainment in exactly the same way as their great grandfathers viewed a public hanging. As early as 1961, the historian Daniel Boorstin in *The Image* described how this void was filled with what he called pseudoevents.[6] These were hoked up to be more dramatic and vivid than the actual event and made to look spontaneous. Pseudoevents are contrived by both the news subject and the reporter. The news leak, the press release, the staged announcement are pseudoevents contrived by the news subject for publicity purposes. When you read that the local ACLU board has announced that they are considering bringing a case against the school board over hair regulations, this is a pseudoevent that lies somewhere between an out-and-out publicity puff and a trial balloon.

Politicians almost continually resort to creating pseudo-events. One state senator in Michigan, who was running for governor, was said to have introduced new legislation every day up to the day of legislative adjournment. He put out a solemn news release on each bill as it was introduced with proper fanfare, though many of the "bills" would never even be considered in committee. Senator Joseph McCarthy became adept at creating pseudoevents. He invented the morning press conference at which to announce that new revelations would be forthcoming at a scheduled afternoon press conference. In that way, both morning and afternoon papers had a pseudoevent story. The news reporters have also had to become adept at creating such pseudoevents in order to keep the news wires busy and so hold their jobs. After any presidential statement they commonly call a series of congressmen for reaction statements in the hope of stirring up some kind of conflict that can be made to appear dramatic; particularly they call members of the President's own party. The "Meet the Press" fox-and-hounds game is this type of random-search expedition seeking to plant seeds that may lead to a dramatic news pearl.

False Events From the creation of pseudoevents it is a short step to the creation of false events. Among the more questionable and depressing examples of this by a political group occurred when, some months before the 1964 election, Senator Clair Engel of California was left barely able to speak or walk after brain surgery. He nevertheless announced his intention to run for reelection, in a carefully manufactured 42-second TV film which was, according to later reports, shot many times and pieced together to hide the character of his physical condition. Those supporting this macabre activity were seeking to mislead the potential competition. Engel died before the primary.

Reporters are also sorely tempted to stage false events. Action at a riot often can be made to occur merely by lighting up and focusing the cameras. It follows almost inevitably that TV reporters will be accused of consciously directing such events in the style of the Communist-invented "spontaneous demonstration against the American Embassy."

Thus we begin with a first assumption that controls modern handling of the news: You have to keep hitting the middle-mass reader or viewer between the eyes with a baseball bat in order to get his attention and you must entertain him to keep that attention.

Interpretive Journalism The second trend in the modern handling of the news has been what has been called "interpretive reporting": advocacy journalism, or what an earlier more innocent age called "slanting the news." The justification has come from schools of journalism and has a basis deeper than one of simply peddling one's own biases in a self-serving manner. Senator Joseph McCarthy at the height of his demagoguery demonstrated that he was able to use the professional news reporters and their objectivity to deliberately distort the news. This was because, following the canons of objective journalism, the newsmen played everything he said straight. If under the protection of senatorial immunity, Senator McCarthy fearlessly charged fifty-three unnamed state department employees with being Communists, it hit the front page. That the evidence for the statements was never presented somehow got lost or was buried at the tail end of the story back in the want ads. Though he rarely delivered on past charges, his new charges were reported as faithfully as if he had been found correct in every one of his previous allegations. The success McCarthy had was repeated by a host of lesser lights using the same tactics of smear by innuendo which the news media also dutifully reported.

But the crux of the story was that the flamboyant Senator was not brought down by careful reporting. Senator McCarthy's end came not when readers formed their own conclusions on the basis of the reporting, but when they were made to view events from a different set of assumptions. This was brought about by as big a ham as Senator McCarthy himself was—a mild-mannered, decent-appearing old lawyer, who looked like a character actor out of an English movie. He had old-fashioned courtly manners and an old-fashioned New England background and a name to go with it: Joseph N. Welch. The Senator's end came in what looked like the climax scene of a gripping movie. Senator McCarthy had just questioned the previous political affiliations of a young lawyer serving under Welch in the televised hearings of Mc-Carthy's mixed bag of charges against army officers and civilian leaders (1954). Welch suddenly faced Senator Joseph McCarthy and his henchmen alone and sadly but relentlessly condemned the wickedness of their reckless accusations of this young lawyer on the brink of a promising career. Then Welch broke down and cried, right there on the television screen, right there in a close-up in front of twenty million viewers. Thanks to the invention of video tape, the scene could be rerun for standing-room-only repeat performances on the 6:00 and 11:00 P.M. news.

What Welch provided was a theme for interpreting events. If you assume, for example, that Senator McCarthy was a sincere patriot, you may applaud his efforts; if suddenly it becomes apparent he is rather a cold-blooded demagogue, you see events differently. The news stories may vary day-by-day, but the theme provides the continuity and plot line. If your theme is that he is really a sincere patriot, you handle the same facts differently.

The news reporters had discovered an important fact and one that has serious implications for news handling. Dead pan or what one called "indiscriminate objectivity" as dictated by professional norms presents no narrative framework for interpreting the news and thus may play into the hands of demagogues who provide the framework. *Time* magazine from the start in the 1920s had argued that news must be presented from a particular viewpoint. It had no separate editorial columns as did its rival, *Newsweek*. At first this view was scorned by the professionals, but the Army-McCarthy TV hearings marked a turning point. At first timidly and then more boldly, the reporters and news editors began to fit the news into a framework to interpret its significance. Just selecting what news to report, they reasoned, was already expressing an editorial opinion. The emphasis given one story over another in a half-hour television news or in its page location was further editorializing that could not be avoided. From this it was a further short step to open interpretive reporting and open advocacy of one interpretation of the news over another.

We are not here concerned with the morality of such practices. At its worst—and in our opinion this is so on national public educational radio and TV—it is like listening to a radio sportscaster of a rival city describing how your hometown baseball team is booting away the game. All you are getting is the announcer's unstated assumptions and somehow what actually happens gets lost. At its best, it can reveal the significance of news events in a way that deadpan reporting can never quite equal. One can only offer slight suggestions to newsmen for ways of solving what is really a genuine professional dilemma. The attempt to present the news objectively to the public is similar to the pursuit of justice for the public in the court system or the pursuit of truth by a scientist. It is an ideal that can never be reached or even quite defined. All one can do in these other situations is to prevent blatant injustice as hearsay or third-degree methods, or by biasing or "cooking" the data in a scientific experiment. The solution, such as it is, has been to develop procedures that will prevent clearly unjust or unscientific practices. Perhaps the proper direction in respect to news handling is also to develop professional procedures that eliminate blatant personal bias in news handling.

The Pattern of Bias What does need to concern us here is whether the themes in the handling of the news have been random or follow a consistent pattern of interpretation. The evidence is fairly clear that they tend to reflect the assumptions and political predispositions of the working reporter. Thus the question of what the underlying assumptions of newscasters and reporters are becomes relevant. Also relevant is whether a political consensus exists at the moment among reporters. We examine each of these questions next.

That a consistently liberal news bias comes through in television is being increasingly documented. Edith Efron, in a book whose title, *The News Twisters*,[7] gives some hint of what her findings are, made a study of tapes of the evening television news on ABC, CBS, and NBC in handling the last seven weeks of the 1968 national campaign. She analyzed each sentence of each broadcast for either a negative or a positive opinion in respect to the candidates for President: Nixon, Humphrey, and Wallace. Most sentences she found contained no such opinion. Those that did were classified as positive or negative. She then counted the words in each of these opinionated sentences. Her procedures were carefully outlined so they could be repeated and rechecked by others. Her underlying assumption, however, is one that, it should be noted, contradicts the commonsense views of many. It is that objectivity requires that the networks should be equal in positive and negative comments to Richard Nixon, Hubert Humphrey, and George Wallace. What she found in terms of words pro and con is depicted in Figure 5-1.

In a perceptive article on the study,[8] Paul Weaver begins by noting that even if Efron made the classification errors or questionable classifications that CBS, for example, alleged in its seventy-page attack on the study, the results would be virtually unaffected regarding the handling of news about candidate Nixon. The ratio for CBS under Walter Cronkite and his colleagues, for example, is about 17.5 negative words about Nixon for every positive word. Weaver suggests Efron's data should be accepted as reasonably accurate. He also argues that the differences in comment can be explained by the tendency of the networks to handle the election as drama, that of underdog Humphrey

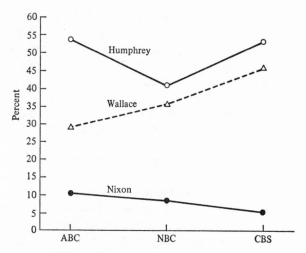

Note: Nixon was given overwhelmingly negative treatment by all three networks; Humphrey the best by all three. Only NBC was negative in a majority of value-laden comments on all three candidates. No network approximated neutrality.

Figure 5-1 Percentage of sentences favorable, major candidates on major networks, last seven weeks of 1968 campaign. (*Source: Edith Efron,* The News Twisters, *Mentor Books, Inc., New York, 1972.*)

overtaking front-runner Nixon. The data do in fact support the notion of presenting the news in dramatic form in order to attract viewers. There are, for example, almost two negative opinions for every positive opinion expressed on all three networks. In addition, the opinionated comments are almost twice as frequent on the underdog network, ABC, possibly as a means of attracting attention and improving viewer ratings.

Nevertheless, we frankly doubt Weaver's conclusions. If Nixon had been the underdog and Humphrey the front runner, we would expect much the same pattern of positive and negative comments. It is more probable to us that the newscasters personally disapproved of Nixon and one may add that given their own assumptions, perhaps for good reason. It is abundantly clear, and we would argue to their credit, that NBC was not enchanted with George Wallace and perhaps less praiseworthy but equally clear that ABC was doing a hatchet job on him— underdog or no underdog. Both seem to have concluded that his formerly expressed racist views and actions did not entitle him to equal pro-and-con comment.

At least one other carefully documented study suggests the underlying predispositions of news gatherers are relevant to news handling. In the February 13, 1971, issue of the *New Yorker* magazine, Edward Jay Epstein investigated the widely reported but erroneous news story of December 7, 1969, that twenty-eight Black Panthers had been killed that year in a genocide campaign plotted by police.[9] He noted that the *New York Times*, which broke the story, printed it without either investigating it or noting that its source for the charge was Charles R. Garry, chief counsel and spokesman for the Black Panther party. Epstein found that after digging for actual names, the list shrunk from twenty-eight to twenty. He did research in newspaper files for biographies of these twenty. One of the twenty, he found, had been murdered by his wife, who claimed he was on a heroin binge. Only ten could be claimed to have died as the result of fights with police and even most of these were involved in criminal acts at the time. The sloppy reporting appears to have been the result of a story that fit a theme which harmonized with reporter predispositions.

The Campus through the TV Eye   One of the sorest points concerning reporter assumptions has been the handling of campus violence, particularly by television. Fred E. Dohrs, chairman of Wayne State University's department of geography, did a study on the press coverage of campus unrest after President Nixon's mining of the Haiphong harbor in May, 1972. As to NBC's evening news of May 9, 1972, he noted:

> The program devoted a ten-minute segment to anti-war protests at Columbia, Harvard, Minnesota, and California at Berkeley. The coast-to-coast roundup by its very selectivity, clearly created the impression that every school in the country had erupted in protest. No mention was made of the fact that the protesters constituted only a tiny fraction of those schools' total enrollments or that the overwhelming majority of campuses had no protest actions whatever.

Dohrs' tabulation based on news stories indicated that of the nation's 2,300 colleges and universities, less than 100 had antiwar protests that could be reasonably described as violent or illegal. Of the more than seven million students on U.S. campuses, he concluded that less than 25,000 demonstrated their antiwar feelings in a manner that might be construed as infringing on the rights of others. In addition, Dohrs criticized TV for uncritically labeling all campus demonstrators as students. He noted, for example, that of the twenty-nine persons initially arrested in the demonstrations in East Lansing, Michigan, only seven, or less than one-fourth, turned out to be students of Michigan State University. (It is not clear, however, whether the crowds divided in the same ratio as those arrested.) Dohrs' conclusion was that events were twisted to fit a preconceived dramatic theme that showed campuses in revolt against President Nixon.

President Robben W. Fleming of the University of Michigan reported an even more clear-cut attempt to fit news into a preconceived liberal TV theme. Here is the description of his reactions as reported in the *Detroit News*, May 24, 1972:

> During one series of complex deliberations with the University of Michigan Board of Regents about adjustments in the school's ROTC program, television reporters with apparent liking for the dramatic, kept casting the discussions as a showdown vote on the abolition of ROTC.
>
> "That possibility never even came up in our talks," Fleming said, "but the television people seemed to need some irreconcilable conflict."
>
> When the meetings ended, Fleming tuned in one television newsman who had been playing the story as a suspense tale about ROTC's future at the university.

The reporter stared seriously into the camera and said:
"And so—for the moment, at least—ROTC is not going to be abolished at the University of Michigan."
"It was hilarious," Fleming recalls. "That man had been pointing to a crisis all week, and was stuck with that line. At the end, he just kept playing it that way, although he knew better."

The Self-Selection of Journalists It becomes relevant to ask what these predispositions that set the themes for many news stories are. Daniel Moynihan has argued that newsmen's assumptions were those of the educated elite found in Ivy League schools.[10] Other commentators, notably to our mind Robert L. Bartley of the *Wall Street Journal* editorial staff, argued against the Ivy League bias, pointing out that many reporters came from what we would describe as tank-town colleges or universities.[11] He makes the more important point that studies of journalism students indicate they tend to be more idealistic than the average student and consciously choose an occupation that permits expression of these commitments rather than a job that may bring higher financial returns. He estimates students who share their views make up about one-half of the 11 percent of all adults who to date have had four years of college education. These 5.5 percent include those recruited into such other expressive professions as the ministry, social work, or even government service. The newsman's assumptions then are those of a small, educated minority of the total population who see themselves as called upon to express their concerns, in their case through advocacy journalism.

Robert D. Novak, a national columnist with Rowland Evans, in a 1972 conference on the mass media, tried to summarize these assumptions. He listed what he called the seven axioms of the Washington news corps, the most prestigious of working newsmen. These he argued are clearly reflected in their handling of the news and are in turn imitated by other reporters.

Axiom No. 1: The Viet Nam War has been a shameful, immoral episode in American history, which blackens the good name of this republic. Consequently, the anti-Communism which as a policy led to involvement in Viet Nam should be subdued and, ultimately, abandoned.

Axiom No. 2: The military-industrial complex is a sinister conspiracy, robbing the nation of its wealth and imperiling its future. To cut defense spending, therefore, is a laudable goal no matter what the international realities.

Axiom No. 3: Severe measures must be taken to prevent the despoiling of the nation's natural resources by pollution, industrial and otherwise. If these stentorian measures result in unemployment, that will be unfortunate, but protection of the environment must take precedence.

Axiom No. 4: White racism, as defined by the Kerner Commission report in 1968, is a cancer that must be removed from the American body. That goal must take precedence over any personal inconveniences caused by such devices as forced busing for the racial integration of schools.

Axiom No. 5: The "forces of repression" in modern America threaten our liberties, a neo-fascist danger becoming a sinister reality under President Nixon and Attorney General Mitchell.

Axiom No. 6: A reordering of priorities is essential and past due, so that great quantities of federal funds can be funneled into the cities for social rebuilding purposes. That a substantial increase in government spending would result in at least some improvement is scarcely debatable.

Axiom No. 7: A redistribution of wealth in the country is similarly overdue through a realignment of the tax system and a general overhaul in tax policy.[12]

One could argue that these assumptions clearly underlay, for example, the presidential candidacy of Senator George Mc-Govern. Some indeed are shared by other candidates of both parties. Their short-run effect, if translated into news interpretation, would no doubt be to help such candidates and hurt those with contrary views. (Yet we should note that the mass media, although initially highly favorable to the McGovern candidacy, turned on him after the convention. This is probably because the candidate appeared to be both naïve and inept. As self-pictured tough professionals, newsmen are not sympathetic to those who wander into a contest out of their league. The fact that the middle masses were not impressed by McGovern indicated to liberal newsmen not that his positions were wrong, but that they were incompetently presented. Admiration changed quickly to contempt and hostility.)

The Effects of Bias   At least one observer is more concerned about the long-run impact of the media. The social commentator Irving Kristol quotes a statement of the CBS TV newsman Roger Mudd:

What the national media, and mainly television have done, is to believe that their chief duty is to put before the nation its unfinished business: pollution, the Vietnam War, discrimination, continuing violence, motor traffic, slums. The media have become the nation's critics and as critics no political administration, regardless of how hard it tries, will satisfy them.[13]

Kristol sees the real danger to democracy not in the short-run bias for particular candidates or causes, but in Mudd's statement that the media will be permanently critical of all who are in authority, that is, "insatiable critics, never to be rendered content by whatever government or whatever policy." Such continued treatment, he fears, would convince most citizens in time that democracy has never worked and never can be made to work. The editor of the Tulsa, Oklahoma, *Tribune* catches this mood in the satire that appears on pages 102–103.

We respect but do not share Kristol's view. We assume that the doomsday mood, characteristic of 1968 onward, will not be a permanent feature in United States reporting. We anticipate the following: (1) Analysis will reveal that rather than being critical of all governments or all policies, the media reporters will be simplistically uncritical of some, as uncritical as they were in the Black Panther story or of Major Andre in the parody. They can be expected to play favorites and when their favorites are in power, to "rebuilding faith in democracy." For example, in 1960 when John F. Kennedy, who was an ineffective President, but of whom most reporters approved, won the Presidency, many found themselves handcuffed. If an Eisenhower had promised in a campaign to desegregate public housing "with a stroke of the pen," as Kennedy did, and then used this as a bargaining chip for two years with Southern congressmen, as Kennedy did, he would have had it forcefully called to his and the nation's attention by an alert press. Somehow Kennedy escaped media crucifixion. (2) Muckraking sensationalism was not invented by television. Many news media seem to have had this initial inclination; it was followed by conservativism. It was the case with political prints (1775–1810), the penny newspaper of the nineteenth century, and the mass magazine.

James Gillray, the first notable English political cartoonist, drew cartoon prints between 1775 and 1810 which were vicious and libelous in a day without adequate libel laws. He portrayed the Prince of Wales (later George IV) surrounded by records of gambling debts and venereal disease cures. His biographer, Draper Hill, sums up his approach to this as "Gillray seems to have had all the manners of a hungry cat in midspring." Hill notes that a reaction against sensationalism set in. During Gillray's time he says "printmakers ran wild" and in the process "made the punishment they meted out exceed the crime and so forfeited the status of underdog."[14]

(3) We assume that newscasting is a two-way process, just as political campaigning is, in which the presentation of the news is affected by the reaction of the viewer. We therefore anticipate a viewer and reader reaction against both sensationalism and personally biased news handling and the disappearance of a credibility gap between masses and journalist. A 1972 Louis Harris poll indicated that such a negative reaction is present already. After Vice President Agnew's blunderbuss attack on the television news media, 56 percent agreed that he was correct "in criticizing the way the TV networks cover the news." Only 40 percent were found by the Gallup poll to agree that the TV networks "deal fairly with all sides in presenting the news dealing with political and social issues." The self-searching seminars by professional news personnel suggest the media are getting the message. One may hope, however, that the liberal bias of the reporters and editors will not be replaced by a conservative one to please the publishers or station owners but rather by a search for more truly professional procedures for newshandling.

SUMMARY

The middle masses are neither greatly interested nor greatly involved in politics because they have convinced themselves that they have better things to do with their lives. They thus generally respond to political appeals in terms of traditional group ties made at some previous time. They can, however, be drawn from such traditional predispositions by the impact of events. In the short run such events are likely to contain an element of moral uplift and be mediated through the mass media or an appealing candidate.

Long-run shifts occur only every generation and a half or so and can be traced to events that have a personal and direct impact on what the individual sees as his own hopes and fears for the future. Such reevaluation of traditional partisan predispositions will result in new or renewed commitments that become the basis

The Detroit News, Sunday, May 28, 1972

Birth of a nation— videotaped highlights

By JENKIN LLOYD JONES

"Good evening, ladies and gentlemen, I'm Fred Flapjaw in Philadelphia, and Transcolonial Broadcasting Co. now brings you Both Sides of the News.

"The nation as you know, has been rocked by the arrest of the brave young Britisher, Maj. John Andre, who seemed to have some plans to West Point in his boot. There has been a second sensation in the sudden departure from his post of Gen. Benedict Arnold, Commander of the West Point garrison.

"We take you now to TBC correspondent Hank Tudor at West Point."

"Thank you, Fred. I have Gen. George Washington here. Gen. Washington, what do you think of Gen. Arnold's so-far unexplained . . ."

"Why, that damned, gold-greedy double-crossing, back-stabbing poltroon. . . ."

"Thank you, general. I'm afraid that's all the time we have. This is Hank Tudor turning you back to Fred Flapjaw."

"THANK YOU, HANK. We are fortunate to have three of our experts here in the studio—Sam Stiletto, Everette Eyebrow and Dirk Smirk—to analyze Gen. Washington's remarks. Everette?"

"I thought the use of the word, 'damned,' on such a distinguished soldier as Gen. Arnold, indicated that Gen. Washington was overwrought. But, of course, the war—let's say—has not been going well, eh, Sam?"

"Right, Ev. Gen. Washington has been under a lot of pressure, but to call

Gen. Arnold a "poltroon" doesn't give him his day in court, does it, Dirk?"

"Right Sam. I mean these are dangerous times and cool heads are needed and in the last couple of days—well, one shouldn't use the term 'irrational' concerning Gen. Washington, but . . ."

"Thank you, Sam, Everette and Dick. And now we take you to Ronald Redcoat at British headquarters in New York, where he has an exclusive interview set up with Gen. Arnold. Ronald?

"Thanks, Fred. Gen. Arnold, what do you have to say for yourself?

"Well, I . . . ah. . . ."

"Are you saying that you were trying to end the war, General?"

"Well, yeah. . . ."

"Are you saying that you are tired of the slaughter of American boys and took this action in an effort to return them quickly to their loved ones?"

"Yeah, that's it."

"Am I correct that you take the position that instead of fleeing for your life you were really riding for peace?"

"You got it, boy, you got it!"

"This is Ron Redcoat in New York returning you to Fred Flapjaw."

"WE HAVE here in our studio Pete Pigeon, the distinguished attorney, who has some grave doubts about the treatment of the handsome and talented young British officer, Maj. Andre. Mr. Pigeon?"

"Justice-loving Americans are hanging their heads in shame, Fred, at the spectacle of a fine youth being stopped on the high road by a group of guerillas without his attorney present, imprisoned without habeas corpus and condemned to death without a jury. We are demanding that Maj. Andre and the papers stolen from him be sent on immediately to Sir Henry Clinton in New York, together with an indemnity of 10,000 sovereigns in gold."

"Thank you, Peter Pigeon. And now for our final item we go to Windsor Hanover on the campus of Harvard University. Take it, Win."

"Right on, Fred. Well, folk's we're in luck. Just as our camera crew reached the campus we happened on a joint demonstration of the Christians Concerned About Conscription Society, the Hell No We Won't Go Club and the Freedom for What Association. They have just set fire to Massachusetts Hall.

"WE CAN'T TURN the camera on many of the signs, but I can read you some—'George, the Hatchet Man,' 'Washington, the Sneak of Trenton,' 'Down With the Butcher of White Plains,' 'Out! The Virginia Aristocrat.' The crowd has torn up a number of striped flags and is chanting 'Free John Andre' and 'Yea, Arnold!'

"Well, ladies and gentlemen, like them or not, here's Young America on the march. Back to you, Fred Flapjaw."

"Thank you, Windsor Hanover. Folks, our time is up. I just want to leave you with one thought. He who ignores the demands of youth is out of touch with the future of America. This is Fred Flapjaw saying good night.

Distributed by General Features Corp.

---

of a new traditional predisposition. There is evidence, given the frequent straying from traditional predispositions since 1960, that Americans are reaching for a new commitment.

The significance of new events for both short- and long-term changes is interpreted for the individual by two major public sources as well as by the private conclusions he reaches. These public evaluators of events are the mass media and political candidates. The first was discussed in this chapter, the second will be discussed in the next.

The mass media, we conclude, will generally only have short-term impact on the least sophisticated readers or viewers and in terms of specific elections or issues. At present, their presentation of the news for several reasons is beamed to reflect the assumptions of a liberally oriented, educated elite. This bias will also appeal to those who aspire to be part of that elite, but is likely to be increasingly unacceptable to other large groupings. The impact will have long-term effect only if it harmonizes with the experiences of a sufficient grouping of the middle masses so as to help them rationalize a new sense of political commitment. In this case, it would aid in the formation of a new political majority through a realignment of traditional partisan loyalties.

NOTES

1 V. O. Key, Jr., *The Responsible Electorate,* Harvard University Press, Cambridge, 1966. On the views of the common man, see Robert Lane, *Political Ideology,* The Free Press, New York, 1962.

2 Eugene Burdick, *The 480,* McGraw-Hill Book Company, New York, 1964. On the uses of public opinion sampling, see George Gallup, *The Sophisticated Poll Watcher's Guide,* Princeton Opinion Press, Princeton, N.J., 1972.

3 Walter DeVries and V. Lance Tarrance, *The Ticket Splitter, A New Force in American Politics,* Wm. B. Eerdmans Publishing Co., Grand Rapids, Mich., 1972.

4 George H. Gallup (ed.), *The Gallup Poll: Public Opinions, 1935–1971,* Random House, Inc., New York, 1972.

5 On the development of thought control and the influence of the yellow press, see George Orwell, *1984,* Signet Books, New York, 1949; John K. Winkler, *William Randolph Hearst, A New Appraisal,* Avon, New York, 1955; Dan Nimmo, *The Political Persuaders,* Prentice-Hall, Inc., Englewood Cliffs, N.J., 1970.

6 Daniel J. Boorstin, *The Image, A Guide to Pseudo-events in America,* Harper & Row Colophon Books, New York, 1961.

7 Edith Efron, *The News Twisters,* Manor Books, Inc., New York, 1972. Edith Efron, *How CBS Tried to Kill a Book,* Nash Publications, Los Angeles, 1972.

8 Paul Weaver, "Is Television News Biased?" *The Public Interest,* 26:60–61, Winter 1972.

9 Edward Jay Epstein, "A Reporter at Large: The Panthers and the Police, a Pattern of Genocide," *The New Yorker,* Feb. 13, 1971, pp. 45 ff. On distortion of campus news events, see John E. Peterson, "TV on Campus Unrest—A Gross Distortion?" *Detroit News,* May 24, 1972.

10 Daniel P. Moynihan, "The Presidency and the Press," *Commentary,* March 1971.

11 Robert L. Bartley, "The Press: Adversary, Surrogate Sovereign, or Both?" in George F. Will (ed.), *Press, Politics and Popular Government,* American Enterprise Institute for Public Policy Research, Washington, March 1972.

12 Robert D. Novak, "The New Journalism," in Harry M. Clar (ed.), *Mass Media and Modern Democracy,* Rand McNally, Chicago, 1973.

13 Irving Kristol, "Crisis for Journalism: The Missing Elite," in Will, *op. cit.,* p. 50.

14 Draper Hill, *Mr. Gillray, The Caricaturist,* Phaidon, New York, 1965.

Chapter 6

Critical Voters
and Uncritical Elections

Back in 1960, Hubert H. Humphrey was doggedly fighting John F. Kennedy in the presidential primaries for the Democratic nomination. Poor and Protestant West Virginia looked like a state in which HHH might make some headway against wealthy and Catholic JFK.

The problem facing Humphrey in West Virginia was finances. The Kennedys had put the squeeze on his donors. He paid the last $750 out of his own pocket so he could have an election-night telethon on a statewide TV network. But he had no funds left to produce a first-rate program, no one to screen questions in advance so that they would fit his main campaign themes, and so he had to wing it.

Theodore White describes the scene. Humphrey is sitting before a TV camera with telephone in hand, pressing a button back and forth for questions direct and uncensored from the viewers. About question three, White writes:

> There came a rasping voice over the telephone, the whining scratch of an elderly lady somewhere high in the hills, and one could see Humphrey flinch (as the viewers flinched): and the rasp

said, "You git out! You git out of West Virginia, Mr. Humphrey."
Humphrey attempted to fluster a reply but the voice overrode him,
"You git out, you hear?"[1]

This was followed by a call from a sweet syrupy woman who
drawled on and on in generalities about American politics. As
precious minutes ticked by, Humphrey repeatedly tried to cut her
off. Finally he succeeded and was just getting back to making
votes when he was interrupted by a telephone operator who
insisted he get off the line for an emergency call. From there on
the program went downhill.

What can we learn from this? We make two main assumptions from it for this chapter: (1) that campaigning is a two-way
communication process in which the voter participates; and (2)
that it is increasingly a communication process in which the
candidate requires the staff help of professionals in order to hold
up his end.

PACKAGING CANDIDATES

Between elections, the mass media and public officials talk mainly
to each other and so dominate the agenda for public discussion
and action. But during the campaign and election period, all kinds
of strange and unexpected things can happen. Appeals that voters
respond to become an important feedback into the democratic
process. This is because most candidates, whether they are
sincere or cynical about issues, come to the same end: They want
to win and the way to win is to get the support of more voters
than their opponent does. You as a candidate begin with your
traditionally committed and try to activate them. Then you either
try to prevent one from straying from your ticket or encourage
one to stray from the other party's ticket, depending on whether
you are ahead or behind. Part of the task of influencing such
potential drifters is being attuned to what they want to hear. Thus
feedback from voters becomes crucial to a well-planned campaign.

Voters have always been easiest to hold or entice away
from the opposition when personal contact is made with them.
Direct contact through campaigning is a form of flattery to the
voter and as De Tocqueville early noted, democratic peoples
enjoy humbling the high and mighty. When Rockefeller ate
blintzes during a reelection campaign, he sent out a message—
that he was not just a Rockefeller but a regular fellow, too.

The Direct Appeal   In former times, it was considered un-dignified for the presidential candidate himself to campaign directly. Personal contacts were made by party organizations or machines through the friendly, neighborhood precinct captain. These party workers were paid off in jobs or in other benefits, but they, in turn, were expected to deliver the vote.

Today the old-style machines are nearly dead because a first-class professional machine can no longer be recruited. In a machine-intensive rather than labor-intensive society and in an age of civil service, you cannot find the government jobs that appeal and without them parties cannot find the professional party workers. And there are few alternatives among the ama-teurs. The notion that very many people in the middle masses want to spend their leisure hours in political organizations does not stand the test of reality. The best you can hope for if you are a Democrat is for some precinct work from labor and if Republi-can, for some suburban Republican precinct organization, based on bored upper-middle-class housewives. Almost everywhere else in the country, the formal party organizations are skeletal blueprints made up of a few eager devotees to whom politics is a hobby. Political parties are in continual organizational and finan-cial difficulties. The state headquarters have trouble coming up with accurate lists of supporters and occasionally carry rural counties where they do not have the names of any party functionaries. For the most part, the organization in either party is hardly worth the postage costs of a direct-mail piece.

This means that the only precinct organization left that is worth considering is ad hoc for a particular campaign and thus depends on the temporarily inspired. In recent years, this has meant the Goldwaterites, those little old ladies in blue tennis shoes working with retired admirals, and energetic college stu-dents. For one or more elections at least, these have demon-strated they have time on their hands plus the energy and inclination to devote themselves to precinct contacts. Thus they are the only "machines" active in recent elections because they have been capable of doing the grubby door-to-door work on a national scale. Their reward has been in enjoying the self-sacrifice of walking around in the rain for an ideological cause and the moral satisfaction of setting their neighbors right. The problem with eager campaign workers is that they fade away when disillusion sets in, which is the inevitable result of either victory or defeat. But during a single campaign they can give a candidate an initial and a formidable advantage, particularly when the vote is light and the competition is a little bored or disgruntled.

The Mass Media and the Campaign Management Firm

The candidates who have no such support—and this becomes the case with most candidates in the end—have to turn elsewhere for help. Campaigning through the media is the substitute for personal contact through the machine. Technology has increased the potential payoffs from such campaigns. The invention of the mass newspaper and magazine, radio, television, and billboards make it possible for candidates to come into direct, though secondary, contact with many more voters than ever before possible and, so to speak, come right out into their living rooms, providing the voter does not switch channels in irritation. Use of the mass media thus is a necessary substitute for the direct personal contact with voters that a good professional party machine was once able to make.

Because of this media dependence, money and especially the efficient spending of it have become a key to electoral victory. Candidates quickly realize they need the help of a new kind of professional—the professional in campaign management. Generally it has been an underdog from the weaker party who has first and most frequently utilized his services. The consultant's goal has been to salvage victory for him or her even if the rest of the ticket goes down the drain.

As with many of the trends in the American culture, good or bad, the state of California pioneered in this effort. The California campaigns for Republican candidates managed in the late 1930s and 1940s by the Whitaker and Baxter advertising agency became models to be copied and sometimes improved upon elsewhere. These agency efforts rested on several assumptions that appear valid for most elections. They assumed and quickly demonstrated that it is a good deal more efficient and therefore cheaper to let a professional "media man" handle media problems than to turn the money over to party amateurs or try to make all the decisions yourself. It is also cheaper to sell style and an image than it is to sell content, and therefore an attractive personality will generally bring in more votes than will a candidate determined to treat the voters to a weighty discussion of the issues. Issues are easiest sold when simplified into catchy slogans that have a nice moral ring ("He Kept Us out of War," "America First," "A Full Dinner Pail," "A Square Deal"). Sophisticated practitioners have built upon what politicians have known for a long time: It is not bad to seem to be discussing the issues, particularly if you can seem to be doing it sincerely and firmly, and so long as you emphasize style over content and do not bore the voter by providing too many details. Finally, agency efforts rested on the assumption that it was easier to differentiate the product by selling individual candidates than to sell the entire ticket as a party team.

Professional campaign management has become a big business in the United States with the packaging of presidential candidates and offering them to the public as breathlessly as the introduction of a new sports-car model. Firms try for records of success and advertise the number of candidates they have helped elect. The consulting industry, just as did the advertiser for soap chips, has borrowed heavily from what social scientists know about consumers, in this case, voters. It is systematically producing campaign strategies that harmonize fairly well with such findings. *The American Voter,* produced by the social scientists of the Survey Research Center, at the University of Michigan, has become their bible. They now poll the voters in advance of the campaign, pretest strategies, study responses to themes in key precincts, and, if there is money left, test everything again against the actual election outcomes.

Organizing a Modern Campaign: A Case Study In *The Ticket Splitter,*[2] Walter DeVries, a political scientist and campaign consultant, provides a classic description of what could serve as a model campaign of today that most such consultants would want to emulate. His candidate was Governor William Milliken of Michigan, who, as a Republican incumbent in 1970, seemed to face sure defeat in what appeared to be a likely Democratic year. The DeVries strategy was to go hunting where the ducks were, to concentrate on those Michigan independent voters who in the past had split their tickets for Republican candidates such as former Governor George Romney. DeVries first isolated the precincts in the state dominated by such voters. Second, he analyzed all past and present opinion data about split-ticket voters in Michigan to find what types of persons these were. He found them, as one would expect, to be middlebrows; suburban more than central city, having a high school education or with some college, Catholic more than Protestant, between thirty and fifty years of age, TV viewers with some interest in politics, viewers especially of TV-news programs and documentaries who also enjoyed the drama and conflict of TV sports.

Third, DeVries aimed the whole Milliken campaign at such voters and concentrated the campaign effort in the nineteen counties in which 80 percent of such voters lived. He put his funds in radio and TV commercials and neatly made the tie-ins to news broadcasts, sports events, and women's daytime quiz shows.

Every TV spot was pretested with samples of such split-ticket voters from these nineteen counties and a continuous telephone survey in heavily ticket-splitting precincts provided day-by-day feedback of the reactions of such voters to the Milliken campaign. The kind of pitch devised was one of selling the candidate as a person who understood the serious public problems facing the electorate of Michigan and as a man who was capable of acting intelligently in respect to these pressing problems. The format was to show slum housing, for example, then have Milliken make a short statement to indicate he was a sincere man who understood that the problem of slums existed and that he was competent to act on the problem, then fade out with an appeal to the thinking independent voter: "Think about it—vote for Governor Milliken."

The ability to handle the job was emphasized by showing the candidate as much as possible with the paraphernalia of the Governor's office, the ever-present flag, the leather chairs and paneled walls, the doodads on his desk possibly presented him by some Rotary Club in the Upper Peninsula. The campaign slogan was "A Leader You Can Trust." Utopian promises were avoided because ticket splitters were found not to trust politicians (or ad agencies either). Solutions were not discussed; stressed only was the idea that the candidate understood the problem and would act in some unspecified way on it and that he was thus worthy of the thinking middle-brow's confidence.

Milliken's margin of victory was hairline at 50.6 percent, but all other statewide candidates elected in Michigan that year were Democrats (the average GOP vote was 40 percent), and the three constitutional amendments on the ballot on which Milliken, perhaps unwisely, had taken a stand all went the other way. He was one of two Republican governors elected in the Midwest. DeVries could with justice argue that his candidate's victory represented the bucking of a trend and would probably not have occurred without his efforts.

Tippecanoe and Tyler, Too—So What Else Is New?
Some have argued that the campaign consultants are introducing "unfair" techniques that encourage the candidate to seem to

adapt himself to voters' views rather than trying to discuss the issues fully and thus to educate the voters. The answer that must be given is that such a view rests on an unstated assumption about what voters want to hear or will respond to. The professional campaign consultants did not invent this kind of campaign nor have they been responsible for it being typical of most elections from the beginning of mass voter participation. Certainly it dates back to the campaigns of Andrew Jackson and before that to Marc Antony's funeral oration. The successful Whig campaign against Van Buren in 1840, might even prove especially worthy of deep study by today's media specialists.

Van Buren, a Democrat who had a visible Presidential record as championing the frontiersman's interests, was opposed by the Whigs, an agglomerate group led by conservatives from the East, such as Daniel Webster of Massachusetts, and those from the newer lands, such as Henry Clay of Kentucky. Unable to agree among themselves, the Whigs adopted no platform at all in 1840; instead, they took a me-too approach. They sought to show that they were the true friends of the common man, especially the frontiersman, by emphasizing style over content. For President they nominated a folk hero, General William Henry Harrison, and called him by the affectionate nickname of "Tippecanoe" (after the site of one of his victories over that frontier villain, the Indian). For Vice President, they selected a renegade Democrat, John Tyler from Virginia. Harrison, who came from an aristocratic Virginia family and lived as a country gentleman on 2,000 acres outside Cincinnati, was sold to the public as a true frontiersman. His supporters toured the country, wearing coonskin caps, speaking from the porch of a log cabin mounted on a wagon, with a hard-cider jug conspicuously near the door. Harrison had been in public life very briefly and was not on record on any of the day's major issues. His party offered the rural working people of the frontier a real he-man, and the expanding urban working populations "Two dollars a day and roast beef."

At the same time, the Whigs made an effort to show that Van Buren did not deserve the vote of the common man. He was an Eastern aristocrat (actually, his father had been an upstate New York saloonkeeper) who lived like a king in the White House and who—of all unmanly things—put cologne on his sideburns. Obviously, if the people wanted a real successor to Jackson in the White House, the Whig "frontiersman" was their man. Harrison won the election.

Issueless Politics: Focus on the Candidate's Image

This is the kind of media-oriented campaign that has always been necessary for an underdog to win when there is really not much difference between the candidates or when the voters are rather indifferent about whatever real differences actually exist.

It is also especially the kind of campaign attractive in today's TV-conscious America that thrives on hokum particularly if it can be made to sound serious and be packaged as intellectual hokum. As noted in the previous chapter, present-day voters have become disenchanted with the traditional differences between Democratic and Republican parties. By 1967, more citizens identified themselves to pollsters as independents than as Republicans. This trend is especially evident among younger voters and this has been accentuated further by the lowering of the voting age to eighteen. The George Wallace third-party movement in 1968 as well as the Eugene McCarthy and peace movements within the Democratic party were further indication of the willingness of many traditional middle-mass Democrats to stray from traditional predispositions. Finally, the mixed results of many elections were symbolized again in 1968 and 1972 when the Presidency was controlled by the Republicans and both Houses of Congress by Democrats. The extent and increase of such split-ticket voting is indicated in Table 6-1.

DeVries and others expect this type of politics to continue through the 1970s, just as it has characterized California since the EPIC (End Poverty in California) campaign of Upton Sinclair in 1934. In that election, anti-Sinclair movie commercials showed pro-Sinclair voters scratching themselves while they explained in bad grammar what a wonderful thing a Sinclair victory would be for Californians. Sinclair lost. One can argue that in times past, when members of the organization made the voter contacts, a team effort was the cheapest strategy. Today when media impact makes the difference, a personal candidate strategy is generally dictated. Some, however, think it may still be possible to revive straight-party voting when a national issue or candidate of sufficient impact divides the voters. We review this prospect next.

CRITICAL ELECTION AND POLITICAL BELIEFS

In the 1936 campaign, President Franklin Roosevelt was pondering with his aide Robert Sherwood what to do about Pittsburgh. In his 1932 campaign he had made a significant campaign speech

Table 6-1 Split Outcomes in Gubernatorial and U.S. Senatorial
Elections: 1914–1970

Year	States with simultaneous elections	Number of split outcomes	Percent: split outcomes
1914	22	6	27.3
1916	24	5	20.8
1918	22	1	4.5
1920	24	0	0.0
1922	22	5	22.7
1924	26	1	3.8
1926	24	4	16.7
1928	24	4	16.7
1930	24	5	20.8
1932	23	3	13.0
1934	22	3	13.6
1936	24	2	8.3
1938	24	4	16.7
1940	26	11	42.3
1942	23	3	13.0
1944	22	6	27.3
1946	24	1	4.2
1948	22	4	18.2
1950	24	5	20.8
1952	22	6	27.3
1954	25	6	24.0
1956	20	3	15.0
1958	22	4	18.2
1960	19	5	36.3
1962	27	12	44.4
1964	18	10	55.6
1966	22	13	59.1
1968	15	9	60.0
1970	24	11	45.8

Source: Walter DeVries and V. Lance Tarrance, *The Ticket Splitter: A New Force in American Politics*, Wm. B. Eerdmans Publishing Co., Grand Rapids, Mich., 1972.

there in which he had attacked Herbert Hoover for having an unbalanced budget and for expanding the federal bureaucracy. If elected, FDR had promised, he would immediately stop these unsound practices. Sherwood's advice to FDR: "Deny you've ever been to Pittsburgh."[3]

The story reminds us of what only the historians seem to

remember: Franklin Roosevelt did not invent the New Deal, rather he stumbled onto it. The same might be said of William McKinley and his Protection program and even of Abraham Lincoln and the Emancipation Proclamation. In the past, at least, the middle mass of voters in some elections were receptive to a discussion of program. All on their own, they did sharply and significantly shift parties over an issue or set of issues. Politicians often responded to such new issues only after they had surfaced and their voter appeal was clear. Such self-generated divisions also had long-lasting political effects. Will voters in the age of professional campaign consultants and TV commercials ever generate issues again? We think it possible, but we cannot be sure.

The Theory of Critical Elections As we noted earlier, changes in political allegiance are the result of new experiences that go much deeper than good government moral appeals or the monetary argument by an attractive candidate. Such new experiences must touch the hopes and fears for the future of a significant number of voters to bring about such decisive shifts in commitment. The candidate who stumbles into such a campaign situation and is able to exploit it to his own advantage and that of his party may even surprise the media consultants, for such deep voter reaction can no more be created than Ford could develop a consumer market for the Edsel.

Political scientists see this kind of change of voter commitments as causing what they call "critical elections." They are critical because the change is from one partisan commitment or from a period of drift to a new long-term partisan commitment in the form of a realignment of factions into a new winning coalition. Thus a new party tradition is established.

In the past, such elections did occur, sometimes in one election, more frequently over two or three national elections. The critical election periods noted by V. O. Key, Jr., occurred one to one and one-half generations apart—at ever-lengthening intervals of from twenty-eight to thirty-two to thirty-six years: 1800, 1828, 1860, 1896, and 1932. Each of these elections signaled the beginning of a period in which most succeeding national elections were dominated by one political party and the other won by default or in some states or localities of traditional strength. By such calculations, we are overdue for another critical election or unknowingly had one in 1964, 1968, or 1972.

Life Experiences and Political Behavior Critical elections are caused by marked shifts in voter belief systems. Let us begin by examining the operation of such belief systems on the personal level and then note the political impact of changes. The kind of change in commitment we are describing could be compared to the way a traumatic event may affect the basic personality of an individual. More frequently, however, rather than coming as the result of a single experience, the change results gradually. The source of change is often a series of new personal experiences. This is likely to have the most impact when the way the citizen lives his everyday life is markedly changed from that of his parents. Perhaps this is the reason why in our country's history, new political belief systems and critical election periods have so often followed after large-scale population shifts, such as the movement of the frontier or of citizens from farms to the big cities, or from cities to suburbs. Each new environment brings its own new set of experiences, which may challenge assumptions long taken for granted and lead to the creation of new ones about how life should be lived. This kind of process occurred for many Southern rural whites who during World War II were drafted out of the boondocks and shipped around the world for the first time.

The network of political assumptions each of us adopts is not necessarily a carefully worked-out set of ideas; it may in fact include inconsistent notions of which we are unaware. These belief systems that grow from a shared set of experiences may be described as a kind of "folk philosophy," or ideology (in the Lasswellian sense of a loose clustering of symbols and concepts). They are not as systematic or as sophisticated as philosophy, and they usually evolve gradually, with no single thinker as their source. In this sense, they resemble folk songs more than the works of serious composers. They are also ideas that we largely accept on faith because they seem to harmonize with the reality of experience. Yet such clusters of assumptions are extremely useful to all of us. They are the basis of how all of us normally determine how we will react to events we observe. These assumptions save us the information costs of looking at every political event or issue from the beginning. We use such loosely related sets of ideas as shortcuts in decision making relative to our work, family, and even leisure time. They serve as a source of motivation for action, a guide and a justification for what we regard as acceptable behavior. They also result in our screening out unwanted information or points of view.

Political Belief Systems   Belief systems are composed of three interrelated parts: (1) assumptions about what exists and (2) how one ought to behave, as well as (3) an emotional reinforcement for the first two. The process of the interrelation of these parts and how change may occur as the result of new experiences can be described in respect to the Southern white. The overriding reality of the rural plantation and village was that blacks were poorly educated and lived at a poverty level. They thus seemed to fit most of the stereotypes of the white as to shiftlessness and irresponsibility. The black's own self-image, as well as his behavior, confirmed the Southern white's image of reality. The reality part of this set of assumptions is directly tied to a moral or "ought" element, which is the most important part of such a set of assumptions. If blacks were in fact as they were described, then one must assume it is right that they should be treated on a par with other domesticated animals for their own good and for society's good, and it is wrong to treat them as if they were capable of intelligent or responsible behavior.[4]

Thus are political programs born. Along with the reality and moral elements is an emotional or "affect" component that reenforces the belief system and holds it together. Thus, to see blacks treated in any other fashion than reality and morality dictate, leads to an emotional reaction that may vary from intense anger to actual physical sickness and revulsion. Note that blacks as well as whites may share this emotional reaction, one that responds most readily and almost automatically to those symbols which come to stand for the whole belief system (the happy watermelon eater).

Belief systems strongly resist change and break down only when new experiences can no longer be ignored. Some people may achieve such experiences through books or from watching television or listening to a sermon. More frequently, it is the result of actual personal experience where its impact cannot be evaded or turned aside. In our example, the change that took place most often was the result of living with capable and intelligent blacks. When the assumption about reality is admitted to be clearly wrong, the moral imperative also begins to change. If blacks are capable of intelligent and responsible action, they are not like domesticated animals and should not be treated as such, but should be treated with the same respect and dignity as other human beings. As the ethical element changes, the emotional component also begins to weaken, but it is the last to disappear and it makes the most determined fight to prevent change. It is also the element that makes the process of change painful. Most reasonable people resist a change in their assumptions until it is clear that their belief system can no longer deal adequately with reality. Some people, however, will go to great length to avoid the pain of change, even to distorting reality or trying to deny its existence. However, once a set of assumptions is questioned to the point where an individual loses faith in it, it is likely to be permanently discarded. Politically, belief systems such as those of the Greenbackers become museum pieces of interest only to antiquarians or historians.

The relevancy of such individual belief systems to politics is, we hope, obvious. These assumptions are the shortcuts we all use to orient ourselves to political events. It is, in fact, the underlying purpose of this book to bring some of these assumptions to the surface so they can be looked at in the light, not of what we wish were the case, but by what appear to be and hopefully are some of the realities we face.

The middle masses have developed innumerable ideologies to deal with small or large issues, anything from the use of "pot" to the problem of the sea lamprey. We argue that they have also developed a series of such belief systems to orient themselves to American politics. It is these assumptions and the political issues related to them that have made American politics so closely conform to the interests of the middle masses. The political agenda of critical election periods sets the scene for political battles in the generation of politicking and legislating that follows. The question of postcritical periods is no longer one of what is to be done; that is a closed issue. It is how much of the what is to be done? Generally the major changes are made immediately after a critical election, as in the first 100 days of the New Deal. Policies of the thirty years or so that followed were only elaborations on the theme.

The Breadth Needed for Wide Appeal The political programs that have had major political impact on American politics have had to encompass a broad spectrum of the experience of the middle masses. They cannot be simply the limited assumptions that emerge from the experiences of, for example, college-educated airline stewardesses or black physicians. Airline stewardesses and M.D.'s each will, in fact, develop a belief system that provides shortcuts for choosing behaviors in respect to their job experiences and some of these may have some political relevance. Such assumptions may also harmonize with a more widely held belief system. However, the kinds of diffuse experiences that lead to politically relevant assumptions, that is, belief systems upon which a major party's campaigns and programs can rest, must be less specialized. We argue that they are most likely to be tied to the experiences of large numbers of citizens rather than to any particular set of experiences. The place where one lives ties together occupation, social status, and income into a special life-style and it is this experience that apparently becomes the source of support for political programs.

We should add that other analysts have argued that one or another aspect of the experience takes priority. The Marxian interpretation is that beliefs result from the societal means of production. Others argue that work experience alone may be the prime source of political views. S. M. Lipset points out that sheepherders and sailors, who work in isolation, are frequently radical in their politics.[5] Some intellectuals and religious leaders have argued that belief is more the result of contact with disembodied ideas and logical argument than of experience. Conversion, then, is the result of missionary work. All these may be true for some individuals and may be especially true in respect to viewpoints of specialized groups, or for views and assumptions that are not politically relevant in campaigns. We contend only that the experiences associated with place of residence tie together the package of experiences for most people. Thus they are especially useful in describing the political belief systems of the middle masses as expressed in political campaigns and it is such belief systems that have controlled the direction of American politics.

BELIEF SYSTEMS AND ELECTIONS

A half-dozen or so belief systems or ideologies have provided the themes for American politics throughout our history. Widely shared belief systems were associated with each of the critical election periods noted by V. O. Key, Jr. It is these we next describe.

The Federalists: Belief in Aristocracy Each of the critical elections of American politics has been especially related to assumptions about how America should be developed socially and economically. Among the most grandiose and perhaps the greatest failure among these belief systems was the first—one developed to rationalize the program of economic expansion put forward by the Federalist party of 1788. It was used to successfully nominate and elect George Washington twice and managed the same for John Adams once before it was junked.

It is instructive to look at this program which proved to be a failure even though it was put forward by the most able, educated, and well-born elements of the population. It was in fact bowled over easily the first time it was really challenged at the polls. It was found wanting because it did not ring a bell for the citizen who wanted to benefit from the new nation's economic growth: It could not capture a mass audience.

The Federalists under the leadership of the brilliant Alexander Hamilton, Secretary of the Treasury, had devised a model mercantilist program of economic development to begin the Washington administration. It was based upon an aristocratic set of political assumptions that fit well the experiences of those in the circles of the Federalist elite. Talent and skill were prized and a man was judged by his ability to carve out a splendid career. Society was cultured and the arts were to be cultivated. From this milieu emerged a political program stressing the prudent planning of bold ventures and calculated responses to challenging circumstances. As Hamilton himself expressed his ideal, "Aristocracy means government by the wise, the wealthy and the good." He acted; to him, it was natural for the elite to assume the burden of creative decision making for the masses.

Hamilton's *Report on Manufactures* was a grand design for quick and effective restructuring of a simple, rural society. It proposed building a great society by using the power of the central government to set tariffs and stabilize currency through a national bank. The method required favoring the merchant and industrial interests in society; a point the critics of Hamilton in the Charles Beard school of historical analysis never tired of stressing. But even if this were so, the criticism misses the main point. More than simple desires to exploit society for one's own benefit was involved. Hamilton was truly creative and his dream impressive. He had a vision of raising America to a first-rate nation by establishing an industrialized society. He assumed it was self-evident that Federalist party leaders were the nation's most able men and these alone had a vision to bring such a modern society into being. He assumed these alone could also effectuate change most rapidly. But mercantilist principles rest on strong central direction and national planning. Hamilton would not hesitate to overrule the majority in what he conceived as the nation's best interests. Like all aristocrats before and since, he argued that the talented had the right and duty to rule; he would have applauded José Ortega y Gasset's phrase describing such an elite as "those who make demands on themselves," while the rest, including Ortega, he classed as mass men.[6] In Hamilton's phrase, "The people, sir, are a great beast," capable of thinking only in terms of short-run interests and appetites. Hamilton's plan was visionary. It might well serve as a model for an Ataturk or an Nkrumah, but it failed as a basis for a majority party coalition in what was beginning to emerge as a mass democracy.

Jefferson and the Yeoman Farmer as Hero Jefferson may be said to have created the first mass-based American political program. He looked to where the voters were and found that he agreed with what they wanted. It was not accidental that this Unitarian deist paid toward the upkeep of the first Baptist missionary in Illinois. Jefferson, the intellectual, pitched his political appeal to the yeoman backwoods farmer, the honest, hardworking, God-fearing stump clearer. He visualized a republic of equals made up of independent and self-sufficient small farmers, with a few crossroads merchants as a necessity. Most would earn their bread by labor on the land and so would develop a national economy by individual effort. He extolled the virtues of rural government. He painted rural citizens idealistically as governing themselves in small republican communities as political philosophers had always dreamed men would. He rejected Hamiltonian dreams of a trickle-down economy or of an economy managed by the experts. It would lead, he argued, to city life such as he had observed in Europe: "scabs on the body politic." This program Thomas Jefferson arrived at intellectually, but the voters arrived at it through experience. They elected him President in 1800. His vision still appears attractive to many who yearn to escape the complications of modern society.

By the end of Jefferson's two terms his intellectualized dream had lost some of its luster and the Virginia oligarchy that followed Jefferson, while mouthing his slogans, was less sympathetic to the egalitarianism that his program had extolled. By 1824, President John Quincy Adams, the son of the Federalist President, but himself a nominal Jeffersonian as was almost everyone else, attempted to revive the discredited Hamiltonian program under a new name. Adams, in his inaugural address, proposed this modernization plan: management of the national currency and finances through the national bank, tariffs to encourage domestic industry, a national university, a naval academy, scientific surveys, astronomical observatories, and a program of domestic improvements including a highway system constructed with federal funds. But a nation in which farmers and small entrepreneurs were the numerical majority was unready to accept any proposals smacking of centralized expertise. Expansion and development were to be sparked by individuals acting on their own conception of the public interest rather than by government planning or direction. With the plowing-under in 1828 of John Quincy Adams and his plan (with some exceptions, such as the now world-famous Naval Observatory), Americans committed the nation for the moment to having the important decisions on economic modernization made by private individuals and reaffirmed its belief in egalitarianism.

Populism Takes Over the Frontier Adams was beaten—resoundingly so—in the election of 1828 by a new champion of egalitarian frontierism: Andrew Jackson of Tennessee. It was he who presided over the first wave of populism and its suspicion of elitism and oligarchy. The anti-Establishment ideas he expressed were those that grew out of his frontier experience, farming in the western Carolinas and in his adopted state. He had faith in the competence of the common man and the possibility of his economic and social advancement through hard work, thrift, and individual responsibility. From these ideas, certain beliefs about government organization and government programs emerged. The following were the most important.

1. Any Man Was as Good as Another in Public Office or as a Voter Jefferson had implied this in the Declaration of Independence (1776), and Jackson had made it explicit in his first message to Congress (1829). One of the objectives of the Jacksonians was to replace their political enemies in the bureaucracy with persons who believed in their version of democracy. By the 1830s, the spoils system, by which federal bureaucrats were selected on the basis of party loyalty, was well established. The rotation-of-offices system was logical if we assume, with Jackson, that the few qualifications needed to run a government are widely distributed throughout society and that those who carry out the policies of Congress and the President ought to believe in those policies.

An assumption in favor of universal manhood suffrage followed logically from egalitarianism. It was a necessary development of Jacksonian thought. Furthermore, it was the natural result of the already existing tendency to broaden the electorate—a tendency that had begun before the Revolution. It appears that at the time of the war with England, about 90 percent of the rural dwellers of Massachusetts could vote, but there was a possibility that property requirements might disfranchise a considerable portion of the urban working class that began to emerge after the War of 1812. During the 1820s, however, property requirements were eliminated in many states, and by 1856 they had virtually disappeared. Universal suffrage (for white men, not blacks or women) had been achieved. Thenceforth, the general public—the vaunted common man—possessed the potential for the control of government in its own interest.

2. Officeholders Must Be Rotated Also part of the Jacksonian system was the populist assumption that officeholders were ever prone to the corruption of oligarchy. This is what had happened to the Jeffersonian system. To prevent it happening again, the Jacksonians provided for terms of office as short as a year, election of as many officials as possible, prohibitions against successive terms for powerful officials like governors or financial officers like treasurers, and as noted, the spoils system of personnel selection.

This political program had an enormous impact upon the writing of state constitutions from the 1830s through the 1850s. In particular, it led to the development of the long ballot, which listed dozens of elective offices and all the candidates for each. The United States Constitution, however, written by aristocrats rather than frontiersmen, had sought to minimize the participation of the voter, and the Jacksonian view became dominant too late to have drastic effects upon the federal electoral pattern.

3. There Were Only a Few Areas in Which Government Could Act to Help the Individual On the question of how much the federal government should be involved in the economy, the frontiersman could choose between the mercantilist's belief that the job of government was to assist in the expansion of the economy and the stump-clearer's conviction that things were not likely to get done unless a man did them himself. In general, pre-Civil War Americans took the position that government could help with very few things and those only so long as the benefit went to the common people of the frontier. In particular, they supported the use of state and federal funds for canal building and the construction of the first "U.S." highway—the National Road from the Cumberland Gap to south-central Illinois (beginning in 1808). On the other hand, for the most part they believed that the functions of the state and federal governments in the domestic sphere should remain few in number, and Jacksonians were quick to oppose legislation they thought would benefit only a favored class. Jackson himself vetoed (1830) the bill for federal aid to the Maysville Road in Kentucky because he was convinced that it was designed more for a few businessmen than for ordinary citizens.[7]

Thus, in effect, the Jacksonians favored transferring to the nation lessons learned from the experience of rural townships on the frontier—government by the common man performing a few basic functions.

The tradition of the Jacksonian frontier farmer represented the mainstream of American political development, but in the southeastern part of the country it had a competitor: an economy of plantation farming and a way of life distinctly elitist. The plantations had begun much as did the small farms of the Northern frontier, but two differences emerged. One was the need for large-scale farming of the cotton crop, the other was the presence of the Negro slave. As the result of these, the small-scale farmer either was squeezed out into the more barren hilly areas or he grew into the large-scale plantation operator. This economic system spawned a caste society with its traditions of aristocracy and chivalry built on a foundation of the use of human beings as property.

The Individual in an Emerging Industrial Society
The next sharp division in political programs reflected the movement of citizens from the frontier farm to the small trading centers that grew up everywhere from New England to the West during the latter part of the Jacksonian period. The emerging small enterprises in these communities met head-on with the slave plantation economy of the South. It was this conflict of economic interest rather than the humane concerns of the abolitionists that appears to have led to the break-up of the major parties, the Civil War, and the Republicanism of the party of Lincoln. A slave economy would wipe out the independent businessman and the way of life of the respectable and largely democratic village crossroads trading center. It was this recognition by the middle masses that led to support of the war and, following the conflict, to championing of the interests of the

small-town enterprise at the expense of the rest of the population. In the years after the Civil War, these small towns began to further industrialize and urbanize and it became clear that America could not become a rich nation so long as it was primarily agricultural. It was during this period that the financing and productive techniques of the large corporation emerged as the effective processes for the accumulation of national and personal wealth. Urban industrialization even in the middle-sized cities began to produce a way of life drastically different from what Americans had been accustomed to; not only the structure of government, but the assumptions of what government's role should be, were certain to be affected.

At first, only segments of the population felt the impact of their new way of life. But by the 1890s the desire for industrial development in the new middle-sized cities became the crucial political question. The issue in an industrial age was not whether the government could aid the frontier farmer in his routine labor, but whether the individual farmer could get a fair hauling rate from a huge railroad corporation; not whether the small-town merchant would deal fairly with his small-town and farming neighbors, but whether a nationwide manufacturer of canned goods would sell products that would not poison those who bought them; not whether Uncle Hiram could find a job as a farm hand through the slack winter months (his brother would take him in and let him cut timber on the back forty), but how thousands of factory workers would support their families if a plant closed for three months; not whether the one-room school that was educating the next generation of farmers should buy a new heating stove, but whether a different curriculum was needed to prepare a generation of professional specialists; not whether the United States should send a high-ranking member of the administration to attend the coronation of a European monarch, but whether it was possible to devise tariff schedules that would serve both industrial and agricultural interests.

In this new age, changing life experiences and life-styles redefined the public's concept of the proper function of government and produced a new set of political assumptions. The political program of post-Civil War Republicanism had been designed to favor the small entrepreneur. But with the growth of middle-sized cities and the extension of monopoly corporations, this belief system reached a new stage of development: one justifying the activities of the large-scale entrepreneur as the source of bounty for himself and the rest of society. The coming of big business, with its large capital investments, ever-increasing mechanization, and impersonal conditions of labor, had produced the new political belief system of industrial individualism. It was a modified and modernized version of frontier individualism, appropriate to the pattern of life in the emerging cities. Americans, in varying degrees of clarity, came to recognize that the future of the nation lay in rapid industrialization.

Challenges to these ideas began with the farmers' protest movements such as the Grangers, Greenbackers, and Populists. The head-on challenge came in the Bryan campaign of 1896 when he called for inflation through the free coinage of silver. The Republicans embraced large-scale enterprise and won with a reenforced coalition that would keep them the majority party for another thirty-six years.

This set of assumptions of the Republican majority included the idea that business (including industry) was the nation's most important institution; that what was good for business was good for the nation; that other institutions, social or political, should play a secondary role and not interfere with the activities of business. Free enterprise and laissez faire became key symbols; government was regarded as inefficient, and its control over business was held to be not only a threat to the progress of the nation, but in fact immoral.

The federal and state courts became the guardians of free enterprise and of the dominant belief system. When these were threatened by federal regulation, the courts turned to the theory of states' rights, and at the same time, they used the due-process-of-law clause of the Fourteenth Amendment to set aside state regulation of interstate commerce. The courts replaced Congress as the dominant branch of government, and the Constitution came to be revered more than ever. In the folklore of the day, the Constitution was given a spirit of its own. It was treated as if it existed apart from the interpretations of it. And although judges often used their personal philosophies in interpreting the document, their decisions were written in a ritualistic language which suggested that it was the duty of the judges not to use their own values in interpreting the document, but to seek to "discover" its true intent. For example, it was found that the doctrine of free enterprise had been the "intention of the framers" even though the men at Philadelphia had in fact been mercantilists.

The middle masses especially in the now-dominant middle-sized cities accepted these ideas in general. They believed that hard work would be rewarded; that government should not interfere with their efforts. They accepted a trickle-down theory such as expounded in Andrew Carnegie's *Gospel of Wealth.* Inspiration for the golden age of individualism came from many other sources as well. Although almost no one reads the works of Horatio Alger today, his stories made great sense at the time they were written. They reflected the folklore of an emerging industrial nation by telling the nineteenth-century youngster that opportunity was his for the taking, that success could be measured in terms of material accomplishments, and that success resulted from virtue and hard work. Perhaps not every boy believed that he could become another Vanderbilt or Carnegie by this simple formula, but he was constantly bombarded with such propaganda by newspapers and magazines whose interests coincided with those of the new titans of business and industry. Undoubtedly these teachings profoundly affected Americans, urban and rural, rich and poor; they had much to do both with conditioning American behavior and with the way in which citizens permitted the giant corporations to create "clusters of private government which first neutralized state powers and then overcame them."[8] They also permitted the building of the mighty industrial nation that Hamilton had dreamed of. And the Spanish American War (1898) gave the nation a standing as an international power.

The Social Service State: Government Evens Out the Bumps The belief system which supplanted industrial individualism was associated with two facts: a continued massive population movement to various metropolises and the widely shared experience of the Great Depression of 1929.

The Northern cities, the places where most Americans lived after 1920, now contained large numbers of working-class people. Some had moved from rural areas, but most were immigrants or the children of immigrants, and they held unskilled or low-skilled factory jobs. The life these people led was deeply influenced by the impact of industrialism; the side effects of an economy dominated by industrial production were brought into sharp focus by the Great Depression.

The kind of life experienced in the city neighborhoods spawned a belief system favoring collective action. The farmer or small-town dweller of the past had provided most of his own household services. His garden, wood lot, and large frame house provided the resources for a self-contained family welfare system. He had room enough to care for widowed or orphaned relatives or retired parents. (Physical disability was the only basis for retirement, and it usually came gradually, without the shock of today's sudden and compulsory retirement at age sixty-five.) If a farmer or small-town merchant became ill, his relatives and neighbors saw to it that his work was carried on for him until his health was restored. Involuntary unemployment was unknown, except for the village idiot or the family black sheep. The farmer and small-town resident, until the Great Depression, favored individual effort on the basis of his experience.

The situation was different in the city, however. Experience even before the Great Depression led to the opposite assumptions. Urban society produced interdependence where independence had once existed. Water and sewage-disposal systems could no longer be provided on an inexpensive and simple basis. Houses were smaller and more expensive—there was no room for retired parents, widowed sisters, or orphaned nephews. Relatively few people could provide adequately for their own retirement independently of their children. Yet the children could not afford to feed or house their parents, not, at least, if they were to maintain what had become their conventional standard of living. And even the elderly person who was willing to work found that there were no jobs to be had—he was too old.

The individual no longer felt confident in his ability to control his own destiny or his environment. The large corporation, with a bureaucracy highly specialized and expert at passing the buck, was too impersonal to be concerned with the individual. Illness or injury spelled economic disaster to the factory worker or the white-collar clerk, whose pay offered little opportunity for saving; business and industrial leaders did not consider such personal tragedies a social cost chargeable to the firm. Unemployment of an involuntary nature became not merely a potential threat—it became commonplace. A man willing—even eager—to work who was employed by another man, or worse, by an impersonal corporation, might be laid off at any time for being ill too much of the time, for growing too old, because the nature of the business was cyclic or seasonal, because of a depression or financial panic, or even because of a personality conflict with the foreman or personnel officer.

These circumstances caused people to look around for a social institution to help them regain the stability and security that had slipped away from them. The most likely—perhaps the only—candidate was government. This view did not come to dominate national government politics until the Great Depression and the mid-1930s, when Franklin D. Roosevelt was President. When industrial individualism clearly failed to meet felt needs, voters turned to collective effort. Increasingly, groups (especially those of the middle masses) saw the government as the institution that could most likely help to relieve the fears and worries of the contemporary urbanite. It could do this by creating services of its own as well as by forcing large-scale industry to assume additional social responsibilities.

A Suburban Life-Style in a Metropolitan, Computerized Society As we have already noted, the belief system of the New Deal that emphasized economic security now seems to have lasted long past the point of its usefulness. Working-class and lower-middle-class people who were forced onto welfare in the 1930s now own dishwashers and sailboats. The poor of the 1930s cannot be compared with the poor of the 1970s. Government domestic programs that gave succor to the desperate then represent only another cause of heavy taxes for today's middle-mass man. America has experienced yet another massive population shift, one that has radically altered the average man's life-style—from resident of the big city to resident of the suburb. The white-collar, middle-management corporation cog has become the typical successful American, replacing the working-class union member. New technologies have made the unskilled worker almost obsolete, forcing him to move—either upward toward a skill, or downward into welfare poverty. The insecurities of urban life are today of a different type. Most of the worthwhile New Deal programs, except for complete medical care and an end to racial discrimination, have been accomplished or have had the basic groundwork laid for their achievement.

The new emphasis is on protection and security in such fields as the quality of the environment, population control, or peaceful international relations. The new experience is one that takes economic security almost for granted—in fact, buffers it through providing insulation for the individual through a niche in the big corporation or the government civil service, with all the accompanying institutionalized benefits. It assumes that government should provide an income for those unable to find jobs. On the other hand, large-scale organization, despite the economic prosperity that has usually accompanied it, also represents threats to individuality. The suburban experience seems to have encouraged notions favorable to free expression and freedom of action, sometimes to the point of irresponsibility, for the old sense of community and social obligation has sharply declined. The combination is very much like the subsidized life led currently by many (by no means all) college and university students. Whether the middle-masses-oriented economic security of the social service state can be reconciled with the need for a sense of integrated community, a chance for the poor, individuality, and free expression into a single political program remains to be seen.

TODAY'S POLITICS

The theory of critical elections discussed above is highly useful in understanding American political events. Its chief weakness is in the lack of dependable advance indicators. Unfortunately, we cannot be certain that a critical election has occurred until one or more elections have passed. For example, we now know that 1932 was a critical election year, leading to the social service state era, but at the time it could well have been interpreted as just a temporary, if massive, protest. Even the great 1936 Democratic sweep did not make it entirely clear that there was a new majority party. Only by the time of the 1940 public opinion polls could professional observers be certain of what had happened.

With this warning on our minds, the authors would put forth this tentative proposition: A new political belief system, one that goes beyond the social service state, is emerging. New Deal liberalism is no longer relevant to present life-styles. A critical election took place in 1968. The Roosevelt New Deal coalition is dead and the Democratic party is no longer the majority party. New coalitions were still in the process of formation in 1972, but their outline would seem to be one of *three* rather than of two groups as in the past. Since the late 1930s and particularly since 1960, there has been a sharp increase in the number of independent voters in the country, persons who feel no emotional loyalty to any established political party. This new group, consisting particularly of young people, is now the swing group. Both the Democratic and Republican parties now fail to command a majority position. For a number of reasons, the new alignment somewhat favors the Republicans in relation to the Presidency and to a lesser extent for congressional elections as will be seen below.

The street brawls between "young activists" and the Chicago police in 1968, the deliberate humiliation of a skillful professional politician, Richard J. Daley, at the 1972 convention, and the disaffection of organized labor leaders that same year were symptoms, not causes, of the disintegration of the winning combination within the Democratic party.

The Old Winning Grouping　The New Deal winning coalition consisted of an unlikely combination of Southerners, urban political machines, blacks, Jews, other minorities, upper-middle-class WASP reformers, intellectuals, organized labor, yeoman farmers, and others. But like every winning combination, and especially one that is larger than it needs to be, the coalition began to fall apart as soon as it reached its peak in 1936, slowly at first, then at an increasing pace (see Figure 6-1). John F. Kennedy

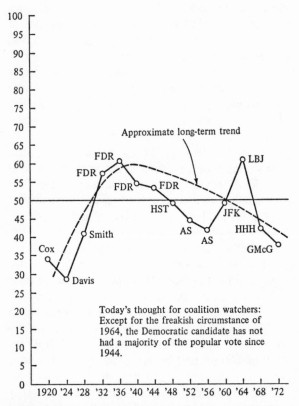

Figure 6-1　The Democratic party vote as a percentage of total presidential popular vote, 1920–1972.

won in 1960 by a margin so thin that we cannot know if he really earned the victory—the margin was by less than the average amount of error in the vote-counting process, as was also the case for Richard M. Nixon in the 1968 election. By 1972, all that seemed to remain dependably in the Democratic fold were the poor, the underprivileged racial and ethnic minority groups, a fair number of intellectuals, and some upper-middle-class idealists and dilettantes. To win, it would appear that the party would need to pull in large numbers of independent voters.

If we are correct in believing 1968 to have been a critical election, it seems likely that the Republicans are in the process of picking up some ex-members of the New Deal coalition, particularly the skilled and semiskilled "hard hats" from organized labor, conservative-moving upper-middle-class reformers, yeoman farmers, and perhaps some others, but not enough to form a new majority.[9] Drifting into the independent category would appear to be many intellectuals, Southerners, labor leaders, Jews (concerned about isolationist trends in the Democratic party that might threaten support for Israel, about the attack upon middle-class values traditionally held by Jews, and the support of employment quotas, as voiced by Senator George McGovern),[10] and young people of every category. Although the Republicans have benefited from the realignment, they have a problem of their own—an aging party that has not yet found an effective way to attract sufficient numbers of young members to keep the party viable in future years.

Evidence on 1968 as the Year　Conclusive evidence, as we have indicated, comes only after several years have passed, but certainly there are plenty of indicators to at least suggest that the above argument is basically correct. Here are some of them:

1. Critical elections took place in 1860, 1896, and 1932, each thirty-six years apart. Political science is not exact enough to say that thirty-six is the magic number, but we have indicated that it has always been something near that number—one and one-half generations. Thirty-six years after 1932 would be 1968. The problems of the Great Depression, with its policies designed to rehabilitate the unemployed members of the middle class and working class, and the yeoman farmers, are far behind us. The dominant groups today are those of the middle-class and "hard hat" suburbanites (a majority of suburbanites are now blue-collar workers). Their concerns, not those of deprived minorities, are the central focus of today's politics, harsh as this may seem to idealists—it was DeTocqueville in the 1830s who wrote of the "tyranny of the majority" as a problem in democracy.

2. The rise of minority parties (one possible result of the 1968 election may be the demise of the two-party system) and especially of the independent voter has meant that only three Presidents have been able to gain the support of an absolute majority of the voters since the end of World War II (1945). Johnson did so in the unusual election of 1964, when the Republican professionals turned the convention over to the amateur supporters of Goldwater. The pros that year knew that the party was up against two popular Democratic candidates— one of whom was a ghost. The Republicans scored majorities in the two Eisenhower elections, 1952 and 1956, which may have portended more of the future than was for a long time realized. Ike said he was a Republican, the Democratic leaders said he was a Republican, but the voters did not believe them. Ike was the prototype Independent, standing well above the level of the grubby political parties. Americans have always claimed to "vote for the man" even when they were staunch party supporters. Starting with Ike, they really did choose man over party. And Nixon won by a majority in the bizarre election of 1972.

3. The Gallup poll has shown a steady decline in party loyalty during the last generation. Only 20 percent of the voters considered themselves to be "independent" in 1940. This figure had increased to 32 percent in 1972. Changing life-styles and the increasing cost of labor have almost eliminated the professional party worker, a cog in the old-fashioned political machines. In most states, political party machinery is now almost nonexistent. Organizations today are created ad hoc about a particular candidate. Television has come to be the dominant factor in the campaigns for President, United States senator, governor, and some other offices. On television it is the *candidate* the voter sees and hears, not the party. The face-to-face relationships of old-time campaigns are gone; so are party organization and discipline. In an age of commercially packaged images, party loyalty is rapidly becoming grist for the historian only.

4. The Democrats won a really big victory in 1964. Astronomers tell us the stars in the heavens often flash brilliantly just as they begin to burn out. So it seems to be with political parties, though for vastly different reasons, we assume. Lyndon B. Johnson won that year by 486-52 in Electoral College votes. The pattern was similar just before other critical elections. Democrat Franklin Pierce won 254-42 in 1852, just before the turmoil that

saw an end to his party's dominance. Democrat Grover Cleveland won 277-145 in 1892, the election before the Republicans reestablished themselves with a bigger and stronger coalition. And Republican Herbert Hoover won 444-87 in 1928, just before the roof fell in on his party. A "one-last-big-effort" to win, or an attempt to ignore the ominous signs of danger, or turmoil within the emergingly dominant party may be factors in producing this phenomenon. Whatever the reasons, it was present, once again, in 1964.

5. Within the congressional parties, many Republicans and Democrats alike are loyal to their party leaders only because the opportunity to advance into leadership positions is through seniority. But increasingly strong attacks are being made upon the seniority system for choosing committee chairmen and ranking minority members. Once these attacks are successful, we can anticipate a large-scale crossover of votes from one party's candidate to another's in forming congressional majorities and determining committee chairmen. What was once the Republican–Southern Democratic coalition could become the formal organizing group in each house. Or after some elections, it could be a bipartisan liberal alignment; the way would be open for Presidents to form their own congressional majorities and to become stronger legislative leaders than ever. Most Presidents would welcome a situation where party labels would be unimportant in determining their coalition of supporters. Abolition of the seniority system, furthermore, would make the life of minor party members and independents far less lonely and would thus probably encourage a further breakup of the two-party system.

This is our preliminary estimate of what is happening in politics today. In all candor, we must add that other patterns may instead develop. For example, there are possible arguments for the theory that after the 1972 debacle, the Democrats will regroup stronger than ever. Or the Nixon victories may be flukes. Perhaps no critical election has yet occurred since 1932 and the Roosevelt coalition is still alive. But we offer here perhaps the most interesting theory.

That Crystal Ball, Again This, then, seems to point toward a new pattern for the future: a new ideology based upon the needs and wants of the largely suburban middle class and upper-working class, an ideology oriented toward security in international affairs and a comfortable, material life-style at home.

Despite the calls for redistribution of the wealth (an old populist war cry), demands for a war not on communism but on poverty, and an end to discrimination of every kind, the dominant electorate—rightly or wrongly—continues to say to the less successful in society: "Come and join us. Find the routes that lead toward upward mobility. We will help you some, but mostly you must help yourself. Certainly, the last thing we will do is to reorient ourselves to accommodate you or to allow government to make you the central focus of its concern." The McGovern strategists misread the ideas of the common man of the middle masses in 1972; the Nixon strategists did not. The majority is indeed a tyrant—everyone wants his own side to win—but at least in an achievement-oriented society, some paths are left open for the children of losers to become winners. That is the lesson that successive waves of dominant American political ideologies have sought to teach us.

NOTES

1 Theodore White, *The Making of the President, 1960,* Atheneum Publishers, New York, 1961, pp. 132–133.
2 Walter DeVries and V. Lance Tarrance, *The Ticket Splitter, A New Force in American Politics,* Wm. B. Eerdmans Publishing Co., Grand Rapids, Mich., 1972.
3 Robert Sherwood, *Roosevelt and Hopkins,* rev. ed., Harper & Row, New York, 1950.
4 See William A. Percy, *Lanterns on the Levee,* Alfred A. Knopf, Inc., New York, 1941. Percy's description of his dealings with his erstwhile attendant, Fo'd, provides an example of the Southern view.
5 S. M. Lipset, *Political Man,* Doubleday Anchor Books, New York, 1963.
6 José Ortega y Gasset, *The Revolt of the Masses,* W. W. Norton & Company, Inc., New York, 1957.
7 Glyndon G. Van Deusen, *The Jacksonian Era: 1828–1848,* Harper & Row, New York, 1959.
8 Robert J. Harris, "States' Rights and Vested Interests," *Journal of Politics,* 15:461, November 1954.
9 See Gallup poll released for publication, July 30, 1972.
10 Norman Podhoretz, "Between Nixon and the New Politics," *Commentary,* 54:4–8, September 1972.

4

**INSTITUTIONS AND
THE CONSTITUTION:
THE POLITICAL RULES**

Camelot

Ask ev' - ry per - son if he's heard the sto - ry;—

—— And tell it strong and clear if he has not:

That once there was a fleet-ing wisp of glo - ry—

—— called Cam-e-lot. Don't let it be for-

got That once there was a spot For one brief shin-ing

mo-ment that was known As Cam - e - lot.

Chapter 7

Fifty-five Men
in Philadelphia

In 1925 an American historian named J. Franklin Jameson gave a series of four lectures at Princeton University that he later published in a slim volume called *The American Revolution Considered as a Social Movement*.[1] His title stated his main thesis that the Revolutionary War was more than a series of military clashes between colonists and Red Coats across New York, Pennsylvania, and New Jersey real estate; even more than an epic documentary with a few dramatic high points reserved for the defection of Benedict Arnold and Washington wintering out at Valley Forge.

Jameson suggested that the war also initiated a social movement, one that encouraged Americans to question the assumptions underlying all traditional social institutions of the day. Once Americans embraced rebellion against their king, other distinctions in rank, property, or status were no longer taken for granted. What the poet and journalist Joel Barlow called the "privileged orders" were under frontal attack and their traditional bases of authority were being rudely questioned.

THE MOVEMENT

While later historians have questioned Jameson's assumption that this social movement began with the Declaration of Independence, few question his conclusion that the Revolution ushered in and encouraged a period of accelerated social change. At Yorktown, the surrendering British band played "The World Is Upside Down" and that could have set the tone for what followed. Those who had successfully practiced treason to the crown were treated as heroes. Loyalists were persecuted and fled the country. The established sentimental and commercial ties to Britain were brutally cut and uncharted possibilities lay ahead for the social order. The symbolic vestiges of a feudal system already on its last legs, such as primogeniture, entail of estates, and an established church, were swept away. The mood of the day was in favor of equality and what the anthropologist Clyde Kluckhohn has called the "cult of the common man" took root.[2] The widening of the suffrage was a subject of debate in most state legislatures. Tory and royal lands had been confiscated by the states and were being redistributed and some of these reached the hands of the formerly poor.

Established ideas were also under scrutiny. Deism and dissent in religion flourished and new experiments were tried in medical delivery systems, penal reform, and education. Phi Beta Kappa was founded in 1776; new colleges and common schools began. The first antislavery societies were organized and laws against this institution and the slave trade were also for the first time being seriously debated in many state legislatures. Vermont became the first state, in 1777, to prohibit slavery. While the American social system had never been as rigid and hierarchical as that of Great Britain, it was in rapid flux. Its basic assumptions as to who had authority to control decisions and how rewards should be distributed were under challenge.

Confrontation politics were also more common. The Boston Tea Party was only the first of a series of incidents. The most notable postwar strife occurred in 1787 in Massachusetts and was called Shay's Rebellion. From a later vantage point we can view it romantically as debt-oppressed farmers marching on Boston merchants and bankers to ask for consideration of their list of grievances and demands. To the Establishment of the day, it was commonly regarded as the prelude to a final breakdown of the social order—a classic law and order issue; one that most state legislatures rather than dealing with forcefully seemed, in the eyes of the Establishment, almost to encourage.

One could apply to that day what the sociologist Robert A. Nisbet wrote about America at the height of the student protests of 1969.

> The most striking fact in the present period of revolutionary change is the quickened erosion of the traditional institutional authorities that for nearly a millennium have been Western man's principal sources of order and liberty. I am referring to the manifest decline of influence of the legal system, the church, family, local community, and most recently and perhaps most ominously, of school and university.[3]

THE GOVERNMENTAL RESPONSE

The governmental situation offered little that would inspire confidence in the middling or upper-class types of citizens. The thirteen state governments were for the most part dominated by the kind of populist reformers who would have regarded slogans such as "all power to the people" as the quintessence of political wisdom. In the period just prior to the Constitutional Convention, even a liberal democrat such as Thomas Jefferson bitterly expressed his disgust with the practices of his own Virginia legislature. In his *Notes on the State of Virginia (1785)*, he concluded that "One hundred and seventy three despots were as oppressive as one . . ." and that "An elective despotism was not the government we fought for." He objected to concentrating all power in the legislature rather than having legislature, executive, and judiciary share power and check each other. (The philosopher Montesquieu had suggested this, but we might remember that Jefferson also wrote as a former Governor of Virginia.) He rejected outright a democratic theory that argued a temporary majority in control could do whatever it wished, as long as it claimed to be acting for "the people." Jefferson, like most other leaders of the Revolution, believed that all majorities must be limited and that some minority rights must be protected from majority decisions.

The new American nation during the period between 1781 and 1788 was also governed, after a fashion, by a national government. This government had many of the characteristics of the present-day United Nations and inspired about the same confidence in its ability to act decisively. Its most significant defect as a government was that, unlike the UN, it could not act on individual citizens but only through the member state governments. Thus it could not tax, draft, or imprison individuals, but only make recommendations for action to the states. This national government had the impressive-sounding name of The Continental Congress, but its legacy to later generations was the classic phrase descriptive of a runaway inflation, "Not worth a Continental Dollar." Its legal basis was a charter drawn up by the states, called The Articles of Confederation, that did little more than establish a loose unity. It had no executive. In its legislative body each state's representatives had only one vote and the main function of the legislature seemed to be that of debate. In its last days it produced one memorable act, The Northwest Ordinance of 1787, but otherwise it was largely impotent. A single state's veto could prevent amendment of the charter.

Twice the Congress, desperate for funds, tried to write in a tariff levy and each time one state vetoed it. The national government, like the UN of a later period, had to settle for member states paying their dues when they felt moved to do so. Day-to-day actions of any significance required two-thirds votes. Under such a system of state vetoes (over such things as army enlistments, for example) the war was barely won and the peace progressed from one minor misery to another, so far as the privileged orders were concerned. *Federalist* paper number 15, one of the series of inspired arguments by Hamilton, Madison, and Jay arguing for the adoption of the new constitution, sums up this situation as they saw it: "To shorten an enumeration of particulars which can afford neither pleasure or instruction, it may in general be demanded, what indication is there of national disorder, poverty, and insignificance that could befall a community so peculiarly blessed with natural advantages as we are, which does not form a part of the dark catalogue of our public misfortunes?"

A COUNTERREVOLUTION IS MOUNTED

It is conventional wisdom of high school history courses to state that the Constitutional Convention resulted mainly from the failures of the national government to act, particularly in respect to commercial quarrels between and among states, the unsound national and state currencies, and the clear inability of such a government to provide much protection in the event of military aggression from abroad. All these tribulations and the inability of the national government to act in respect to them no doubt contributed greatly to the movement for a new constitution. They do not, however, we believe, fully explain the rush of events that culminated in an illegal overthrow of the then existing government.

Neither do the self-serving tendencies of some of the Founding Fathers. In his book *An Economic Interpretation of the Constitution of the United States*,[4] the historian Charles Beard demonstrated that the delegates to the Convention were heavily recruited from young men on the make in the first flush of success of what they hoped would continue to be impressive public and commercial careers. More than half were college-educated, a truly impressive number, given the general level of education of the day. Most were businessmen or large-scale planters. A number held government bonds, at the time of the Convention worth considerably less than face value. Many would profit directly from putting the national government on a sound financial basis by refunding the national debt at face value, creating a stable currency, encouraging trade and manufacture by clarifying the commercial regulations, especially in respect to tariffs, and by providing defense for international trade. (For example, within the first generation after the new government was established, the Marines were to make their first landing—on "the shores of Tripoli"—to protect American commercial shipping against the Barbary pirates.) But while we may be somewhat chagrined to find some of the Founding Fathers were perhaps motivated by private gain, we should not therefore lapse into cynicism about them (any more than we do about ourselves). Their actions and the result for us, more than justify whatever personal, material side payments a few of the Founders derived from the new government.

Motivation for Change   If all the reasons discussed so far are important and contributory but are not the most basic, then what did inspire the document composed in Philadelphia in the summer of 1787? The central fact of the Constitutional Convention was that *it was a counterrevolution* as impressive in its impact as the Revolution itself. For the moment, the Constitution brought to a screeching halt a social movement that seemed to those who wrote the document to be getting out of hand. It slowed down the momentum of a populism that assumed that the essence of democracy was to be unchecked majority rule which could refashion the social order in any way it wished. It established the authority of traditional institutions and of a legitimatized new leadership elite. Not all pressure for change was deflated, but henceforth it would be channeled through accepted institutions and would be piecemeal, and gradual.

The political scientist Gottfried Dietze states the case for the counterrevolution theory. He writes:

> The convention wanted the Union mainly for the preservation of free government from democratic despotism. While the adherents of absolute democracy conceived of freedom [as] . . . freedom of the majority to infringe upon minority rights, [to the Founding Fathers it meant] freedom from absolute democracy for the protection of those rights, among which the right of property played a prominent role.[5]

Dietze marshals considerable evidence to support his case. There is little question that the assumptions of populist democracy prevalent in many state governments were being increasingly questioned among the educated classes. John Adams, one of the authors of the Declaration of Independence, in his *Defense of the Constitutions of Government of the United States of America* challenged head-on the assumption of unrestricted majority rule. Benjamin Rush, liberal, revolutionary patriot, and the father of American medicine, was equally blunt. In his *Address to the American People*, in January 1787, he called for a second American Revolution against popular despotism. Dietze also points out that the commercial problems cannot fully explain the need for a convention. The Annapolis Convention of 1786 could by treaty or state compact have dealt with some of the most distressing commercial situations then troubling the nation. Instead of doing so, it disbanded with almost unseemly haste, recommending to Congress a convention representing all the states to consider revision of the Articles.

Dietze, of course, comments in addition on the composition of the Constitutional Convention with its aristocratic-commercial bias. He asks why the Constitutional Convention should have had to meet in secret with guards at the door if only matters of commerce and common defense were to be dealt with. He assumes that the Founding Fathers had early resolved to do more than revise the Articles and to set aside the right of only one state to veto their changes. He points also to the evidence of Madison's notes of the Convention debates. Even liberal delegates such as George Mason (who in the end refused to sign the document) and James Wilson, who argued for direct election of the President, expressed the need for checks on majority rule. But most importantly and transcending all other arguments, he looks to the result of the deliberations as found in the Constitutional document itself. It was not a revision of the Articles but a new government and if ever a constitution met the kind of objections Jefferson had expressed about unlimited popular rule, this one did. The widespread tearing apart of the social fabric by what the Founders saw as demagogic leaders of transitory populist majorities would be ended, once this document became law, and so it was.

THE FOUNDING SKEPTICS

Before the Founding Fathers are dismissed as selfish villains of the Establishment bent on grinding down the masses, let us look at some of their basic assumptions since these, more than direct personal interest, seem to have led them to act as they did. Let us grant them the same kind of hearing concerning their idealism that we do self-proclaimed "Friends of the People."

The Assumptions of the Founders Their most important assumptions are those about the nature of man and society. Refreshingly unlike most persons at most periods in history, the Founding Fathers attempted to dredge deep for such assumptions and bring them up to the surface for examination. It is this characteristic that makes *The Federalist Papers* such a clear-cut defense of their position, worth reading two hundred years later; that and their willingness to have those assumptions weighed in terms of empirical data.

The Founding Fathers assumed as self-evident that every society will have an aristocracy based on distinctions of property, status, and political power. The notion that a community of equals could last very long, they rejected as naïve. They would expect to find pecking orders arising naturally in any social system short of that of the angels in heaven. They would have expected this as well in a modern commune. They were skeptical about the evenness with which abilities and talents were dispersed. They also assumed thus that social, economic, and political hierarchies had some relation to competence and performance. They believed in a natural aristocracy of talents among men and wanted a government that built upon such ability. Governments that failed to give such recognition, they felt, would be continuously unstable. A government could not remain perpetually under attack in the state of questioning of assumptions and uncertainty that characterized the postwar era of the Articles of Confederation. For it to remain so, they confidently assumed, would lead inevitably to dissolution of the social order and a drift to some type of despotism. Man could not long exist under such conditions of uncertainty and unpredictability without coming to hunger for some kind of stable order. Though they predated such leaders of revolutionary change as Napoleon, Stalin, Hitler, or Mao, they would confidently have predicted the tyrannies that arose from their social preconditions.

On the Nature of Man   These assumptions were complemented by a deeper skeptical assumption about the nature of man; one that generally separates conservatives and reactionaries from liberals and radicals. The Founders were skeptical about human altruism and man's potential for change. Their assumptions about man can, if one wishes to, be interpreted religiously. They talked as if all men were prone to guilt for commission of one or more of the seven deadly sins: lust, gluttony, sloth, envy, anger, pride, and avarice. But most Founders could be more accurately classified as confirmed secularists who had seen enough of life not to be astonished by man's tendency to error and egotism. The Founders would, in later days, have been at home discussing with Freudians the aberrations that flow from the id. Yet as conservatives, they did not see man's state as totally hopeless, but saw all men, even the most humane and idealistic, as occasionally weak and subject to backsliding.

Most important is the assumption this led them to make about themselves. Many self-righteous reformers can ably detect the evil or error in those with whom they disagree, but see in themselves the embodiment of purity and wisdom. To their credit, the Founding Fathers were able to fit themselves into their own pattern of assumptions about man's proneness to error. They could not be accused of assuming the pharisitical stance of an elite of truth bearers pointing out to everyone else that they were poor sinners in need of salvation. They could admit their own frailty and that of their kind of people and build into their constitution safeguards against it. They trusted no one completely, not even themselves.

They were also skeptics about man's perfectability. To check man's proneness to error and selfishness, the best they hoped for was enlightened reason to be achieved only as men were forced to deliberate before acting about long-term possible effects. Thus they favored some measure of social control through institutional constraints. They wished to avoid rash or unconsidered action. They borrowed from Adam Smith that most attractive of social inventions, the assumption that institutions could be arranged so that man's selfish tendencies might interact and cancel out each other for the public good. Limited government and governmental restraints were their only hopes in forcing men to look at long-range interests.

An additional and also very skeptical assumption the Founding Fathers held was of a limited community of interest in society and the limits of man being able, even with the help of enlightened reason, to discern it. Given the shortage of resources of status, power, and wealth, they did not assume that everyone's desires could or should be satisfied. They did not expect to teach the world to sing in perfect harmony, but rather expected a great many frustrated second tenors who would believe they should take the solos. Self-serving individuals and groups they saw as inevitable and as the greatest danger to free government. In *Federalist # 10*, Madison summed up their views in a classic statement. They expected antagonistic factions to be endemic to any society. One could destroy the faction only by destroying liberty and free government, a route, it should be noted, that they rejected but one that is commonly taken by totalitarians attempting to create an artificial harmony of interests. The only remedy the Founders saw was to control the effects of faction. They proposed to do it by creating a republic composed of many factions whose influence could offset each other. No one, as a result, could be completely satisfied.

Contrast with Liberal Assumptions Before examining the kind of society and government the Founding Fathers assumed to be desirable and possible, we will pause here to contrast these assumptions with those of the traditional liberal or radical leftist of that day and today. Their assumptions inspired populist democracy and what after the French Revolution of 1789 was called "Jacobin democracy." These assumptions found expression both in the Declaration of Independence and in the Bill of Rights and have also contributed a great deal to the development of the American system. Generally the assumptions of the left take for granted the goodness and improvability of man. In this sense they are idealistic. Their definition of justice moves to equality rather than a hierarchy based on ability or performance. The left assumes the hierarchy the Founding Fathers saw as inevitable was instead artificially created and preserved and not a natural development. What the right sees as natural and inherent differences, the left sees as pathology, created by environment. To them, a new environment would change these differences. Institutional constraints and regulations thus are frequently seen by the liberal as unnecessary and even occasionally corrupting.

At the left extreme, where the belief in the perfectability of man is strongest, is the assumption that by destroying such restraints and providing absolute freedom, man may fulfill himself to his own improvement and that of society. The liberal who shares a bit of the conservative skepticism would favor only relaxing somewhat such constraints. What those with a skeptical view of man see as constraints needed to restrict potentially corrupting actions, those with the alternative assumption see as chains that limit man's potential for beneficent actions.

The left often assumes that change may best be achieved by providing a new environment that will bring out the potential good in man. Thus liberal experiments with the mentally ill, prisoners, the poor, the education of children, and in many other areas have attempted to bring social improvement through environmental change and education. Finally, the left assumes the sense of community and common interests will override the selfishness found in factionalism. In this view a natural goodness will lead to a sense of community rather than having a lack of goodness lead to competing interests and the hierarchy that emerges from such competition.

One might suppose that those at the extreme left would want no government at all (anarchy), while those at the reactionary right would opt for authoritarianism. In the middle, where liberals and conservatives are found, some recognition of the mixed nature of man would lead to preferences for a government of moderate restraints. Liberals would argue for more majority rule, while conservatives would stress the need for restraints on transient majorities and the recognition of the established order to insure stability. Reasoning leads to two bull's-eyes and one miss. The theory holds fairly well at the middle for liberals and conservatives and at the right extreme, but not at the left extreme.

The earnest leftist seekers after community without institutional restraints have often tried valiantly by a quantum jump to create a new society based on the brotherhood of man. From Brook Farm through the modern large-scale Communist national experiments, such as those in Russia and China, the great leap forward has generally been too great for the average man with his kinks and orneriness. It occurs even for a short period only where a deep commitment bordering on religious fervor is present. Psychologists call it the "Hawthorne effect." (Mao remembered it as the mood of The Great March and later unsuccessfully attempted to recreate it in the Cultural Revolution.) Once crisis and the initial fervor it brings are over, the backsliding elements of man or as some would have it, his previous institutional socialization, bring about the threat of dissolution and leaders see the need for an imposed order to bring about their desired community of interests. Generally the latter has been a totalitarian despotism rationalized by an enlightened elite as capable of reeducating the masses so they may be capable of true freedom, after they have been taught what their real interests really are (or should be). At that point, the state will wither away, it is said.

We can thus isolate three general assumptions made by the kind of prudent conservatives who wrote the Constitution in order to slow down an idealistic social revolution: (1) Some men were more naturally talented than others and if competition were permitted, the social order would reflect these natural distinctions in a hierarchical order; (2) all men were prone to selfishness and error; and (3) there was no natural harmony of interests, but rather a natural state of conflict. These assumptions led the Founding Fathers to conclude that the best government is one that permits a certain degree of freedom while exercising enough control to hold conflict within reasonable bounds.

THE GOVERNMENT THE FOUNDING FATHERS CREATED

The Founding Fathers, with their somewhat jaundiced (or realistic) view of human nature, set about fashioning a government to reflect their skeptical assumptions. Given their competence, they succeeded reasonably well, as one would expect. They wanted the following: (1) national and state governments with sufficient power to be stable and capable of keeping order. At the same time they also wanted (2) a limit on the power of government to act, since they could not completely trust the rulers; and (3) a government led by the natural aristocracy of society. Recognizing their own fallibility, they compromised what seemed possible to compromise and swept the rest under the rug.

The Distribution of Power   Their Constitution thus began by creating centers of governmental power capable of taking action on major problems. Creating the national government they saw as a principal need. It was to have a strong executive plus a legislature that could legislate on national issues without state vetoes. It was to have a national court capable of overruling state actions on some matters while leaving considerable power to the states. It was to create an armed force as a national unit but with a civilian, the President, as commander in chief. Few more powerful national governments have been created and its very existence would serve as a check on the power of state governments. To give it stability as well as power, the Founders set the terms for President, Congress, and court of different lengths, so that they would not coincide and would thus encourage gradual change.

The Founding Fathers tried to limit this potentially powerful government in a number of ways. The first way was, of course, through a written constitution which specified, in eighteen clauses, the powers the national Congress could legally exercise. Next they built in the separation of powers (assigning parts of governmental power to legislative, executive, and judicial branches) in which the inherent drive for power and control in each of the three branches of government would serve as a check and balance on the other two. An additional division of power, called "federalism," was made between national and state governments. Each level of government was, in theory, granted independent arenas of action and control.

Finally, the Constitution writers opted for a mixed system rather than either a democracy or an aristocracy. Thus all elements of society were to be given some influence in the selection of their governmental leaders, but none exclusively so. The people, by direct election, would choose representatives and state legislators, but the state legislators were to choose the senators. It was assumed such indirect election would handicap demagogues who were irresponsibly capable of stirring up popular support. A two-step process was also used to bring into the system the influence of what the Founders considered the more able and talented. The people would directly elect eminent personages at the state level to a College of Electors and these in turn would select the President. Federal judges would be chosen by the President with Senate approval. No major element was excluded, but none was given unchecked power. No transient majority could quickly achieve its purposes.

Compromise, the Art of Government Three major policies were compromised in the final constitutional agreement. The most significant, that in respect to slavery, provided for an end to the slave trade in twenty years and instituted an artificial formula which considered slaves both as property for taxation and as people to be represented (without vote). The Founders compromised justice for peace. This issue came out from under the rug only at a later date. The equality-of-states issue was compromised in the two-house legislature patterned after England's parliament with states represented equally in the upper house. The Founders' fear of unbridled liberty had left them open to charges of tilting their government too far in the direction of restraints on citizen action. To get adoption of their Constitution they were capable of political compromise that rose above principle: They added a Bill of Rights based squarely on the assumptions of the left about the goodness of the ordinary human being.

What was the result? First, the architects of a new government had created almost miraculously a system that quickly gained legitimacy in the eyes of the nation, for it offered something for nearly everyone and at the same time conveyed the stable feeling that someone was in charge. George Washington, aristocrat and born leader, led it while following sound conservative doctrine. The Whiskey Rebellion of 1792 was no instant replay of Shay's, but was speedily and efficiently repressed, with some strong complaints from the left. Tom Paine said of President Washington: "The world will be puzzled to decide whether you are an apostate or an imposter, whether you have abandoned good principles or whether you ever had any." A degree of certainty and predictability once more became characteristic of American social and economic life.

Second, it was a government that, as was quickly demonstrated, permitted a tolerable degree of freedom, for all policy was based on compromise. Significantly the opposition press could not be stopped from criticizing it because anti-Federalist partisans could organize politically to take over the regime peacefully. Third, it was a government that could be accommodated to incremental change. This included surviving a takeover by the Jeffersonians, who were its initial critics. Yet it was a government that required compromise on all policies over victories of principle. There were payoffs for anyone who wanted to work within the system. Finally, it permitted the new nation to establish its basis. The questioning of basic assumptions slowed down and confrontations on the most serious problems were for a time avoided.

The Results   In summary, the Founding Fathers succeeded in creating a constitution which to a tolerable extent fulfilled the promise of its rather high-sounding Preamble composed as propaganda to offset that of the populist reformers: "We the People of the United States, in Order to form a more perfect Union, establish Justice, insure domestic Tranquility, provide for the common Defense, promote the general Welfare, and secure the Blessings of Liberty to ourselves and our Posterity, do ordain and establish this Constitution for the United States of America."

One can also judge its success by the alternatives that seemed to be available at the time. One may, if one wishes, rule out as overpessimistic the possibility of the infant nation blowing apart into thirteen or a half-dozen nations, falling to a foreign conquest, or drifting into despotism, though all these have happened to other former colonies shortly after gaining independence. Yet one may still conclude that whatever other alternatives were possible in 1787, none would probably have been much preferable to the government that emerged from the Philadelphia convention.

A government based on skepticism about human abilities and goodness has weathered reasonably well. But it has also changed and the kinds of changes and how they came about will be considered next.

THE ONE THE FOUNDING FATHERS LOST

Perhaps the government established by the Founding Fathers survived precisely because it underwent change to accommodate itself to the assumptions of the egalitarian liberals, if not the radical leftists. Certainly the liberal takeover symbolized by the Presidential victory of Thomas Jefferson in 1800 established once and for all the government's general legitimacy. It could be used to implement liberal policy. Since then, it has co-opted other former policy critics into the Federalist system. Taking power has also exacted a price for such liberals and radicals: acceptance of a politics of moderation and gradualness, because of the Hamilton-Madison system of checks and balances.

A Miscalculation of Assumptions Ironically the first important casualty of the federal system was the notions of zealots in the ranks of the aristocratic Federalists themselves. Several pieces of evidence suggest the government they created did not turn out in practice to be as aristocratic in policy matters as they hoped it would be. The Federalists in power thought themselves justified in suppressing liberal but loyal dissent as if it were revolutionary action. The successful suppression of the whiskey rebellion in 1794 went to their head. By 1798 a Federalist Congress scared out of its wits by the Jacobins of France passed and signed into law by President John Adams an Alien and Sedition Act. But instead of French fifth columnists, critical Jeffersonian editors went to jail.

The Jeffersonians were handed the next election because the government the Federalists had created was not as authoritarian as some of them had supposed. The fate that befell the Federalist party itself is instructive. The clique of notables, which was to rule wisely for the masses, fell apart in its first confrontation with a mass-based party. Its final gasp was at the Hartford Convention of December 1814–January 1815, where a clique hoping to move the body to secession or for a new constitutional convention, lost. The Federalist cause and that type of aristocratic conservatism, it was clear, would lose further as new western states would be created and admitted into the Union on an equal footing with the original thirteen. And so the party of the Founding Fathers lasted at best only a scant twenty-seven years; only twelve of the Fathers held office. Their policy proposals landed in the ash heap. They lived to see New England commerce handicapped by an embargo under Jefferson and the nation under Madison embark on a fruitless war of almost total disaster with an England then trying to win a war against the despot Napoleon.

Moderation in All Things If the government in operation disappointed the more aristocratic conservatives and reactionaries, however, it has not in turn overjoyed radicals of the barnburner inclination or of the New England abolitionist variety. It proved to be a government resistant to the building of majorities for programmatic goals. Reform through it would come, but only gradually. As one part of the system, President, Congress, or courts moved on their own to achieve programmatic goals; it was almost like clockwork checked by one of the other two. Thus by 1938 the Roosevelt New Deal program was dead in Congress just as the conservative court of the 1920s fell before the attack by the same President. Great power could be exercised for a short time by men as diverse as Joseph McCarthy, Lyndon Johnson, or Earl Warren, but almost immediately the Madisonian system reacted like white corpuscles rushing to an open wound. In this sense the assumptions of the framers about policy making thus far held: Ego would offset ego and power would remain checked and limited by countervailing power.

At only a few times in history did men of principle on the right or left achieve full control, for even a short period. One such time was in the South just prior to 1860 and nothing in the Madisonian system prevented a bloody Civil War over programmatic goals that would not be compromised. More often, groupings of zealots had access to some decision makers and provided an initiating force for a short time which more pragmatic and opportunistic politicians of the liberal or conservative camps used to further their own electoral ambitions. Prohibition provides a dismal example.

To the disappointment of aristocratic reactionaries and radical reformers, the American system could be best operated by not very inspiring coalitions of pork choppers—some liberal and some conservative. The first concern of such successful politicians has generally been for the short-run payoffs of office for themselves, and a full dinner pail for their partisan supporters. Inevitably they have bid for middle-mass support or at any rate tolerance. The crudeness and crassness of this politics were somewhat muted under Thomas Jefferson, but came into full focus under the leadership of Andrew Jackson. Ideology gave way to pragmatic selfishness dressed up as a moral crusade. Nor did slavery stir the Northerners very deeply, until it became apparent that the free labor and industry of which they were a part could not compete effectively with a slave economy. And the wealthy bent on making more money could adapt themselves very easily to the pork-chop politics as long as they disclaimed aristocratic polish and were thoroughly vulgar in their aspirations.

Those who succeeded best in operating the system wanted mainly the chance to make a buck in a nice, tolerably comfortable, middle-class society. But if one reserves judgment by results rather than purity, it has not worked out too badly. Given the influence of popular opinion, the system has moved progressively leftward; farther to the left than the initiators of the Revolutionary war social movement would have dared to hope for. Under such politics the middle-class welfare state was inevitable and it too in time arrived.

This policy trend was first discerned by that perceptive French visitor during Andrew Jackson's Presidency—Alexis de Tocqueville. In *Democracy in America* (1835), he saw the inevitable result of the nation's politics as an egalitarianism which would level off to a general middle-class mediocrity in the arts, religion, education, or politics. He would cheerfully have predicted Muzak, the Western comic strips, Montovani, or the TV commercial had he known the potentials of technology. The basic assumption held by successful democratic politicians, he argued, was that most men were generally equal in talents, weaknesses, and potentials and thus should be treated with wrought equality.

But De Tocqueville also reechoed the fears of the earlier Federalists—that of a popular despotism based on public opinion. He foresaw the best and worst suppressed in a kind of middlebrow culture. Senator Joseph McCarthy before his cheering crowds would have scared him as much as Franklin Roosevelt, George Wallace, or Andrew Jackson, or the latest rock star. De Tocqueville anticipated modern social scientists and even the people who created "All in the Family," by concluding that the common man was not given to tolerance of deviant opinion or behavior that he did not quite understand.

If liberals have generally had the long-run edge because votes were the major political currency of control, conservatives have not been without short-run policy influence in the American system. Part of that influence has been through Madisonian checks on liberal majorities. Reform of policy is slow. Part has also been through informal checks not envisaged or at least not mentioned by the Federalists but blossoming out in the system like wild weeds in a craggy rock wall; i.e., the filibuster, congressional seniority, judicial review, or senatorial courtesy. Finally the system has encouraged inaction as the result of the inertia that in time appears to affect even the most politically activist of citizens when faced with Madison's design.

Thus the overall policy trend of American politics has been toward an egalitarian welfare society designed for the middle masses. But the progress has been slowed by governmental forms or habits so that much of the struggle has been over structure just as it appears the Founding Fathers intended it would be. It is that struggle—the playing out of the Founders' assumptions—that we review next.

THE ONE THE FOUNDING FATHERS WON

Many battles over policy have boiled down to battles over the governmental structure established in the Constitution that the Founding Fathers bequeathed us. Since at least the Civil War, if not before, the American political battle has been joined by a group of scholarly idealists whose sympathies generally have lain with the left but whose methods have stressed structural reform. Men such as Woodrow Wilson (as a political scientist) engaged in this reform effort. Ironically their goal has been to make the American system more like the British system that the Founding Fathers revolted against. The central assumption of the reformers rests on a faith in the people.

The American system would be improved by streamlining it into a centralized bureaucracy immediately responsive to the will of the people. A first assumption is that the policy goals that the majority of citizens want or at least should want are the same as those of the reformers. A second assumption is thus that this majority should never be frustrated in its genuine desires by the limitations on the exercise of political power built into the federalist system. A third is that given control, the majority can be trusted to preserve minority rights. From these assumptions have issued a variety of academic reform programs aimed at making the governmental system more responsive to majority views and more efficient and uniform in its behavior.

Intellectual Goals for a Democracy   One of these goals has been to build up the prestige and power of the President at the expense of Congress, both in foreign and domestic affairs. "Strong" Presidents have been those who echoed the desires of "the people" and forced Congress to act. A second goal has been to reduce the power of fifty states to the benefit of the central government; to recognize what Harold Laski called "The Obsolescence of Federalism,"[6] by creating arrangements through grants-in-aid whereby the states functioned more as administrative units for national governmental programs than as independent entities. A third goal is to consolidate small governmental units into larger ones. This is true within the federal bureaucracy where ex-President Herbert Hoover added his stature to the reorganization movement as well as at the local level where the desire to coordinate has led to proposals for consolidation. A fourth movement was to streamline and professionalize bureaucracy so that it will react as a disciplined hierarchy to demands from the top.

Reform movements also attacked those check-and-balance encrustations that seemed to spring up and adhere with no particular effort to the Founders' system. Party conventions in the states were replaced by party primaries so the majority wishes might be heard more clearly and the movement for a national presidential primary continued. Party reform to open up the national conventions was pioneered with disastrous and somewhat undemocratic results by Democrats in 1972. Political scientists proposed a series of changes to bring about a more responsible party system—one that would take stands on issues and carry them out. The seniority system of Congress and the power of certain of its committees and their chairmen are subject to Nader-like scrutinizing. The lack of apportionment of state legislatures and even city councils was called into question as was the system of electoral college voting. As long ago as 1914, selection of senators by state legislatures was abandoned for direct election.

A parallel and complimentary movement flowing readily from these reform assumptions was to expand the electorate to include every citizen who conceivably could be justified as being eligible. Through constitutional amendments blacks, women, and eighteen-year-olds were added. Through court action property qualifications and residency and literacy requirements have been altered or eliminated.

Reforms and Constitutional Continuity The methods used to achieve these reforms have been by interpretation of the Constitution as well as by amendment. Most important have been the interpretations of the Supreme Court, especially when, in exercise of judicial review, the Justices have declared unconstitutional legislation of Congress or an act of the President. But Presidents, Congress and party activities, governors and state legislators have all contributed interpretations that have remained the law of the land. Change has also come by formal amendment which requires two-thirds favorable vote in each House of Congress and approval by three-fourths of the state legislatures. Such formal change has generally been reserved for actions in which the words of the document cannot be twisted out of shape even by the Supreme Court or when a recalcitrant court refused to accept the interpretation of an overwhelming majority in Congress.

The aristocratic structure of the framers with its checks and balances has to a great degree been dismantled. A good many of the checks have been eliminated and the electorate has been expanded from the select to include almost everyone. On balance, few, even of the most conservative, disapprove of the result. Some reforms, such as administrative efficiency, were needed if the system would survive at all; others like the party primary can be manipulated with relative ease. But most importantly, the system of checks and balances survives and will continue so as long as Presidents are elected independent of Congress.

Thus far the Founders' system still frustrates a uniform effort to create the kind of egalitarian and responsive society the scholarly idealists envisioned. Minorities, sometimes those observers would consider the wrong minorities, continue to throw their weight around, and slow down and for a time check majorities. The conflicting arenas still keep getting captured by differing groups, and as one oligarchy is rooted out another grows up in its place. The once conservative Supreme Court and Senate fell under the same liberal dominance as the Presidency and the checks in the federal system were overcome by systems of federal grants. But countervailing trends almost immediately popped up. The increased conservatism of court and Presidency and the experiment in revenue sharing with the states suggest a system still resistant to neat planning. If these roadblocks are ever overcome we may some day test the basic assumption of the scholarly liberal reformers—that popular majorities can be trusted to respect minority rights without special built-in structural restraints. In the meantime it appears we are stuck with a government that is only partially democratic and that is the way the Founding Fathers wanted it. But it is also a government responsive in policy in a rather uninspiring way to the desires of the middle masses. That may not be what the aristocratic Founding Fathers wanted, but that too is what we are stuck with.

NOTES

1 J. F. Jameson, *The American Revolution Considered as a Social Movement,* Beacon Press, Boston, 1956. Originally published, 1925.
2 Clyde Kluckhohn, *Mirror for Man,* McGraw-Hill Book Company, New York, 1949.
3 Robert A. Nisbet, "The Twilight of Authority," *The Public Interest,* 15:3-9, Spring 1969.
4 Charles A. Beard, *An Economic Interpretation of the Constitution,* The Macmillan Company, New York, 1913.
5 Gottfried Dietze, *The Federalist, A Classic on Federalism and Free Government,* The Johns Hopkins Press, Baltimore, 1960, p. 65.
6 Harold Laski, "The Obsolescence of Federalism," *New Republic,* May 3, 1939, pp. 367-369.

Chapter 8

And $X_1 \ldots X_n$ in Washington Today

The Founding Fathers wanted to establish a government that would guarantee freedom by making sure no one could exercise unchecked power. They banked on the selfishness of each set of political officeholders to offset that of others, rather than on the good intentions of any one. What the Founding Fathers assumed about the human nature of politicians and officeholders has been nicely borne out in the practice of American government.

They established an open system of government and assumed that policy would emerge only after it had been hacked away at by many governmental warriors and whatever private ones cared to try a jab or two. Few would deny that reality. They assumed, secondly, that government officials who made up the corps of regular combatants would seek to aggrandize their own units at the expense of all other governmental units. The title of this chapter suggests the result—that from the fifty-five men of Philadelphia, we have experienced an infinitely expanding bureaucracy.

A third assumption they were too prudent to state openly or even hint at, but it would not have astonished them to find it an integral part of their systems. The more influential members of each unit have come to assume that it is their privilege to arrange matters so as to benefit themselves at the expense of others of their unit as well as at the expense of those outside the unit.

The first aspect of the system then is that, in broad outline, it consists of planned clashes among the branches of government; of built-in conflict among governmental policy-making units over the making of policy, the tendency for each unit to seek power for itself at the expense of the others, and finally the tendency for the most influential in each to attempt to expand at the expense of their colleagues.

The Political Process: A Simplified Version

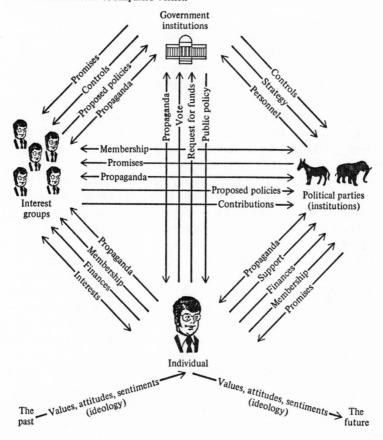

Figure 8-1 Politics consists of many interrelated activities.

THE FOUR LEGISLATURES

The root of what makes the federalist system so conflict-ridden is that the Founding Fathers provided it with four legislative branches—five if the House of Representatives and Senate are counted separately. Each of these branches, the Presidency, the courts, the Congress, and the bureaucracy, has an important policy-making role. Each also is different in composition and in the assumptions it holds. Each has its own set of exclusive legal powers, its own independent methods of organization, its own pattern of recruitment, and its own separate, special constituencies. One may thus anticipate disagreement.

The above description even oversimplifies because it reifies these institutional bodies; that is, it treats them as if they were individuals. But they are not individuals or if they were, they would often be Hamlet-like in their general inability to act with decisiveness. The branches themselves are always potentially splintered by inner conflicts over leadership and policy. Seldom are all the members of the House of Representatives united on a legislative policy; seldom even, for that matter, are all those associated with the presidential office. In each, a dominant grouping emerges from time to time, to give that institutional body a policy direction and emphasis. But there is always a loyal opposition in the branch potentially ready to undercut it.

The leaders of each branch and their coalition of supporters organize that branch around a set of common assumptions about what is desirable among the possible policy alternatives and work through a set of formal and informal rules which help them make this choice. Sometimes the mobilization of power in a branch is well handled; at other times the elite on top is so divided within itself in fighting for supremacy that the branch is largely ineffective. Thus the very effective Warren Court of the 1960s championed a liberal policy position whose impact went shuddering throughout the whole governmental system. Alternatively the office staff of President Eisenhower displayed publicly the inner struggles for control of Presidential office policy. Its members voiced contradictory tendencies illustrated in the Harold Stassen attempt to dump Richard Nixon for Vice President in 1956 or Treasury Secretary George Humphrey's pointed contradiction of the President in a press conference on the 1958 budget.

Fortunately, for the nation, mobilization is most difficult to accomplish in respect to the whole of the bureaucracy, where the fight among the many conflicting interests and units keeps the administrative system always a little off balance. It is most readily achieved in the presidential office or the courts, although some congressional leaders, notably Lyndon Johnson as Senate Majority Leader or Sam Rayburn as Speaker of the House, have been able to mold each of the congressional branches into a formidable organization.

But the picture of five legislatures competing with each other in prolonged conflict over policy is only part of the story. The Founding Fathers also had a prescription for avoiding long-term stalemates and giving a sense of direction to the system.

THE CHIEF LEGISLATOR: INSTITUTION, NOT INDIVIDUAL

How can all this conflict, as valuable as it may be for getting many points of view expressed, achieve any consistent direction on policy? How can it result in anything but chaos and stalemate? This was the second problem the Founders solved.

In the short run, two things occur: Conflict does result in a draw or standoff; or depending on the issue, for a time the Congress, the Supreme Court, or the bureaucracy may be independent initiators of national policy and will manage for a while to carry it out on their own. But the gyroscope of the federal system is the Presidency. This office, over the long run, draws the rest of the system toward the course it pursues. It in the end can break the stalemate or cancel out the independent action of any of the other branches.

This is because over each of the other branches, the Presidency holds legal powers which can stop it dead, sometimes in the short run but almost always over the course of two presidential terms in office. The President replaces Supreme Court justices as they die or retire, and the Court will thus in time begin to veer off into his preferred policy directions. The political and military heads of major agencies are appointed and, as General Douglas MacArthur discovered in Korea and Secretary of Commerce Walter Hickel discovered closer to home, may be removed by the President. Agency budget and organization are directly influenced by the Office of Management and Budget under the President's direction. Over Congress, the President has a veto which requires for overriding it a two-thirds vote. The President is thus potentially equal to the voting power of 67 senators or 290 representatives, since it takes this number to cancel out his veto if all legislators are present and voting. If his party overflows a phone booth, he can generally depend on that much support and so even by threats of vetoes can bring policy more closely into line with his desires. He may also use his vetoes more directly. Franklin D. Roosevelt occasionally vetoed minor bills sponsored by individual legislators just to remind them that they might be behaving too independently. In addition, the President has areas of policy making in which he can act nearly with independence of the other branches, notably in foreign affairs. He can recognize new nations or break off diplomatic relations, send troops to a foreign country to fight without a declaration of war, and meet with the representatives of foreign nations to make executive agreements.

In all these cases, the presidential office can be checked, especially if it is held by a one-term President or one who is politically inept. But there is no way the other branches singly or together can do this very easily or very often. The checks on the Presidency are weaker than those the incumbent possesses and are generally more difficult to execute. The Court can declare his actions unconstitutional, as they did in respect to Harry Truman's seizure of the steel mills; Congress may override his vetoes or propose constitutional amendments such as that limiting the President to two terms. The Senate may refuse to confirm his nominees or reject his treaties. Congress may refuse to appropriate money or pass legislation he desires or may investigate his administration in a glare of publicity. The bureaucracy may sabotage or slow down his programs. But most of these are guerrilla tactics aimed at wearing a President down and perhaps creating stalemates. Seldom can any other branch deliver a knock-out punch to the man in the White House and those who act on his behalf.

Still, the President (and perhaps his top staff) must always remember that they are not omnipotent and cannot become so by the very nature of democracy. The Watergate scandal of the Nixon administration, like the Teapot Dome scandal of the Harding administration fifty years earlier, offered good insights into why the President's staff and agency heads cannot do as they please or act with impunity. The overenthusiasms, arrogance, and stupidities of the higher and lower echelons of the Nixon staff could not be covered up, even though a foolhardy attempt was made. (The apparently power-drunk planners of the cover-up seemingly forgot one of the most unbendable rules of politics: "If more than two people know about it, expect to read the story in the press.") The Watergate scandal could not be hidden from an honest federal judge who was outraged by what was obviously perjury being committed in his courtroom; or from the chairman of a special Senate investigating committee who had his personal image as well as his party's interests at stake; or from a suspicious public press, one already stung by administration criticism. And as the facts came out, public policy leadership passed from a defensive White House into at least temporarily a limbo.

The legal powers the President holds thus do not make him the inevitable winner in a conflict over policy, but they insure that usually in one term and almost certainly if he serves two terms, no one else can win without his consent. Inevitably, to get action over the long run, the other branches know that they have to strike a bargain with the presidential office. Thus compromise and cooperation and also direction are forced upon the system. The President gets at least part of what he wants and puts his stamp of approval on the overall policy direction of the system. Most frequently, the way is smoothed for this because Congress and the Supreme Court are manned by the same political partisans as those who control the Presidency. But even when this is not the case, the other branches, including even the potentially powerful bureaucracy, must either wait him out, hoping he is not reelected, or they must come to terms. He will have to give some ground also, but it is he who ultimately decides whether a bargain is to be made.

Thus the other branches generally wait for the President to take the lead in proposing policy and then they react to it by trying to shape it as much as possible to their own desires. He sets the agenda and pronounces what the major issues will be. In this way the system struggles along, producing considerable conflict and occasional harmony and some battle-tested policy.

FITTING THE PARTS TOGETHER: THE SEARCH FOR A METAPHOR

Students over the years have tried to visualize how this complex system looks in practice. They have generally tried to find analogies by comparing it to some kind of organic process or to a piece of machinery. Such attempts at system analysis lead to confusions because they sneak in implicit assumptions about how the system *should* be operating. Inevitably both organic and mechanical analogs build in the human-robot assumption—that the government should be operating like a neat input-output system that functions with flawless efficiency.

The Gall Bladder vs. the Colon Let us examine an organic analogy. The human digestive system seems at first glance to provide an attractive comparison. Opinions and pressures from specialized publics can be seen as roughage swallowed up as inputs to provide energy. The analogy does have the advantage of calling attention to the fact that not all output is desirable, but some is waste products of no use to the system and even of potential harm, a point that systems theorists with their penchant for neatness often overlook. The comparison breaks down because the various stomachlike organs are supposed to cooperate willingly together in a common effort to keep the organism from starving. No digestive system has the liver attempting to sabotage the pancreas or only reluctantly going along with the spleen.

All organic analogies are misleading because they assume that the various parts should always be acting in interdependence rather than with considerable independence. Such analogies at times invite thoughts of sacrificing one of the vital organs, such as the gall bladder or colon "for the good of the system." Independence of the liver is treated as treason rather than being a planned part of the way the system is supposed to operate. Systems analysts visualize making all the parts fall into line, marching along like good, docile, little vital organs on orders from the brain or central nervous system. Thus the system itself comes to have a life and purpose of its own that overrides the wills of the parts, and the real model comes closer to an authoritarian leviathan than to our own form of democratic government. A good many systems work like the flow along the alimentary canal, but the United States government is not one of them.

The Plugs May Show Little Spark The same difficulties exist with mechanical comparisons. One can imagine public opinions collecting in huge garbage cans which sit along the curbstone. Soon, one of those efficient rubbish-and-garbage packer trucks, representing the United States policy-making machinery, rolls up. The opinions get dumped in by garbage handlers who are really the interest-group leaders and the mix is ground up and pounded together. A new product is formed which in its broad outline is perhaps predictable, but is unnamable in terms of its exact composition. Many systems operate like machines and perhaps even some governments grind out policies like so many little link sausages on an assembly line, but the United States government is not one of them.

The Problem with Analogies: A System, Yes, but One of Conflict The difficulty with both the organic and the mechanical analogies is that they lead one to assume that the system the Founding Fathers created is always suffering from acid indigestion or stripped gears. They discount the value of building conflict into a system so that whatever policy is proposed gets a sometimes unexpected going-over from many points of view. Such analogies lead one to assume that a policy-making machine can be built that has the efficiency of an automatic washer working over a load of dirty laundry while still being democratic. They assume that what should be done is already known and self-evident to all and need only be proclaimed by the system's brain or central nervous system (generally conceived of as the President or Supreme Court) or by whoever designed the machine, that is, the creator of the analogy. The Founding Fathers, with little optimism about human motivation or behavior, thought policy for a great nation, before it would be proclaimed, should be worked over fairly thoroughly by many people who held different points of reference and who had selfish reasons of their own for challenging any such attempt and had a measure of independence from the proclaimer which enabled them to make their challenge effective.

Achieving Order out of Chaos If the organic and machine analogies emphasize the need for order too much, other analogies can overemphasize the conflict. The recognition that the best analogies require a high degree of freedom and independence in the parts may tempt one into Alice in Wonderland comparisons which dismiss the whole policy process of the United States government as a form of exhibitionist egotism in a lunatic asylum with no overall purpose or direction. In that strange but familiar world of Alice, individual power seekers each seek their own self-aggrandizement with a rational purposefulness and independence that seems to satisfy the participants despite its overall aura of logic run amuck. But this analogy is also tilted. It neglects the order that emerges from the federal government's policy making. The Alice in Wonderland analogy overlooks the point that the American government, like many other institutional arrangements of long-term vintage, does despite certain aesthetic, philosophical, and perhaps even moral defects, produce results that make life bearable and even sometimes enjoyable for a great many individuals besides the official participants. It neglects the fact that the Founders provided limits to the conflict. They thus designed an institution which like most other long-lived human enterprises (a family, a business, a church, or even a college classroom) was a precarious balance between order and anarchy; a balance that includes tendencies to unite as well as to disintegrate. They recognized that this is normal in human institutions and accepted it as such, rather than calling it sickness or pathology.

The United States government can perhaps be understood a little better when one makes the comparison to a system that our government policy making really does resemble to some degree—that of a three-ring circus. The surface similarities are obvious: the egotistical demands for attention by competing acts, the high-wire type of thrillers, the antics of many clowns, the sideshow freaks, the caged animals and their trainers, the tinsel and glitter, and the high-sounding dramatic pronouncements through a megaphone by a ring master; all of which sometimes cover rather sordid private activities and private lives. In a good circus, however, a rather admirable human effort and a kind of order-out-of-chaos come shining through—one that makes it a remarkable human achievement. Participants and viewers alike recognize that a circus is a serious business that requires individuality along with some measure of cooperation among extremely disparate elements. To dispense with the ringmaster is to invite anarchy and confusion. To make him a tin god who can dictate completely to the human and animal zoo with which he deals is to stamp out the diversity and contradictions. Most importantly it is to destroy the life and spirit of the circus. Whatever results in either case may be more free or alternatively more efficient and machinelike, but it is no longer a circus.

Thus the best analogies are not those that lead one either to make efficiency assumptions or to surrender all hope for overall direction. The best analogies are those that lead one to recognize that the American policy process is a human organization made up of many imperfect and conflicting and yet cooperating individuals. The fairest judgments are in terms of results in this imperfect world rather than in terms of results in imaginary utopia where everyone marches along together in lockstep because they love each other or because they act as if they were all high on the same mind-molding drug.

THE BUREAUCRATS

Every branch and unit in the United States government are prone to arrogance and self-glorification. He who desires to admire humility must usually look to the private sector, where it is hard enough to find.

If No One Else Will Love Them, They Will Do It Themselves
The special temptation of the bureaucrats is that of the religious zealot—the secret assumption in their heart of hearts that they fight in the cause of righteousness. This is because their basic assumption is that the professional values, standards, procedures, and goals to which they give fealty are the only true religion. All else is compromise with Lucifer—that is, compromise with uniformed assumptions of the laymen or the selfish interests of knaves.

There is much to be said for these professional values. They do hold up a standard of service and demand a degree of disinterested performance to goals beyond the self. They also attempt to fit procedures to these goals so that once the mission of service is defined, the tested methods for accomplishing it will be chosen. And they demand from the individual bureaucrat a minimum level of professional performance if he is to maintain his self-respect.

They also lead, however, to three perversions; the tendency to judge behavior by the good professional intentions of the bureaucrat rather than by the performance that results; and second, the inability of one set of bureaucrats to see the effect of the single-minded pursuit of one set of professional values on the attainment of other values. This is the problem of opportunity costs, in that the choice of one set of values limits therefore the possibility of achieving others. Third, the substitution of professional goals for citizen desires occurs.

The Road to Hell Is Traveled by Bureaucratic Intentions
Let us examine these bureaucratic perversions. To have professional motivations can become a great shield and a rock of ages behind which one can find shelter from the cold reality of being

judged by results rather than being praised for one's good intentions or methods of operation. The professional soldier knows how to fight battles so well that later West Point classes will study them in detail to fully admire the fine points, even if the Vietnam village has to be destroyed in order to save it. The highway engineer knows how to upgrade the quality of life for all Michiganders by cutting another three minutes off the interstate to Chicago, even if it means relocating a few thousand more citizens out of their sordid ranch homes and trailer parks and destroying just a few hundred more farms or roadside businesses. The welfare worker can cheerfully and with good conscience sentence social rejects to a condition of perpetual dependency in order to build up their self-respect. The FBI helps preserve civil liberties of the citizens by bugging private conversations of those who they think might destroy these civil liberties. These examples suggest that not only may professionalism encourage action being judged by motivation rather than by result, but also that the result may deprive citizens of values they also cherish because one value is being pursued too single-mindedly at the expense of all others.

All this is to suggest that, as admirable as they may be, professional values can be interpreted so narrowly as to be turned against the citizen. It does not deny that complex, difficult tasks are accomplished only by professionals; admirable and needed roads are built by professional highway engineers, welfare clients are helped to independent self-respect by professional social workers, and potential destroyers of our liberties are apprehended by the FBI. But too single-minded a pursuit of any of these professional values at the expense of all other values can also lead to monstrous rather than humanistic behavior and even destroy the value it hopes to achieve. The tendency to judge behavior by adherence to standards prescribed by the professional dogma rather than by results encourages that tendency.

The Mysteries of Status   Professionalism frequently leads to the substitution of long-range professional goals for direct service goals in the work and reward systems of a government agency. Professional bureaucrats act in ways not immediately comprehensible to the layman. Thus citizens think they hire professors to teach students, but the greatest rewards at universities go to those who publish research in their areas of specialty. Professors have worked out an elaborate rationalization for this which is eminently reasonable and convincing to us, but we find on occasion it is sometimes less so for the layman, even including sometimes the students in our classes. Professionals also bestow great rewards for what seem to be only minor elaborations and refinements on the agency's main function. Again, the public often fails to see the importance of the distinctions. Detectives are given higher status than policemen and laboratory technicians status above them. The cop on the beat, the one who risks his life by stopping the fellow about to mug you, is given the lowest status and rewards.

The organization and recruitment of bureaucrats encourages a single-minded adherence to the professional assumptions over all others. It emphasizes that self-interest in terms of bureaucratic career advancement is linked to these values. The professional school that trains its students in these values is the key to entrance into the middle and upper levels of the bureaucracy for all but the highest political appointments. The FBI and the Office of Education demand and get only the best trained. After that promotion depends upon ratings of superiors, with tenure guaranteed to retirement. One can prosper as an undistinguished professional; only unprofessional behavior is an overriding sin.

The separate specialized constituencies of the bureaucrat also accentuate this commitment, since they are the colleagues of his professional specialization including especially those who lead its national associations and the special interests in the larger society concerned with his specialist function. The national association professionals, like the university teachers, applaud those who innovate in the direction of the professional commitment and reward them with honors and attention. The special interests in the larger society learn to frame their demands in terms of professional goals and values like so many natives earning beads from a nineteenth-century African missionary.

Even the political heads of agencies appointed directly by the President can be disarmed by insistence on professional goals. The President continually battles lest his Secretary of State be captured by the Foreign Service mentality of the State Department or his Secretary of HEW begin talking like a professional social worker.

Power Obstructs The legal powers of the bureaucrat are vast. It is he who almost always interprets the law for the average citizen. When the citizen says, "You can't fight City Hall," he is not talking about a political oligarchy that rules the city council as much as the administrative one that collects his trash or gives him a traffic ticket for overparking. He is remembering the sympathetic attention given to preserving his time and patience that is expressed in putting together the long form 1040.

Resistance to Attack Presidents have found the best way to influence an administrative program with whose professional underpinning of assumptions they disagree is to starve it and then if possible bypass it by creating a new competing program built on different professional assumptions. The notion that it can be changed quickly by sending out different signals from the top is doomed by the bulwark of professionalism that has grown up. If one is in doubt, one should consult the court-martial record of General Billy Mitchell, whose major sin was pointing out in the 1920s that airplanes were potentially a useful weapon of war against things like battleships and infantries.

Rival Bureaucrats Only occasionally can an agency be mobilized into an effective initiator of broad policy. J. Edgar Hoover was able to achieve this in the FBI through long life and the single-minded commitment of a bachelor to professionalization of police work. Other agencies, like the military, the State Department, or the Office of Education, have been captured by a value system that overrides any individual in its rigidity. But such single-mindedness becomes a weakness for the whole bureaucracy because it sets professionals to fighting each other like so many Protestants and Catholics engaged in a holy war. Park and forestry specialists see things differently. One sees forests as so many trees providing shade and campsites for vacationing tourists. The other sees forests as lumber, a valuable natural resource to be nurtured and protected at all costs against those campers who so carelessly start forest fires. This leads bureaucrats to seek allies in the other branches such as Congress or the presidential office rather than with their fellow bureaucrats.

The Search for Personal Goals There is, however, also an unprofessional dry rot in the bureaucracy based on the assumptions championed by civil service and the unions of what should be professional workers. Unlike the assumptions of professionalism, which turn workers outward and encourage them to live up to a standard of service, these assumptions turn the bureaucrats inward to matters of personal satisfaction with job conditions and even on occasion to self-indulgence. Carried to its ultimate, the assumption is that the job was created to satisfy the needs and wants of the employee rather than to provide a service to the general public. Where workers have been financially exploited or treated shabbily, or the professional work effort has been marginal and professional morale is low, unionism is natural and logical, and one might add, probably a desirable outcome. If there is no alternative set of assumptions that stress service and give the worker professional satisfactions, one may expect him to demand mundane job satisfactions. It is not astonishing that the major beachhead of unionism in federal employment has thus far been the formerly patronage-ridden Postal Service, whose performance has often fallen short of any imagined professional goals. It is likewise not astonishing in local government to find unionization in the educational system, where teachers have been treated with all the respect and generosity generally accorded inept eccentrics.

The Job That Is Done The bureaucracy, though more conflict-ridden than the other branches, continues to exercise an important role in policy making, especially in respect to details. Its thrust is to implement policy advanced by professional specialties, whatever the actual law may say. Its achievement falls something short of its vision. The process of specialization and professionalization sometimes breeds a petty tyranny of the mind alongside some very benificent results. But neither the land flowing with milk and honey envisaged by utopian liberals who championed professionalized administration, nor the bureaucratic police state so feared by conservative polemical writers, has resulted.

THE CULT OF THE ROBE

The judiciary, a particular type of bureaucracy, is highly professionalized, but it is a specialization with a difference. Having a written constitution encourages legal wrangling within a nation because someone has to be the final authority on what the document means legally. The judges thus come to have a vested interest in legal hairsplitting in order that, by their special knowledge of legal lore, they may set policy for the rest of the government. For the display of sheer self-righteous arrogance, no other branch of the United States government has ever been able to match the courts.

The formal doctrine is that the judges merely interpret the Constitution or the laws passed by Congress and President. In practice, they legislate their own assumptions about the direction in which they feel the nation should be heading. Judges in the past as well as today have been quite willing to place their own assumptions above those of the other branches, public opinion, and the election results. All this is done from the highest of motives.

When the courts make decisions so as to set policy, we have what is known as an "activist" court. Yet, in fact, a majority of the United States Supreme Court has been nothing else since Chief Justice Marshall, in *Madison v. Marbury* (1803), proclaimed the Court's right to be the final interpreter of the Constitution. Even earlier, the Supreme Court had had enough confidence in its own infallibility to explain to President George Washington, who had asked for one, what the Founding Fathers had really meant in respect to legal expressions known as "advisory opinions," even though he was the Founding Father who had presided as chairman of the Constitutional Convention while members of the Court had not even been present as delegates. Justices have performed the same services for Presidents and Congresses ever since. One can hardly point to a clause of the Constitution or a major piece of legislation that does not have the tooth marks of justices upon it. To the layman, the interpretations of the Court have often seemed farfetched, to say the least.

The Scope of Power   A legal precedent can be found for almost any position, and judicial interpretation is thus permitted a wide latitude. For example, in order to regulate business operations through congressional law, the judges developed the legal fiction that electricity was a form of interstate commerce. This is not unlike the actions of nineteenth-century judges, who applied the Fourteenth Amendment, designed to assist ex-slaves, for the protection of monopoly corporations against hostile legislatures, or those judges who more recently (and before the constitutional amendment) declared unconstitutional state laws against eighteen-year-olds voting for national offices, even though the Constitution in its first article says that "the electors in each state shall have the qualifications requisite for electors of the most numerous branch of the state legislature." A useful technique of the Court has been to argue that the first Ten Amendments (the Bill of Rights) or the Thirteenth through the Fifteenth Amendments, which dealt with slavery, turn out to have overruled what the main body of the Constitution clearly states. To the layman, it may even appear that those who proposed and adopted the amendments did not know they were making such policy at the time, and if they had anticipated the judicial interpretation of later days would probably never have offered the amendments in the first place.

The Effects of Judicial Review Henry Steele Commager, the historian, has pointed out that championing judicial policy making sets up bad habits for a democracy. It takes policy out of the hands of the elected legislators and puts it in the hands of an undemocratic oligarchy which holds office for life. It also assumes that the pronouncements of the past are more important than are present-day concerns—a doctrine that would usually benefit conservatives. It can lead to a real crisis in the political system as judges attempt to legislate against current public opinion, as they did in the Dred Scott decision which favored the South, prior to the Civil War, or in the recent school-bussing decisions.

Judicial policy making, however, does have several other clear advantages: (1) It is an effective, though not the only, way by which to maintain the supremacy of national policy making over state policy making; (2) it can also provide a useful way for maintaining broad congressional representation by decreeing reapportionment of the House of Representatives on the basis of "one man, one vote." Thus the nation has been able to avoid the kind of constitutional apportionment crises that wracked Great Britain in 1832 and 1867 and led to the battles over the House of Lords in 1910. (3) The arrogant judiciary provides an American substitute for a hereditary aristocracy and monarchy. The justices solemnly set a stamp of legitimacy on political acts just as does Queen Elizabeth when she reads the Prime Minister's message to the assembled Parliament. This symbolic act is important, for it can be seen as the granting of legitimacy to the law by someone symbolically (though not necessarily in fact) above the political battle.

The policy-making activities of judges do not, however, go on unchecked forever. Peter Finley Dunne, in the character of Mr. Dooley, made the widely quoted observation that the Supreme Court follows the election returns. It would have been more accurate of him to observe that the man who appoints the members of the Supreme Court and the federal judges of the lower courts follows the election returns. Thus, until someone does the government of the United States the disservice of unlocking the secret of human immortality, the nation is safe. Judges, like the common ruck of humanity, also with the passage of time, begin to slow down, falter, and eventually retire from the scene. New judges appear to have little hesitation in bending policies proclaimed by previous judges, with all their high-sounding phrases, into new shapes to fit new assumptions. And thus the court rejoins the nation, if sometimes a generation late, though rarely more so.

In Defense of Judicial Policy Making If one looks at results rather than judging in terms of ideals, the case against judicial policy making is also not as dark as it might first appear. The policy that results from judicial pronouncement on balance seems to be clearly to the good. If the court sometimes lags a generation behind, it also pioneers and hurries up trends that are only beginning to develop in the electorate. Few would deny it accomplished this needed result in respect to legal racial discrimination. The court in recent years has also championed other very liberal upper-middle-class positions in civil liberties and civil rights. Many conservatives believe the judges have over-emphasized concerns for the individual at the expense of the larger interests of community and society, but at least the actions of the court have raised to the level of debate the question of the preference of its position as compared with that of the more cautious and traditional legislative bodies.

The basic assumption of the judges is that democracy as expressed through public opinion cannot always be trusted. This assumption was certainly shared by the writers of our Constitution, as well as by many Americans since. If it is qualified with the notion that no one (not even a majority of the Supreme Court) should be trusted completely, it is not a bad guide for action. In the courts more than in the other branches, the above assumption is often combined with a disinterested idealism that assumes officials should act for the peoples' own good, even if the people themselves do not appreciate this attitude of "Papa knows best." This is because the courts are shielded more than any other branch from the pressures of public opinion. In the courts, idealistic assumptions may remain relatively pure because they are not subject to the immediate pressures that torment other public officials. The courts can enjoy the luxury of being a generation ahead or behind the rest of the country. Their special methods of recruitment and organization encourage this result.

All federal judges are appointed permanently, with no further review unless they are clearly caught with both hands in the till, a rare event. They hold office for life, more specifically, "during good behavior." They are selected from a very special population, that of law school graduates who have been indoctrinated with the professional mumbo jumbo of law professors. Especially in the appeals courts and the Supreme Court, the judges isolate themselves from the hurly burly of society. They surround themselves with a ritual that emphasizes bowing and scraping before the majesty of the presiding judge. While this excessive decorum, required of all, is said to show deference for the court rather than the individual presiding, it is not too difficult for the individual presiding to allow a little of the deference to rub off onto him personally and come to assume that Providence—or something—has blessed him with unusual acumen.

The constituency of the court reinforces this shelter from rude blasts. At the highest levels, the judges write opinions that are studied by fellow professionals, the law students and law professors of the future. In addition, along with their colleagues on lower courts, they take actions which are judged by their professional peers in the legal game. Whatever assumptions about policy dominated the law schools of a generation ago come to be applauded in the judiciary of today. Around the beginning of the century, these assumptions, as Justice Oliver W. Holmes pointed out in a dissent, were those of the laissez faire social philosopher, Herbert Spencer, the belief that if the individual in his economic role were left unhampered, the result would provide the maximum possible production of goods and services which would be distributed according to one's contribution to society. Professional standards of the day applauded judicial constructions of the law and Constitution which would indicate that this is what the Founding Fathers really meant. During the 1960s and 1970s, the basic assumptions were those of the generation of Franklin D. Roosevelt, when the present justices struggled through the law schools under the conditions of the Great Depression, the belief that if the individual in his social role were left unhampered, the result would provide untold social benefits for the rest of the citizens.

The Limits of Power When the views of the Supreme Court majority lose in two presidential elections, the courts are in line for change. Indeed, the change will most likely be acted out with all the fervor of a team of high-pressure salesmen out to beat the firm's record. No precedent will be too small to be overturned by a new and more "enlightened" reinterpretation. And so the system grinds on as new zealots and reformers become part of the judicial establishment and, in time, also turn defensive about their interpretations as another set of presidential elections overturns the dominant pattern of judicial assumptions.

THE WORLD'S MOST EXCLUSIVE CLUB

In a political world in which equality is the byword, it is strange that the United States Senate does not receive more adverse attention. Its representativeness, either on the basis of one-man, one-vote, or in terms of mirroring with any accuracy the groupings within the population, is poor. Yet almost no one proposes an "affirmative action" program for it.

The ready answer is that the Senate's basis of representation of two senators per state is determined by the Constitution itself and can never be changed, even by constitutional amendment. Courts, in other respects, have dodged constitutional obstacles as formidable as this one and a determined public opinion led by a popular President has done the same. The reason for inaction on Senate reform is more complex. It is that the groupings that sniff out every nonegalitarian practice in state legislatures, national primaries, national party conventions, or universities have not wanted to consider the unrepresentativeness of the Senate. The reason is that, for the most part, senators say what these groupings want to hear and so at least for the moment practical politics triumphs over logic and egalitarian enthusiasm. The relatively unpopulated tundra of Alaska gets the same representation as do the teeming tract developments of California.

The Self-Image   Without regard to the political content of what individual senators advocate, their basic assumption about themselves is clear. They see the Senate as the body that will ventilate the great questions that stir the nation and will deal with them in broad terms, emphasizing moral principles above individual cases. Its whole organization is designed to achieve this end and, to a large measure, the Senate has been successful in achieving it.

The key word in respect to the Senate is debate. It is not in the profundity of what is said or even in the aptness of the oratory. Few senators become phrase makers the way Presidents with their platoons of speech writers do. It is that the Senate is the forum for many opinions, including critical and potentially unpopular opinions, whether they are the views of segregationists or of those who favor amnesty for draft dodgers. Every senator has a vested interest in keeping the Senate that way, for few are excluded from the spotlight when they want it.

It is more difficult than with the courts or the bureaucracy to state what the political assumptions underlying the Senate are, because it is a more diverse body, chosen on a less rational and more hit-and-miss basis. The general inclination of the Senate today is to embrace liberal and egalitarian political assumptions, but this has not always been the case, nor will it necessarily always be.

The things senators express depend always to a large extent on the constituencies from which they are recruited. Because an entire state is a senator's constituency, almost every senator has one or more large and a number of middle-sized cities within his district. The political facts of life make it impossible to win a Senate seat in most states without support from these areas—or so at least most politicians probably correctly suppose. Thus both parties in recent decades have nominated for the Senate candidates they feel will appeal to what they suppose is a liberal-labor constituency. Champions of the small-town virtues have had a bit rougher going since the Great Depression, while those who would feel at home with the youth group in an up-to-date suburban church have an easier time of it. If the opinions in these constituencies change markedly in the direction of a blue-collar conservativism, as may be the trend of the 1970s, one may anticipate changes in the Senate's outlook and perhaps a new look at its representativeness.

Rules to Feel Good By The organization of the Senate encourages the individual senator to cultivate his sense of self-importance. The committee system based on seniority, as in the House, gives leaders positions of power. The Senate also has its system of elected leadership through the majority leader who schedules legislation and debate. But the power of such leaders is looser than in the House, and the presiding officer is the Vice President, not a member of the Senate. The individual senator thus is less easily put down by the system than is the representative.

The individual senator's self-esteem is nurtured by other aspects of Senate organization, most notably in the filibuster which permits as few as a single member to dominate Senate business until this minority gets its way or collapses under strain. Cloture, a rule to cut off debate, does occur on rare occasions but even then not with the brutal effectiveness with which most other organizations cut off self-advertisers and willful obstructionists. Only after considerable delay, much hand wringing, soul searching, and efforts at compromise can the individual senator be told by his colleagues to cease and desist.

The other aspects of organization emphasize the chumminess of belonging to what has often been called "the world's most exclusive club." The significant assumption in the eyes of all who are senators or are part of their staffs is that this body has great prestige and each of its members should be respected, if not for himself, then at least for the office he holds.

As a result, members come to feel a sense of reverence for the privilege of being part of that body. The internal rule of the Senate, as in the medical profession, is to encourage the awe and respect of the public. Thus someone as ambitious as Senator John F. Kennedy wrote a book extolling the courageous profiles of past senators.[1] Almost every senator is in the national headlines at some time or another and many have names that become the proverbial "household words" throughout the nation. A few senators in this heady atmosphere have veered toward exhibitionism. When this happens, they may get their wrists slapped, on rare occasions even to the point of being socially ostracized by their colleagues. But opportunistic demagogues such as Huey Long in the 1930s or Joseph McCarthy in the 1950s have been allowed by other senators to cut a broad swath through American society before any real notice was taken by their colleagues. It is notable that, in Senator McCarthy's case, his fellows took action against him only after he turned on other members of the Senate. It was for this that he was censured, rather than for activities that those outside the Senate may have regarded as more significant unseemly behavior.

The prestige of senators should, in their eyes, clearly be distinguished from the likes of the other legislative body, the House of Representatives. The legal and organizational rules encourage that distinction. Senators are far fewer in number, have greater legal responsibilities, and have a six-year term instead of the two-year term that requires continuous campaigning. As one would expect, the career ladder goes upward from House to Senate. Few go the other direction, and so far as is known, no one in full control of his faculties has done so willingly in this century. The only approved way out of the Senate is upward, that is, to the Presidency or Vice Presidency. Like judges, senators seldom die and rarely retire. Unlike federal judges, however, they do have to stand for reelection and defeat is a dramatic, if uncommon, end for a few. The success of senators in capturing the highest offices from the days of Senator Harry Truman onward attest to the Senate's continually growing status. (Between 1948 and 1972, five out of seven Presidents, and an equal number of Vice Presidents, were former senators, a batting average of .714.)

Special Powers for Special People   The legal powers of the Senate add greatly to that body's attractiveness as a platform for moral pronouncements. The Senate, in effect, sits as a judicial body giving its advice and consent as it reviews the qualifications of most of the significant appointments that a President makes either to the bureaucracy or to the courts. A President whose party is a minority in that body, such as was the case for Dwight Eisenhower and Richard Nixon, can expect the advice and consent to be proper moral admonitions combined with politically motivated rebuffs. The technique of avoidance, developed to a high level, but not originated by Nixon, in respect to the bureaucracy, is to have the real work done by personal appointees who do not require Senate confirmation—the Patrick Moynihans and Henry Kissingers. But this is not always possible with the bureaucracy and never with the courts.

A second major legal power of the Senate is that of ratifying treaties. On secondary matters, the President may make executive agreements, but major treaties require concurrence of two-thirds of that body. The Senate has built this legal power into the right to speak out on all matters of foreign relations. Since America became a world power in 1898, the Senate has become the major governmental forum for discussion of the President's foreign policy, whether in respect to arming merchant ships in World Wars I or II, the League of Nations or United Nations, the draft, Pearl Harbor, isolationism, war profiteering, or the Vietnam war. This function is an extremely useful one for the nation as a whole, even though individual senators sometimes spout nonsense during foreign policy debates. It is true that Senator

William E. Borah of Idaho assured President Roosevelt publicly in the summer of 1939 that there would be no European war. But senators are not always this wrong nor are Presidents always so right.

The Senate has also generally made a better thing out of the legal powers it shares jointly with the House of Representatives. This is again a direct outgrowth of its greater status in its own eyes; a line that has been sold to the general public as effectively as either the Marine Corps or FBI publicity campaigns. The discussion of legislation in the Senate becomes a matter of open debate with arm and leg twisting and all the political drama that can be milked from an issue. This is something that Roger Mudd can get his teeth into for the nation to follow with interest on the 6:30 news, in contrast to the rather mechanical counting of noses and votes, such as in the eyes of the public generally characterizes law making in the more humdrum House of Representatives. Also, when the Senate investigates something, it usually does so with flair and more eclat than does the House. People pay attention and senators are even invited to explain themselves on TV programs, such as "Meet the Press" and "Face the Nation," or to unbutton their minds at greater length for Johnny Carson and the late-night intellectuals.

All this forms a very useful service for a government that was built on the assumption that no one's action should go unchecked or unobserved. The initiative for legislation does not have to come from the Senate. It is even better if it comes from the outside, from the White House. What the Senate supplies is the publicity. Whatever even a few of its members get interested in gets a going-over in the press and the TV news. Sometimes it even stirs the public. The nation, while it may not always accept the status position senators feel they should be accorded, would be a grossly poorer thing without such a body.

THE ORPHAN OF DEMOCRACY

The House of Representatives is the little orphan of the national policy-making system. It was originally designed to furnish the democratic impulse for the whole system. It was the only body the Founders wanted to be directly elected by the voters. It should have developed like the English House of Commons, which in the course of a century swallowed up most of the powers of the sovereign and the upper house (though it can be argued that the Commons was, in turn, consumed by its own executive committee, the Cabinet). But this has not happened and it is useful to begin by asking why.

Limited Opportunities, Limited Status It is not because the House is not mathematically more representative of citizens and voters than either the Senate or the Presidency. It has not been an absolute mirror of democracy, but has been closer than the other branches. It discriminated against Negroes for nearly two hundred years by the denial of an equal opportunity to vote, but that characteristic disgrace of the South (and also a good deal of the North) was also to be found in Senate and presidential elections. The House did not get pushed into fifth place because of this characteristic.

The failure of the House to serve as the focus of democratic hope was because it offered fewer career opportunities for talented politicians than does the Senate, the courts, the bureaucracy, the Presidency, or even the Vice-Presidency. Its handicaps are several. The term is only for two years; an incumbent in a competitive district must be forever campaigning and his risks of meeting disaster are greater than in other government careers. There are no special legal powers attached to House membership as compared to the Senate or Presidency, except for the technical and not actually important power to introduce revenue bills. While the rule on tax-matter priority gives the House first crack at financial matters, the power has been exercised effectively by committee chairmen only in bargaining with Presidents, senators, and other House members.

Furthermore, the House member is only 1 in 435. He does not get a desk on the floor or even his own special seat in the House chamber. He files in and takes a seat the way you do at a movie. Because there are so many House members, debate has to be severely limited and few representatives make page one very often, even in the home-town newspaper. It takes a real flair for showmanship to rise above the herd, as Richard Nixon or William Fulbright once did.

All this would suggest to the ambitious politician that he run for the Senate or a governorship as soon as possible. But there is also another way out. The weakness of the House as a political body is partly overcome by its organization. Much more than the Senate, the committee chairmanships of the House offer a hope, in fact almost the only hope, for achieving prominence and power. The seniority system of passing out chairmanships and important committee assignments assures that only those who have few worries about reelection biennially secure these positions. Although the seniority system has been criticized by Common Cause, Herblock, and generations of editorial writers, it has at least two attractions for the membership. First, representatives place great emphasis upon the House being a collegial body. Among equals, how does one choose a chairperson? Length of service as a criterion maintains the illusion of equality. Secondly, using seniority avoids embarrassing intraparty conflict. Having a liberal Democrat fighting a moderate Democrat for a chairmanship could be highly divisive for the party.

While it possesses no special constitutional powers, the standing committee chairmanship carries with it a great many informal political powers. The chairman or even the chairman of a subcommittee can try to hit pay dirt with an investigation. And legislation can be bottled up by the chairman using such techniques as holding interminable hearings or even of failing to call the committee in session. What the House gets to vote on is thus the result of bargains struck with those who control its committees. This government by gerontocracy is added to further by the Rules Committee, all of whose members are especially experienced legislators. This body is supposed to act as a traffic cop to schedule action on legislation for the whole House and decide whether amendments and how much debate are to be permitted. In the past these powers have led the Rules Committee to act as a super legislature for the House, delaying or crippling legislation of which it disapproved.

The Pieces of Power   What the committee system and the prerogatives of its chairmen accomplish are the placing of the political power of the whole House on a particular subject, in the hands of one man or at most a few men. Thus, Presidents have had to bargain directly with Wilbur Mills, the Chairman of Ways and Means, on such matters as tax policy, revenue sharing, or medicare, or with the Rules Committee or other committees who have administration legislation bottled up.

Parallel to the committee system is the House organization of whips and leaders, headed by the Speaker, who is the presiding officer. He is elected by his party's membership in the body rather than succeeding to the office on the strength of a well-functioning liver. Before the reforms of 1910, the Speaker could act as a virtual dictator over policy because he selected all committee members. Today, he is rather like a tough field manager for a team of all-stars, the chairman. Besides making rulings on parliamentary matters, he still has powers of recognition of individual members, assignment of bills to standing committees and appointment of special committees, and the appointment of members of conference committees who meet with senators to work out differences in similar bills passed by each house. But in using these powers he has to bargain with the rest of the team, namely, with the veteran members of the Chamber. Some Speakers, such as Sam Rayburn, were able to maximize the whole House's power potential by threatening to use the votes of the less important members to gain concessions from the more important chairmen of standing committees. More commonly, the individual committee chairmen with sympathetic committees overpower the Speaker or form an alliance with him and so exercise most of the power in respect to specific legislative areas.

The Constituent Is King The neophyte member, then, faces the problem of looking for something to fill up his time while waiting for the years to pass. Immediately at hand are the needs and demands of his constituents. Unlike senators, most representatives have constituents packed into districts of manageable geographic and population size. A House member's motto could be borrowed from that of a small weekly newspaper, The Boomerang (Missouri) *Gazette,* which proclaimed itself as "The only newspaper in the world that gives a damn about Boomerang." So, too, a congressman may be the only federal official to care much about a particular stretch of swamp and stumps, or fireplugs and storefronts. Many districts have a composition that somewhat approaches homogeneity in terms of race or ethnicity, occupation and industry, or urbanization. This, too, encourages the representative to identify with his constituents. He becomes the errand boy, ombudsman, hand holder, and humanizer of the federal government operation for those who live in his district and have the uncommon common sense to continue to elect him. Such services can vary from providing interesting information about hogwarts or rosebud rot, to making extensive contacts about pensions with the Veterans Administration, to providing information about civil service jobs, or to assisting businessmen in contacting any of the numerous governmental agencies that can add to the treasure of local industry, agriculture, or labor.

The House, then, wears two faces, one for the policy-making effort and one for the public. For policy, the veterans exploit the newcomers and mobilize the support of the whole House to fit the assumptions of a handful of leaders. Such assumptions, it is often noted, are those of a bygone age and may suffer from a lack of timeliness.

For the individual congressman, the major assumption is that of any patronage-type operation, that blood is thicker than whatever flows through the veins of strangers. The significance of this as a humanizer of government for the average citizen can hardly be overemphasized. Even when the service performed is haphazard or inept, it serves a needed psychic function. There is someone who cares at other than election time. That it is almost always election time for the representative may not be realized by most of his constituents. Just to know that there is someone in all that buzzing confusion in Washington who will listen to what a citizen in the northeast corner of the Fourteenth District wants or needs is perhaps as valuable a contribution to our nation's ongoing democratic experiment as many of the more publicized theatrics in the other branches of government.

LADIES AND GENTLEMEN: THE PRESIDENT OF THE UNITED STATES

Traditionally, the President of the United States is treated like royalty and given no introduction beyond the nine words that head this section. Around him is much of the aura of kingship but with a distinct difference. Kings go on until they die or, rarely, are deposed by a revolution. Presidents last only four or at most eight years. Thus citizens can pay homage to the President and the effort is more easily accomplished because one knows the man holding the office and being honored serves but for a short time. One need only note the way ex-Presidents are treated to realize the honor attaches only to the office and not to the person.

The office of President, of course, gives more than just temporary rewards to the ego. It is also an office of great legal powers and their exercise brings additional honor, as well as criticism, opposition, grumbling, and inevitably some hate and envy. This is especially true since, as we have noted, those powers can be used effectively to check the officeholders in the other branches. Most of all, however, the presidential office gives its occupant the opportunity to do something about the way the nation is heading.

The Only Constituency: The Historians A President is encouraged to have what the British Prime Minister Benjamin Disraeli called "heroic ambition," that is, the desire to wield power toward some important purpose. This is emphasized by what a President imagines will be the reaction of the major constituency, which increasingly comes to dominate his actions as his term progresses and time runs out. This constituency is not his most dedicated partisans, or even all the citizens. As Edmund Burke noted, a nation may be conceived of as being made up of those citizens now living, those citizens who have died, and those yet to be born. A President makes his main appeal to all these, but especially to the judgment of future citizens. He thus makes his appeal to historians and those they write for.

This appeal, which is essentially an invitation to make history, can be ennobling as well as frustrating and even disastrous. Perhaps this, more than anything else, can explain how Lyndon Johnson's general prudence was overcome in respect to the Vietnam war when he was faced with the nightmarish thought that he could go down in history as the first American President ever to lose a war. At the same time, the sense of history inspired a rather run-of-the-mill Missouri politician, Harry S. Truman, to achievements far beyond what his contemporaries expected of him. The challenge may also overwhelm the man. President James Buchanan seems to many historians to have been unable to cope with the political situation that soon after he left office deteriorated into the Civil War. Whatever the result, we can be sure that this appeal to history will be a major motivation of most Presidents of the twentieth century.

The President, however, in order to accomplish these higher purposes, must work with the politicians currently in office and with present demands and needs. The way in which he is recruited emphasizes this involvement. The process begins with presidential primaries and state conventions and ends in nomination at a national conclave. Few emerge from these experiences without some political commitment to others. Election by the winner-take-all method embodied in the Electoral College system emphasizes the power of large states and of the minorities within them that can swing all the electoral votes of a state to one candidate or the other.

Diplomat, Not Commander The President's day-to-day activities form a pattern that encourages and rewards the development of negotiating and diplomatic skills. If forced to, a President can make his term a fight of a single man against superior political forces, gaining whatever is possible from a belligerent Congress and recalcitrant bureaucracy. This is the stance of all inept Presidents or of those others who face one or both houses of Congress dominated by the opposition party: Harry Truman, 1946-1948; Dwight Eisenhower, 1954-1960; and Richard Nixon, 1968-1976. A President's strategy under such circumstances is to concentrate on foreign policy, where freedom of action is greatest, and to champion by making them his own, whatever planks of the opposition party he considers worth appropriating.

Much more satisfactory is the role of presidential leadership when both houses of Congress are not dominated by the opposition party but by the party of the President. Even then the result is far from smooth sailing, as John F. Kennedy discovered, but the President at least operates with better odds. The skills required are those of the balance-of-power diplomat, in which Franklin Delano Roosevelt and Lyndon Baines Johnson excelled. It requires building a coalition of supporters in Congress and selling the assumptions of the President's proposed program to the public. From the Johnson administration, like that of Roosevelt thirty years before, issued a parade of domestic programs on which the next generation would have to chew in an attempt to digest them into the American society and economy. The ill-fated Vietnam adventure obscured the accomplishment of LBJ to the point that by 1972 his own party could only with great reluctance bring itself to hang up his picture at their national political convention where TV cameras, they themselves, and the rest of the nation might see it. But the breadth of his accomplishment, whether one agrees or disagrees with the thrust, cannot be so easily brushed aside by the historians of the wanderings of the American nation toward whatever destiny awaits it.

How one builds such coalitions is both a science and an art. The science deals with organizing the staff of the presidential office and acting in accordance with such simple precepts as isolating your enemies, appealing to the public in prime TV time, accepting half a loaf, rewarding friends and punishing enemies, and a dozen other such conventional tactics. The art comes in breaking these precepts; knowing when to do so and for what effect. Each President follows an individual pattern dictated by his own strengths and weaknesses, as well as by circumstances. Commentators of the day and future historians may "cluck-cluck" and "tsk-tsk," scratch their heads, whistle long and low, or cheer depending on their own perceptiveness and their own assumptions and prejudices. Presidents Eisenhower and Kennedy seem to most observers to have wasted what opportunities they had. President Nixon is treated as if he always exercises consummate political skill, which is at this time still debatable.

Yeah, Team   Most important in this operation is the building of what may be called the presidential "team." This cliché, borrowed from a salesman's Monday morning pep meeting, became popular during the Eisenhower years. For the team, the President must recruit effective alter egos for his Cabinet, liaison persons for Congress, as well as people for special missions, such as that of Henry Kissinger. The Cabinet choices are often dictated by the payment of political debts and the balancing of various interests, but they also at times signal significant policy directions and emphases. Most importantly the President needs to find a few completely trustworthy and perceptive advisors. He must also organize the presidential administrative office. Here are the people who help with the more mundane tasks that a President needs done for him, from checking facts and digging out information and ammunition, to preparing stories for the reporters, and writing inane proclamations for Mother's Day. No President can keep full control of such an operation, for leaks, blunders, sabotage, or in-fighting are bound to occur (the Watergate incident is a prime example). What he must aim for and achieve to some extent is the recruitment and molding of a reasonable cadre of persons loyal to his set of assumptions, persons who also have the skills needed to achieve the goals that flow from those assumptions. His effectiveness depends much on these recruits.

The Ship Does Have a Rudder   The President thus provides some measure of direction for American policy making and he assumes, correctly, that on this history and as yet unborn citizens of the nation will judge his success and accomplishments. Building such heroic ambition into the Constitution and at the same time restraining the occupant of the presidential office was one of the master strokes of the writers of the Constitution, even when one takes into account the presidential disasters that have resulted on a few occasions and are likely to happen again in the future. The United States system may provide for better checks on the abuse of power than do many others, but no system yet devised has been found to be foolproof.

MEANWHILE, BACK IN POCATELLO

Those who live elsewhere but have some job in government, often speak of "that mess in Washington." This is not only a form of self-indulgence or self-delusion, but most importantly is often pure envy. The problem with "that mess in Washington" that is apparent to most governors, mayors, and state legislators is that they are not there to take part. Despite all the sentiment about life back on the hustings, few politicians are without the ambition to join the Washington scene. What they most generally lack are the abilities or the votes. Either one will suffice, but you must have one. Some will gladly swap a shopworn governorship for a Cabinet or sub-Cabinet office as both Governors George Romney and G. Mennen Williams of Michigan have done in recent years. Others struggle to join the United States Senate. The ambitions are laudable ones, but they color the operation of the federal system: Few politicians fail to recognize that Washington is the big time.

The Inferior Partners The Founding Fathers had no choice in granting some independence to the states. Even the degree of centralization they proposed was greeted by cries of "tyranny!" They made a virtue out of necessity and created the Senate with equal representation. Senators were assumed to be representatives of the states, but it soon became clear they were far from such in practice. Just as the President bypassed Congress and appealed directly to the voters, so Senators bypassed state governments and campaigned directly. The Seventeenth Amendment, which provided for direct election of senators, made official what was already the fact: The government of each sovereign state did not have in Washington its own representative who would dance as it pulled the strings.

The result of the Senate representing people rather than governments was more built-in competition for the American system. But it was a competition among unequals. It was not only that the leaders in the states could be bought off with federal offices. It was also that whenever a dispute found its way into the courts, it was the federal judges who made the final decisions. Predictably, the men in black performed just as if they wore the uniforms of the Washington Nationals. A third reason for the shift was that the national government had the resources which could be translated into power. The Civil War decided that a state or even a group of states were no longer free to pick up their marbles and start a different game. The Sixteenth Amendment, which started Form 1040A, gave the federal government vast potential financial resources. Starting with the administration of Theodore Roosevelt but gaining momentum under Franklin Roosevelt, the federal government through regulations and what a Supreme Court justice irascibly described as dangling financial lures before the states (Presidents call it the "grant-in-aid system"), states were pulled in directions desired by those who held the strings in Washington.

Up until recently the state governments contributed to this trend by their general venality, amateurishness, and backwardness. It was hard to swing a dead cat around a state capitol rotunda without slapping in the back of the neck either a knave or a fool, or both. Only since the beginning of World War II have a great many states begun to seriously professionalize their staffs and eliminate some of the incompetence and corruption. They have been aided in this effort by their own organization, the Council of State Governments, and its many offshoot organizations, such as the Conference of Governors and similar groups for legislators, attorneys general, and other officials.

The same kind of story is true of local government, except that professionalism reached the cities earlier. The efforts of the good government reformers, who were denounced as "goo goos" by professional politicians, taught city officials how to clean their finger nails and act like good middle-class citizens about a generation before the message got to the state legislatures. The movement was aided by the invention of the city manager system and its widespread adoption from the early 1920s on.

Power to the People Who Can Do the Job—But Who Are They? Having reached this point, government officials had two options. One was to manage the whole thing from Washington, or at least from the Maryland and Virginia suburbs. This was the solution pushed hard by Lyndon Johnson and aided and abetted by a series of Supreme Court decisions such as *Baker v. Carr,* which insisted on reapportionment of state legislators on the basis of "one-man, one-vote."

This approach floundered for several reasons. The assumptions underlying the Great Society programs were often poorly thought through. (We examine these in greater detail in the chapters to follow.)

Equally important, the Great Society programs were necessarily designed to shake up the local status and power systems. The effect was similar to some Methodist's missionary efforts among the cannibals; the cannibals who did not like it were the ones holding the knives and the stewing pots.

A third reason was an administrative one. While it could be conceded that the localities could benefit by being pulled away from selfish parochialisms, it was not clear that a central direction system could be devised to do it.

A number of administrative analysts are taking a second look at the federal system. Not all have concluded that a complete centralization is possible or even desirable. In competition among governments, federal, state and local, in the same metropolitan area, the same city, county, or state, they have discerned some positive benefits. They note the communications snarl that results from overcentralization. They argue alienation is directly tied to the thought expressed in the phrase "You can't fight city hall." They see a complacent, tenured, and little-challenged bureaucracy as the definition of mediocrity. For all these reasons they propose a reexamination of federalism in terms of results produced rather than buying the underlying assumptions of the administrative centralization model.

The problem is similar to that of supplying food for the city of Albany, Georgia, for September 30, 1981. One method of accomplishing the result would be to plan the operation centrally just as the invasion of Iwo Jima was planned down to the last can of C rations put aboard the ships. The other is to set up an ecological process in which individuals following their own selfish desires produce a useful social result, i.e., an abundant supply of okra and other edibles at the A & P store in Albany on September 30, 1981.

Each approach presents difficulties. The first requires a formidable bureaucracy with considerable sagacity and some means of getting feedback. President Johnson's plans were something less than satisfying in this regard. The second requires a framework of regulations to insure that the system does indeed provide social benefits along with satisfying the selfish needs of those who hold the knives and stewing pots.

President Nixon has opted for the second solution and calls it "revenue sharing." Instead of a variety of federal programs that march the states along to the tune of "Stars and Stripes Forever," he proposes a grant of money for the states to see how well they can handle some of the social problems they face.

Like the first income tax, the first shared revenue grant is a modest one. Its continuance and increase are dependent on the political power those with the knives and stewing pots can muster. Already critics are saying that giving money to the more incompetent local governments is as effective as pouring water down a gopher hole. Others say that the plan will benefit unneedy suburbs relatively more than the problem-plagued inner cities.

The contribution of the rules of the federalist system is to introduce additional confusion and conflict, and to offer invitations for persons and groups to pursue their own ends within certain limits. This is an aspect of what is called "pluralism" and it is in bad repute with those who go around with neat little blueprints in their heads. But it is the way our federal system is likely to continue to operate until a breakdown creates demand for more changes.

HOW POLICY GETS MADE

In this chapter we have emphasized that policy in the United States emerges from an arena of conflict and bad blood. No one set of assumptions or of interests dominates the whole process, but many views and actions effect the final result. The presidential office attempts to bring some order out of this chaos and has the best chance of doing so.

Whether the policies that emerge precisely mirror the "will of the majority," or the "national spirit," or any other spooky kind of reformulation of Jean-Jacque Rousseau's notion of the "General Will," seems to us an unanswerable question. What may be asked is whether the result is tolerable enough to live with. Most past generations as well as present ones have answered, "yes, it is." We anticipate that future generations may decide in the affirmative as well. A few years ago, a radical college student commented disdainfully, "Splitting the difference is not justice." Maybe it is; maybe it is not. It *is*, however, a necessary part of democracy.

NOTE

1 John F. Kennedy, *Profiles in Courage,* Harper & Brothers, New York, 1955.

5

COMPROMISE AND BARGAINING:
THE POLICY RESULT

Camelot

Chapter 9

Civil Rights
and Civil Wrongs

How sweet it is to do one's thing. And to be able to tell others about it is half the joy. Such freedom is a bedrock minimum for individual satisfaction with life.

Our sweet land of liberty also reaps some social benefits from free expression. Only when citizens are able to express themselves does responsive government have a chance to flourish.

Thus freedom of speech, religion, press, and assembly, and the right to fair and just treatment without intimidation when we run afoul of the law, are listed in the Bill of Rights. These first ten amendments to the Constitution were the price liberal critics wisely exacted of the Founding Fathers for the document's adoption. Related guarantees are found in other provisions and in judicial, congressional, and presidential interpretations of the document.

EVERYBODY'S TALKING AT ME

Occasionally some zealot or egocentric will argue that neither society nor government has a moral or legal right to control his or anyone else's mode of expression. This assumption is both as visionary as the unicorn as well as being dangerous nonsense for this imperfect world. It pretends that the bud of unchecked free expression can never blossom into ugly weeds in the form of the methodical exploitation of oneself or of one's neighbors. It forgets that the heckler who is booing down the speaker deprives others of their rights, or that democracy can thrive only in an atmosphere of civility.

Anyone in authority comes to recognize that while the individual and society can benefit from free expression, he or she as well as other people can also get hurt by it. Limits on individual freedom in a democratic society are supposed to reduce this probability to reasonable risk levels. This is the kind of morality every public official who has to worry about votes applies.

Civic morality differs from copybook maxims that stress only good intentions. Free expression of opinions or acts, like all behavior, cannot be judged only by the proclaimed purity of the expresser's motives ("I'm really a good guy"). It also has to be weighed by the outcomes for everybody concerned. One begins by looking at the possible harm or benefits to others, either immediately or in the form of less direct but still present risks or costs.

Furthermore, we must also look at the possible harm to the expresser himself. Even that defender of liberty John Stuart Mill would have questioned the want ads in the *Berkeley Barb* since he doubted that an individual should be free to sell him or herself into slavery just because he or she could argue no one else was really harmed. Modern students, such as James Q. Wilson, ponder an equivalent problem: Should anyone be permitted to stay hooked on drugs even if he wants to, since society by standing by is in effect encouraging a form of human degradation?

For this reason, civic morality plays down motives and arguments about how sincere people are, and tries to figure out the effects of their actions. Snake handlers who claim they are leading all of us to new religious insights are restrained; publishers, who in print assassinate the characters of those they have concluded are too evil to exist unmolested, may find themselves slapped with a libel action; and those political spellbinders whose gospel is so seductive as to turn a crowd into a mob may discover themselves stopping the swing of a police stick with some tender part of their anatomy. The Bill of Rights is not a license to do anything that one pleases either to oneself or to others, nor does it excuse an individual from the consequences of his actions. Justice Oliver Wendell Holmes put it well in two of his famous decisions: "Freedom of speech does not extend to the right to shout 'Fire!' in a theater when there is no fire"; and (to a policeman who had been dismissed for making political speeches), "The Constitution gives you the right of freedom of speech, but it does not give you the right to a job with the Commonwealth of Massachusetts."

The strings attached to individuals are not only those of government. If they were, it is doubtful that life would be possessed of any sense of civility. Freedom, to work at all, also requires the individual to exercise some restraint on himself. If everyone pushed his inclinations to the limit of his legal rights all the time, society would take on the look of a continuous football scrimmage. The folkways and mores of society are also restraints enforced by social sanctions. These are customs, including etiquette and good manners, which are supposed to prevent exploitation of self or others, as in the delicate prohibitions against getting ugly drunk in public. Organized private groups also limit freedom of expression, as when the Missouri Synod of the Lutheran Church puts accused heretics on trial and perhaps excommunicates them, or the Democratic party refuses to seat the Illinois delegation of Mayor Richard Daley, as occurred at the National Convention of 1972.

These controls mesh. The minor social controls make a society of civility possible. But the controls which carry legal penalties are usually the most important since they set the limits for what private individuals or groups may do. The not unreasonable reaction of Mayor Daley to the Democratic party action of 1972 was to take his case into court and it would not be unusual for a convicted heretic to do the same. Freedoms in the matters people consider important are ultimately determined by the judges.

INNOCENT AND NOT-SO-INNOCENT BYSTANDERS

Early in 1972, a former student of government and a one-time governmental official, Daniel Ellsberg, released to American newspapers some secret United States government papers about the Vietnam war. His action was right out of the cloak-and-dagger spy stories. After a little fidgeting, American newspapers, led by the *New York Times,* began to print probably more than most of their readers could easily digest, and in a short while, the whole collection of secret papers was published commercially as *The Pentagon Papers.*

Ellsberg's defense was the traditional one about the citizen's right to know in order to form reasoned opinions. A number of civil liberties groups and individuals including the American Civil Liberties Union came to his defense. The ACLU in its court brief would only grant that "the government 'could conceivably' prevent publication of secret codes, designs of new military equipment, and plans for military operations—but not if their publication would be 'of value in permitting citizens to render an informed judgment on public issues.' "[1] The government's response was a traditional one—the release of secret documents by an individual acting on his own violated the law and endangered the national security.

While Ellsberg went to trial, the rest of the nation settled back waiting for the dust to clear. The *New York Times* had operated at about the same level of morality as does the receiver of hot overcoats or stolen TV sets. On the other hand, after a little closer examination of what were supposed to be military secrets, most citizens concluded that the nation's defense structure had not been irrevocably shattered. The government's action in starting procedures to further declassify documents confirmed what many had assumed ever since they saw their first Saturday afternoon movie serial—governments keep a great many things secret that are about as startling and significant as the fact that the sun is gradually cooling or that President Grover Cleveland in his virile young manhood fathered an illegitimate child.

Do as I Say, Not . . .   In October of the same year another civil liberties event occurred. The ACLU went to court again, this time to challenge a provision of the newly adopted Federal Elections Campaign Act which required political parties and all "issue-oriented" organizations to disclose the names of contributors of $100 or more. This time it was Congress proclaiming "the citizen's right to know in order to form reasoned opinions." But this time the ACLU argued such disclosures would endanger its own security.

One can, of course, reject the assumption that the security of the ACLU is more important than the security of the United States and nevertheless see logic in the ACLU position. The ACLU argued that the disclosure of financial contributions of over $100 "when imposed on controversial organizations like the ACLU, will deter persons from joining and contributing." One must choose between citizens suffering the costs of living in abysmal ignorance or of some discomfort falling upon the ACLU and all other such controversial organizations from the John Birch Society to Women's Lib, Gay Lib, or the Trotskyites.

Whose Costs? Whose Benefits? This question is the old familiar one of opportunity costs. Making a choice of one value over another, putting the preferences of one group ahead of another, choosing one type of freedom over another, is as much the essence of this civil liberties case as is deciding whether to fire a couple of salvos at the Viet Cong from battleships in the South China Sea, or to spend the same money underwriting the interesting activities of the P. Blackstone Rangers. One man's civil right may be another's civil wrong and choice is a weighing of such social costs and benefits.

A second aspect of this problem is that the costs and benefits are not limited only to the two adversaries directly involved. Negative externalities may exist for everyone in the neighborhood of a civil liberties conflict just as they do when a factory puffs out sulphur smoke into the air that everyone in the neighborhood breathes. A typical case is the familiar newspaper story, the innocent bystander. The latter is found on a corner waiting for a bus when a figure darts by, and along comes a policeman, who is dutifully chasing a mugger and purse snatcher. The wrongdoer gets collared, but the innocent bystander gets clobbered in the fracas. Here the fallout is dramatic. In other cases, it can be a good deal more subtle in its impact. The Supreme Court has found externalities in such curious places as those parlors in which attractive women are advertised as giving massage treatments to men, the public schools, and on a crowded street in a New Hampshire town on a Saturday afternoon. To protect innocent bystanders, it ruled local governments could prohibit massage parlors, teachers could not read a nondenominational prayer to kick off each morning, nor could Jehovah Witnesses parade up and down that crowded street in New Hampshire without a permit.

These problems of negative externalities are getting worse. Innocent bystanders are much more common in big cities than on the open prairies. More people get sucked into any event as society gets more organized and individual actions get more tangled together. Down on the farm you can feel free to light smudge pots or practice yodeling without it being very much anyone else's business. But when suburbanites and exurbanites begin to renovate old barns into residences, externalities start to appear. The newcomers complain about the noise at 5:30 A.M. when the farmers are revving up the tractor to get an early start out in the fields and the newcomers do not like the smells or the junked cars and miscellaneous rusted farm machinery out next to the shed (it is useful for spare parts). The farmers in turn are not too happy about the way school taxes begin to skyrocket, nor do they always see the full value of inviting in progressive educators to address the PTA. The thicker the crowds, the greater the externalities.

Externalities are also likely to be more grating on people's sensibilities when a mixture of life-styles inhabits the same area. Permanent residents typically are not happy with the way summer cottage owners carry on, teenagers turn up the stereo decibels too high for their parents or for the neighbors, and the man who fails to cut his grass or weed out the dandelions in Rolling Meadow Estates is in for some deep-freeze treatment from other residents in that otherwise friendly community.

To summarize, freedom of expression is a necessity for government based on informed opinion. But such behavior needs to be judged by effects, not by the actor's good intentions. When the government permits the exercise of freedom of expression by one citizen, it may result in social benefits, but it may also result in opportunity costs for someone else who is directly involved and not able to do what he wants to do. It may also result in harder-to-trace externality costs or benefits for many others. The impact is more extensive as people herd together into metropolitan areas; it is more likely to be perceived negatively as different life-styles rub shoulders with each other.

HOW FREE IS FREEDOM?

The problem involved in weighing costs and benefits of any action is that consequences cannot always be figured out with absolute certainty. Choice is on the basis of assumptions, and these assumptions often flow from the job responsibilities of particular groupings within society.

The police have the job of preventing or apprehending those who seem to them to have committed what the law defines as a prohibited act. They are human enough to expect that those who they are sure in their own minds are guilty should pay the social costs of their behavior by serving a little time. They are also human enough to be tempted by a few shortcuts that lead to convictions. These can be accomplished by using such handy new technical inventions as sophisticated wiretaps, or by turning to the more old-fashioned illegal search, or the third degree. Either one can frequently turn up clear evidence that connects a person with a crime. Courts, more concerned with preserving an area of citizen privacy not at the mercy of the police, have in recent years tended to cut down drastically on police use of such shortcuts by refusing to admit evidence collected by such means.

Professional civil libertarians, such as the ACLU, on the other hand, hire themselves out as the self-appointed guardians of freedom. They are apt to see control of individualism, in any form they approve of, as repression that will blow our society apart. The externalities, such as those that occur when more ordinary citizens get mugged or intimidated because known criminals are freed on procedural grounds, they tend to see as costs, which society's citizens should be glad to pay, or are regarded as trivial.

The picture is even more complicated than this. In former days the ACLU concerned itself with the administration and validity of police procedures in respect to all citizens. More recently a number of critics—and we certainly agree with their criticism—have seen the ACLU as being more concerned with protecting radicals per se than in preserving civil liberties for all kinds of people. One can point to the sorry record of the ACLU in largely overlooking the invasions of the civil liberties of others such as occurred on campuses in 1970–1971 when college administrators were intimidated, shouted down, or physically attacked by students, or in the occasional black intimidation of whites that has also occurred in the stress of radical conflicts. (The ACLU prides itself on having defended right-wingers in the past, but in recent decades it has seldom defended a reactionary or attacked a left-wing demagogue.) The ACLU seems to have accepted the implausible assumption, left over from World War II days, that only the right and center and never the left can endanger the civil liberties of others. This is despite the evidence of their senses, or of present experience in those Communist nations of the world today, such as Poland and Czechoslovakia, where civil liberties like the last embers of a fire are being drowned out.

This putting on of blinders has been accelerated since the

ACLU as an organization recently began to express policy preferences of its own. Like any other pressure group, it now also is committed to some policy ends over others, rather than playing the role of an umpire among contestants, to make sure that just rules are followed. To accept the ACLU view over that of the police today, is rather like substituting a hanging jury recruited out of the local Unitarian church for a crowd of Mississippi redneck Baptists. It does not seem a particularly desirable way of preserving civil liberties for the rest of us.

HERE COME THE JUDGE

A major question facing a government in the civil liberties area is how much it will intervene in the marketplace of competition among opinions. The governmental stance may vary from an absolute free market, one with a belief in the hidden hand of God making everything come out right, through a mixed system, to a controlled society. Which choice is made depends on whether one assumes the major need in society is for stability and peace, or for more opportunity for spontaneity and creativity, or for a compromise between the two goals.

How Much Latitude?   When authors set up choices on a continuum such as this, the reader can generally expect them, like the carnival pitchman, to be selling hard the middle choice, no matter how wild or improbable it may be. This, you are warned, will be the case as you read on, with but one caveat: Only a few knaves or fools do not at one time or another argue for the appropriateness of the assumptions at one end or the other of the continuum, depending upon the circumstances and the degree of knowledge about the probability of impact of the externalities involved. But a position in the middle, in which the scales of justice have a tilt in favor of taking some risks for freedom, is the most suitable one for a democracy. Let us review each of these assumptions in more detail.

The people, convinced of the need for stability and peace, become very sensitive to the known evils of opportunity costs and externalities, that is, the trouble that free spirits cause others including innocent bystanders. They, like old-fashioned prudes, insist that the individual who wants to do his thing should pay all the costs. They frustrate him by rigid regulations and controls over his freedom to act if they see any risk of anyone getting hurt, and punish him later if he goes ahead anyhow. Such a view wants an end to what is called "mollycoddling criminals and eccentrics."

This is the policy of Castro. Once he was established in power in Cuba, he behaved in accordance with a familiar puritan tradition, acting a good deal like a "support your local police" John Bircher. Homosexuals, drug addicts, malcontents, and other social deviants including American hijackers found themselves in a four by four by four box in a jail or mental institution. It helps, in holding this assumption, to have firm convictions about the depravity of those who disagree with you.

While totalitarian systems, whether communist, fascist, or just old-fashioned, self-serving despotism, generally adopt this kind of governmental action, all societies take this position about some acts. All forcibly restrain a citizen who goes around peering down the sights of a rifle while playfully aiming it in the direction of other citizens. Even before the trigger is actually pressed and intentions are clear, most citizens favor repression of such behavior and many take the same view concerning the freedom to seriously advocate or plan butchery of fellow citizens.

At the other end of the assumption continuum are those who view the civil liberties of the individual as sacred because society so badly needs innovation and experimentation. In the tradition of the Bohemian artist or the nineteenth-century capitalist entrepreneur, they are apt to view the rights of any innocent bystanders who get in the way as irrelevant, either because they will not notice the impact if the negative externality is too trivial, or because the philistines involved are not important enough to bother with. They believe the result of such a system is a natural harmony. If this assumption is carried through logically, those holding this view believe that an anarchistic or libertarian society, with few or no controls, will best suit everyone's needs. It helps in holding this opinion to have a sanguine view about human nature and other people's motivations.

The libertarian view may be degraded by delusion and rationalization. One may conclude that only a few really deserve to act freely while the rest should welcome bearing the costs and waiting for their reward in the world hopefully to come. The system is justified by survival of the fittest and is accepted by all believers in their own superior virtue. Generally such führers have not found it too difficult to persuade themselves of their own worthiness.

The Guilt-ridden Dilettante A fashionable and faddish latter-day variation was found in what the writer Tom Wolfe called "radical chic."[2] It assumed that members of any group that in the past has suffered injustice may now exercise their rights of self-expression without check and everyone else should accept whatever consequences occur with good-humored resignation. A defense-fund raising cocktail party given on behalf of the Black Panthers for a selected group of white liberals by the symphony conductor Leonard Bernstein provides Wolfe's main example of this aberration. The first crisis these guilt-ridden humanitarians had to cope with was the maid problem. At most Park Avenue penthouse parties before this, maids had been black hirelings, wearing neat little uniforms with white headbands. The Bernsteins rose to the occasion by recruiting Puerto Ricans so their black militants would not be embarrassed by seeing soul sisters behaving in submissive roles. The party consisted of a rather unsatisfactory interaction between white guests, all part of the nation's most respected cultural establishment, and some rather crude and unfeeling self-proclaimed black revolutionaries who, at any rate, acted as free individuals deserving of respect.

What led the whites through this kind of orgy of self-hatred? They judged their actions by motivation rather than result. Like the Indian fakir who lies on a bed of nails, they reasoned that display of excessive guilt is a mark of virtue since their motivations could only be simon pure. This view required that because blacks have been and still are discriminated against by whites in our society, blacks deserved to be treated henceforth as if they could do no wrong. The ends pursued by the pure of heart would justify any consequences that resulted. Externalities suffered by any white or other black bystander, none of whom could be regarded as innocent, were largely irrelevant.

Most citizens cannot afford to be so high-minded as can the upper-middle class, for they cannot as easily avoid the consequences of negative externalities caused by revolutionaries. They judge behavior by probable results, not by the loftiness of motivations. Nevertheless, in some matters they also conclude absolute freedom is necessary. Even Nazi Germany and the Soviet Union could not march everyone in their lockstep. Some scientists, generals of the army, or even artists such as Solzhenitsyn, demanded and, with reluctance, were granted some freedom of action.

The Middling Approach The "clear and present danger" compromise tries to take the costs and benefits into account and through governmental policy strike a balance which tilts toward freedom. It substitutes a situational ethics for an absolute standard. Some degree of externalities, it assumes, must be borne by members of a free society as the admission price. At the same time, it holds that the behavior by one individual that presents costs to others may under certain circumstances be controlled by the government and even prohibited and this too is part of the admission price to a civilized society. But to control behavior, the probability for harm must be high and must be now; not some time in the indefinite future.

The doctrine is far from a sure guide. The definition of danger remains ambiguous because people differ about the significance of probable costs and risks. Justice Oliver Wendell Holmes, revered by civil libertarians, first enunciated the doctrine in the Schenk case in the 1920s, when he was arguing that speaking and writing against the draft during World War I and encouraging young men to avoid the draft presented just such a clear-and-present danger to the nation and could be stopped. He might well have clapped in jail all those who in the 1960s manned draft advisory centers, set up coffee houses around army bases, and circulated underground newspapers to servicemen. To adopt the clear-and-present danger position thus also means one accepts the probability of an endless and sometimes bitter debate.

In former years, most of the civil liberties cases that arose were the outcome of government suppression of freedom. In 1798, in the Alien and Sedition Acts, the right to make speeches or publish reports critical of the government was prohibited. As late as the 1920s and 1930s, such basic freedoms as prohibition of prior censorship of newspapers and the use of third-degree methods, or the right to wave a red flag, had to be protected by the Supreme Court against action by state governments. But the climate of opinion has changed.

Government continues to intervene through the courts, legislative and executive acts, but its recent intervention has been to expand the free market of opinion rather than contract it. Only at two points in recent years has government for a limited period intervened to seriously contract freedom: in the Nazi-like Japanese internment program of World War II and the Communist witch hunts of the early 1950s.

The Supreme Court handles most governmental intervention and does not have an easy job in mediating among private
individuals and groups. The balances of costs and risks it has
recently reached in a few illustrative areas will be examined next.
Each of these areas involves a conflict between groups that either
by choice or involuntarily live different kinds of lives that come
into conflict with each other generally in highly urbanized areas.
They are the civil liberties conflicts that result between criminals
and the rest of society, white and black, swinger and straight. We
depend heavily in the sections that follow on recent newspaper
clippings.

CRIME PAYS MUCH BETTER THESE DAYS

Right-wing reactionaries have long argued that our society is too
permissive, especially in respect to criminals. They feel the
freedoms of law breakers are overprotected at heavy costs to the
rest of society. One need not look very hard at recent crime
statistics to conclude that the present-day protective system is
like the dike about a half hour after Hans took out his finger and
went home. Today, some poor American victim is murdered
every thirty-three minutes, instead of about once an hour as in the
idyllic days of just twelve years ago. Other crimes show similar
upturns. A 1973 Gallup poll indicated that one person in three in
the core cities of metropolitan areas had been the victim of
mugging, robbery, or theft within the last year. Even in the
suburbs, the figure was one in five. Some 28 percent of the
persons in the sample had been victims two or more times.

The obvious reason for this upsurge is that it is becoming
more and more apparent that crime, while always a profitable
business, now has a high probability of success, since the risks
involved are considerably lower than they once were. In Chicago
in 1968, if you committed a burglary, the odds were 23 to 1 that
you would not go to jail. These are much better, the economist
Anthony Downs has noted with some chagrin, than the odds for
success if you opened a new small business.

The Courts Overwhelmed   What then reduces the risks of
crime as a professional career choice for a young man willing to
work at it and serious about rising in life? One cause is that the
courts are unable to handle the number of cases the police bring

them and look for shortcuts to clear the docket. Most often prosecutors and judges resort to "plea bargaining," that is, lowering the charge to a lesser crime if the suspect pleads guilty. In New York City in 1970, out of 94,000 persons arrested for felonies by police, only 552 came to trial. The others were disposed of by either having the case dismissed outright or having the charge reduced, if the accused pleaded guilty.

Commenting on the externalities involved in this introduction of the free-market system into judicial decision making, former New York Police Commissioner Patrick V. Murphy said, "No doubt certain honest dedicated policemen who made these 94,000 arrests came to the belief that conscientious police work is a waste of time, a waste of effort, a waste of devotion." He then noted the effect in one specific area of crime.

> We did a study of every fourth arrest on gun charges. This amounted to 156 cases, of which 136 were felony arrests for criminal possession of hand guns. Not one of these 136 criminals was convicted on the original felony charge.
>
> Now is it a serious felony to carry an illegal hand gun or is it not a serious felony according to the law? If it is a serious felony, how do we justify a record like this?
>
> If they had been convicted on the original charges and sentenced to maximum terms, they could have gone to jail over 952 years (seven years per man). In other words, the law would have permitted 952 years of jail but the court system, in its wisdom, meted out five years and four months, an average of a little over one month per man.
>
> No wonder so many people of criminal intent carry hand guns in New York City. They know the penalty for carrying a gun is a joke.[3]

The Courts Overboard The risk is also reduced because the Supreme Court has put much of its recent effort in a much-needed tightening up of police procedures so that the protectors of law and order are considerably less free to throw their weight around. The police, like the rest of us, have difficulty adjusting to new rules. But this is only part of the problem. Some critics, including justices appointed to the Supreme Court by President Nixon, have argued judges have also gone too far in permitting the release of known criminals for what are sometimes described as technicalities. At the same time, it is argued, the

Court, out of sympathy for born losers, is openly trying to undermine the thin blue line of society's protectors by not supporting reasonable police action. Such commentators regard as characteristic the decision of March 23, 1972, in which the United States Supreme Court declared a Georgia curse-and-abuse statute unconstitutional on its face.

Justice Harry Blackmun, in his dissent, argued:

> It seems strange indeed that in this day a man may say to a police officer, who is attempting to restore access to a public building, "White son of a bitch, I'll kill you" and "You son of a bitch, I'll choke you to death," and say to an accompanying officer, "You son of a bitch, if you ever put your hands on me again, I'll cut you all to pieces," and yet constitutionally cannot be prosecuted and convicted under a state statute which makes it a misdemeanor to "use to or of another, and in his presence, opprobrious words or abusive language tending to cause a breach of the peace. . . . "
> This, however, is precisely what the court pronounces as the law today.

A Grab Bag of Sentences The risk of a life of crime has also been lessened because an aura of uncertainty exists among the judges themselves as to what should be called a crime. One might reasonably describe the situation as a crisis of basic assumptions. A basic symptom of this state is the widely divergent sentences handed out by different judges or by different levels and type of court. Equality of treatment for the same acts is as much a problem in the courts as it is to professors attempting to grade fairly the assorted student responses that turn up on essay examinations. But it becomes a really serious problem when widely differing standards of evaluation are being applied —and that seems to be the case in the courts today.

A 1972 study of the Detroit Recorder's Court by the Detroit Bar Association showed the difference in average sentences among fourteen judges for the felony of armed robbery with intent to rob varied from 3.3 years to 8.9 years. The maximum penalty for such an offense is life imprisonment. The two most lenient of the fourteen judges, a fact that appears related, disposed of 358 and 428 cases each, while the less lenient disposed of 123 and 214 cases each. A prominent Brooklyn judge, Irwin R. Brownstein of the New York Supreme Court (a trial court, not the state's highest court), who at about the same time testified before a New York state legislative committee, asked for a law that set mandatory minimum sentences for some criminal acts, thus removing from judges a large measure of discretion that he felt they were abusing.

That the problem of rising criminality is not found in the United States alone is evidenced by a 1972 report of Great Britain's fourteen-year-old parliamentary Criminal Law Revision Committee, which recommended drastic changes in British criminal procedure because "in recent years, the balance of advantage under the present law has swung too far in favor of the defense . . . the law of evidence should now be less tender toward criminals generally." Among the changes suggested were that wives could testify against their husbands, the protection against self-incrimination and hearsay evidence be relaxed, fourteen-year-old witnesses should be treated as adults, and other similar suggestions.[4]

If respect for the law and the courts had declined among criminals, the same may be said about many ordinary citizens. Perhaps as concise and to-the-point statement on the turmoil of the judicial system in the United States was that of an outraged citizen writing his local newspaper during the period of George Wallace's "Send them a message campaign." Note that he did not even bother to indicate the case that stirred his wrath:

To the Editor:

Our judges should wear clown suits.

[Name withheld][5]

WILL THE REAL CRIMINAL PLEASE STAND UP?

The "hard-hat's" assumption about crime has been that the convicted criminal should pay the major share of the costs for his antisocial behavior since he is morally responsible. Those holding this view want custodial facilities that will take the convicted criminal out of circulation so that he stops creating externalities for innocent bystanders. This attitude has often been coupled with a lack of concern over the conditions that have characterized many American jails. A second implication flowing from this assumption has been that punitive action serves a social purpose. The certainty of some inconvenience or even some punishment may help reform the criminal; the death penalty may restrain other potential criminals, as well as giving the needed assurance to the law-abiding that going along with the system pays off, or at a minimum, does not penalize you.

What Chance for the Criminal? This assumption treats the convicted criminal as an outcast, puts little hope in reform of people seen as not deserving of anything more than a good swift kick in the teeth. The prisoner, under such treatment, not unnaturally lives up to expectations. When contemplating his release from prison, he resolves to do a more workmanlike job so he will not be caught again. His fellow inmates during the long evenings in the cell block can often supply him with training in the necessary skills that he appears to need so badly.

A do-gooder or prodigal-son assumption is that held by those who like to think of themselves as progressive-minded. They conclude that the costs involved in rehabilitating those committing antisocial acts are worth it and should be largely paid by society itself, since it is the unhealthy social environment that manufactured the criminal and he is not really to blame. There are three implications flowing from this assumption. The first obviously is that social policy should be aimed at the deviant 5 percent rather than for the conforming 95 percent. The second is that since environment encouraged antisocial behavior, a new supportive environment can create socially acceptable behavior. Incarceration thus is only a way of isolating the client in order to achieve rehabilitation. The third implication is that some of what society defines as crime is mistaken zeal and should perhaps not be so defined since a crime must have a direct victim.

The proponents of this assumption are plagued by newspaper publicity that plays on their failures, since innocent bystanders frequently pay the costs of their experimentation. For example:

JACKSON, MICHIGAN (AP) (October 18, 1972): A 24-year-old inmate of Southern Michigan prison allegedly committed murder while home on leave but acting Warden Charles Egeler still defends the prison's furlough policy.

Columbus Thompson, Jr., serving time for assault with intent to commit murder, was indicted Wednesday by a Detroit federal grand jury for the October 4 holdup slaying of Daniel Czarnecki in the Inkster Post Office.

"I hate to see something like this happening," Egeler said today. "This definitely has been a successful program."

. . . Egeler said 2500 men have been granted 48-hour passes since the program was started and "This is the first serious thing that has occurred." . . .

In Warden Egeler's eyes, the potential good gained by a procedure that has contributed to the rehabilitation of 2,500 men is worth continuing the program. To him 2,500 to 1 are reasonable odds, though these are not likely the real odds.

Who Is a Criminal? The attempt to redefine what is criminal by eliminating allegedly victimless crimes, would remove from dockets such currently defined criminal acts as adultery, performing abortions, homosexuality, prostitution, alcoholism, the smoking of marijuana, or hard-drug addiction. While these may be viewed as crimes without victims, they are not acts in which externalities are absent, and they are acts in some cases in which the person involved may be degraded. The families of such free spirits undoubtedly suffer most frequently, but even the driver of a Volkswagen sharing the same highway or the parents of small children in the neighborhood may feel the impact. Two lines of argument are presented regarding such behavior. One is that these acts should be redefined as illness rather than crime, and their perpetrators should be treated psychologically or medically if they agree to such treatment. A second argument is that until a child is molested or a Volkswagen reduced to scrap, such persons should be treated neither as being ill nor as criminals. Both arguments leave unsolved the problem of determining potential risks to those who may become innocent bystanders of such so-called victimless behavior when and if it does turn clearly antisocial.

Recent court rulings suggest that in criminal cases, the pendulum is swinging back to considering more carefully the civil rights and liberties of that forgotten man, the innocent bystander. More citizens than it was once supposed seem unwilling to pay the full costs of rehabilitating high-risk offenders or to put up with many of the externalities they now read about or see fellow citizens suffering from. They are looking for ways to reduce such risks and one assumption is at hand that seems consistent with what we know about crime and criminals: Certain types of criminals cannot be rehabilitated easily. Ergo: These should be handled differently from others.

Today's crowded court dockets are largely the result of drug-related crimes. (About one-third of all arrests, counting the serious and the trivial charges, are for being drunk in a public place. Some alcoholics have been arrested hundreds of times, at great expense to the taxpayer, but with no effect upon the behavior of the person arrested.) Such criminals cannot easily be rehabilitated using present psychiatric techniques or medical treatment and certainly will not be brought back into useful social life by a confiding slap on the back or the opportunity to write for the prison newspaper. Such addicts are similar to the criminally insane, who are currently incarcerated as much to protect themselves as to protect innocent bystanders. We could in the same way incarcerate drug addicts and pushers at the expense of markedly expanding our prisons. An alternative is that of giving addicts a full share of the drugs they desire, thus making a life of crime unnecessary and at the same time encouraging them to kill themselves more quickly than would otherwise be the case. This is what some see as the "humane" British solution, where the death rate among addicts supplied with drugs by the government is twenty-eight times greater than that of the average citizen. Alternatively, though less effectively, the government might set up clinics which through the use of substitute drugs attempt to wean the addict from a life of crime as well as from hard drugs. These have to date a success rate about equal to the probability of winning a free trip to the Caribbean in the next *Reader's Digest* sweepstakes.

Whichever route is chosen is presumably preferable in the eyes of many citizens to giving such criminals full civil rights and treating them as we would the nonaddicted criminal, that is, as if they were capable of responding to the rehabilitative stimuli found in the usual prison and parole procedures.

The Career Crook A second and related reason for crowded dockets is that antisocial behavior for some becomes a career choice or for psychological reasons an impulse whose gratification they cannot deny. It is questionable that such criminals as mobsters, the criminally insane, repeat rapists, con artists, or habitual muggers and robbers respond to the usual rehabilitation techniques. Indeed, prison life works against rehabilitation and psychological counseling has been of little help. Criminals who are rehabilitated have done so as a do-it-yourself project. Possibly we could learn about rehabilitation from

France, which has the lowest rate of recidivism in the world. It also has the harshest prison conditions and no psychological counseling whatever. Judge Brownstein, mentioned earlier as desiring minimum mandatory sentences, noted that of 326 cases then on his calendar, all but 12 (96.4 percent) involved multiple offenders. He argued that if recidivists were imprisoned for lengthy terms, "the crime rate would drop so sharply as to stagger the imagination."

Chuck Stone, a black political commentator, well aware that a rape charge still is a favorite technique used to railroad "uppity" blacks into long prison terms, reflects the view of crime that is becoming increasingly common:

> A 17 year-old youth was charged with the attempted rape of a 19 year-old girl. Although he had confessed to four previous rapes in 1971, he had been wallowing in freedom because of two technicalities in the law. One technicality involved the failure of two victims to appear because they had moved out of town. The other was based on a statute requiring state police to take a juvenile into juvenile court immediately on his arrest and prior to questioning. . . .
>
> There is absolutely nothing in my allegiance to our present system of laws that persuades me of the constitutional right of a four-time confessed rapist to walk around free. . . . [6]

If we may hazard a prediction, it is that the constitutional rights of victims as well as of innocent bystanders to common criminal acts will receive more attention in the future by the courts. Only a society that feels relatively secure can take the risks involved in trying to rehabilitate criminals. One that continually sees innocent victims exploited by criminals whose arrogance for the law is apparent, is likely to veer to harshness. Leniency for hardened criminals becomes cruelty to those who are trying to live decent lives and also to those who have committed a crime and now deserve a chance at rehabilitation.

OUR MISERABLE FAILURE

No one in America has had less freedom to act as he or she pleases than a black (except for Oriental-Americans until recent years, people who were once not even allowed to own land in California). Freedom of expression for all of us in an urban society has meant the setting of more irksome limits and boundaries and some frustration for all, but this has been doubled and redoubled for blacks.

One assumption degrades their existence and it dies hard: that we should discriminate *between* blacks and whites rather than *among* blacks as we do *among* whites. The assumption was weakening to the point that in the early 1960s the middle masses seemed about to catch up with the *Plessy v. Ferguson* decision of 1896, that is, they seemed almost willing to grant separate but at least equal treatment. This was the period when one showed one's progressiveness by attending a Harlem Globetrotters game and cheering Meadowlark Lemon, since progressivism meant encouraging what one thought was the black entrepreneurs. The great urban riots of the late 1960s changed all that.

For the educated white elites, the riots indicated that the time for granting blacks the high privilege of sitting at the same dime store lunch counter had arrived. And this movement was expanded to other equally significant areas. The advertising media took over selling the black with all the clumsy skill and subtlety that they had applied to other public service campaigns. Everyone from characters in TV spy stories to Archie Bunker endorsed the product and no brassiere ad was complete without at least one black girl striking a ballet pose. (It should be noted, however, that part of the new advertising appeals to blacks reflects the increased purchasing power of the expanding black middle classes.)

With all its occasional vulgarity and its patronizing airs, this effort is still to be applauded since it has produced some desirable results. It is especially to be cheered in a world where the overwhelming number of nations, white or black, royalist or republic, communist, fascist, or democratic, indulge themselves in some form of ethnic discrimination as accepted national policy. (The Japanese discriminate against the Ainu, the Russians against several Asiatic ethnic groups, the Swedes—always eager to denounce "racism" in America—against the Lapps, to name only a few cases.) But like the campaign to give up smoking cigarettes, to wear seat belts, or to put your extra money in Savings Bonds, it leaves a lingering notion with many customers out front that something must be odd about the product if it has to be pushed that hard.

A good many people appear to have concluded that was indeed the case. The riots and their aftermath seem to have led the white middle masses to what the ad men, who sum such things up so well, would probably characterize as product resistance. The riots resulted in a dropping of restraints within segregated black communities so that what was called a "ghetto" became more like a zoo without keepers, that is, a jungle. The old Southern police technique of allowing a black to commit any crime he felt inclined to, so long as it was against one of his black brothers or sisters, was made police policy in many Northern cities as well. Anyone else who strayed into these black areas after dark was also fair game, including the police themselves.

When such behavior was extended further into the white community under the banner of "black power" and "black separatism," it looked to the white majority a good deal like what old-fashioned liberals meant when they talked about racial prejudice, only with a reverse twist. It seemed that the underlying assumption of this new race relations was that freedom of expression would be extended to anyone strong enough to grab it out of the hands of their neighbors. The worst fears and prejudices of the thrifty white burgher were confirmed: "The blacks don't know how to be middle-class." When judges turned to the big yellow school bus as a solution to racial problems and proposed to bus the white cheerleaders and their male siblings daily from suburbia into the inner city schools, the response was predictable. The overall result was a tragic stalemate.

One enterprising social scientist turned to a polling of what he claimed were America's seventy top intellectuals. These delphic oracles, he reported, had reached a similarly dismal conclusion about the present state of affairs. While they were filled with many suggestions about the problems of youth and capitalism, they "most frankly admit they do not know how to solve America's race problems."[7] Some may regard this as an encouraging sign, that we have turned a corner. At any rate it suggests that a look at consequences has replaced the sentimental indulgence that accompanied high-minded actions—actions that produced only adverse consequences for black and white alike.

Hope Still Springs   Three responses seem promising. They are based on the assumption that discrimination should be *among* blacks and *among* whites rather than *between* blacks and whites. One response is to treat black criminals with as much lack of prejudice as we do white; that is, apprehend and prosecute them to the limit of the law even if their crimes are against other blacks, and even if we feel tortured with the sweet satisfaction of knowing society in the turn-of-the-century rural South or the big city Northern slums made them what they are today. Criminals, whatever made them, are now a luxury neither blacks nor even guilt-ridden whites can any longer afford if the 90 to 95 percent of blacks are to gain the freedom they deserve.

A second response is to continue to tear down the walls that keep blacks from a middle-class way of life. The most important are those that buttress racial exploitation in housing and jobs. This means paradoxically insisting that blacks be treated with the same tenderness and toughness that personnel men and mortgage lenders apply to whites. Initially this means continued lower payoffs for many blacks who are only beginning to achieve the education and skills needed. But this is no excuse for holding back the many who are ready to live in the middle class.

A third response is among scholars, some of whom are beginning to wonder if we should not reexamine the assumptions upon which we seek to develop public policy relative to race relations. Some scholars, most notably perhaps Edward C. Banfield,[8] have questioned the common notion that "racism" is the root cause of the problem. He points out that all the difficulties blacks have could also be seen as stemming from lower-class status. The problem is cultural, one of attitudes much more than race, granted that skin color makes the anti-lower-class discrimination all the easier.

The Banfield thesis is that the problem is one of a disproportionate number of blacks being committed to a "culture of poverty." They "think poor" and so remain poor, a subcultural attitude that is not limited to blacks, however. The poor of whatever color, according to this approach, live for today; they are present-oriented rather than future-oriented, as are the middle masses, and they are discriminated against because of their life-style.

One reason to believe that Banfield may be right is to look at the destinies of Chinese-Americans and Japanese-Americans. Both groups suffered violent discrimination, equal to and in some cases more harsh than that accorded blacks; both came to this country as poor as slaves, and both were "color coded." But the subculture of Oriental-Americans has always emphasized future orientation and especially, from Confucius, discipline, respect for those in authority, and the importance of education. Only a generation ago during World War II, 100,000 Japanese-Americans were thrown into concentration camps—for being of Japanese descent. Today Oriental-Americans probably encounter less prejudice than do Jews—and they are overwhelmingly middle-class.

If this new thesis is approximately correct, the desirable public policy in order to overcome the problems of race relations becomes clear: Policy should include anything that will encourage the rapid movement of large numbers of upwardly mobile blacks into the middle classes.

MY GRANDCHILD IS A UNIVERSITY FRESHPERSON

The following is from a daily newspaper question-and-answer column conducted by the Right Reverend Richard S. Emrich, Episcopal Bishop of Michigan:

> QUESTION: My granddaughter is a university freshman. Her roommate has a boy friend who sleeps in the same room with her. Why is this allowed? All the money paid for dorms, and for what? My granddaughter told her roommate, "He moves out, or I do," and was told "You might as well go." E.K.
>
> Dear E.K.: We live in a strange day that has little respect for traditional wisdom, that believes moral codes are simply subjective and man-made preferences and which is condemning itself to live through all of the pain and disorder that comes from breaking the moral law. In the name of "freedom" the obvious rights of your granddaughter to her room and privacy are treated with selfish contempt. It isn't just the sexual conduct of the roommate and her boy friend which is wrong, it is their arrogance which is also offensive.[9]

The conflict between the swinger and the straight becomes a conflict of life-styles similar to radical and criminal divisions. Each side, well aware of the externalities, feels put upon by the other. The libertine and even the moderate drinker shudders at prohibition and the Sunday blue laws of a former day. But equally common is the deep distaste the respectable churchgoer of today experiences as he shuffles through the movie ads and sees what is playing at the local drive-ins.

Class Values and Social Strife The social scientist Herman Kahn, taking time out for the moment from his calculations of when a nuclear holocaust is due, sees the conflict of today in class terms. To a newswoman he described his written comments in the *Intellectual Digest* as follows:

We are having a kind of religious war. The upper middle class is forcing its religion—call it secular humanism—on the middle class which is basically nationalistic and fundamentalist. The result is that the middle class has begun to feel it has lost its country. The middle class does not mind elitism so long as the elitists leave them alone. But elitists have made public fun of their values. Take the movie "Joe" of a couple of years ago as an example.[10]

Kahn would lump together all who live the upper-middle-class jet-set style or copy it, against the more traditional life-style of what is described as "keeping respectable" or "living in a nice neighborhood." But the conflict between lace curtain and shanty that he describes is not a new one. The historian Lee Benson, in his study of the Andrew Jackson period, argued that the political struggle of the day was not the economic one as claimed by Arthur Schlesinger, Jr.[11] Rather, it was a conflict of life-styles between those trying to civilize the gaudy frontier towns, that is, the solid Main Street merchants and community builders, and the drifters with their saloons and pool halls, and what have been described euphemistically as their dance-hall girl companions. The one emphasized a life-style of thrift, sobriety, and hard work with a good mixture of evangelical religion thrown in. The other emphasized a more charming and irresponsible life of living it up and gambling for a quick killing with a good mixture of wine, women, and song thrown in. The political scientist Alan Grimes has similarly argued that it was this struggle that brought women suffrage its first victory in 1869 in Wyoming. The leading citizens, in a clever male ploy, doubled their votes at the expense of the prospectors and drifters.[12]

In our day, the clash occurs over the same kind of work ethic vs. hedonistic issues; abortion, gun laws, homosexuality, pornography, capital punishment, respect for the flag, sex education in schools, amnesty for draft dodgers, and all the rest of what some have called the "greening of America" and critics have interpreted as America going to seed.

Kahn's formulation is useful, though like all categorizations, exceptions pop up that suggest the conflict is not always between class life-styles. Women's Lib furnishes one example. The Playboy male consumerism which preaches a Victorian view of male dominating female, finds the upper-middle-class female objecting to having her sisters tiptoeing around with bunny tails on their behinds for the gratification of what they perhaps suspect are often repressed mother's boys who have not quite grown up. But they could escape the logic of their position if they were to redefine the problem in class terms rather than sex terms and require the lesser to provide the gratification for the superior. Essentially, this is the Women's Lib stance toward the workaday world, which has the lesser breeds of each sex taking care of home and children while the more dominant of each sex bring home the bread. Whether they will adopt the escape clause we male chauvinists are offering so freely and thus make the battle a class one rather than one of sexes is to be doubted, however.

The issue is further complicated because the class lines on life-style blur class lines on economic issues. Thus George Meany, who is head of the AFL-CIO, seemed to have every economic reason for supporting George McGovern over Richard Nixon in 1972, correctly assumed that his blue-collar followers would support Nixon because of the espousal of upper-middle-class issues by McGovern and their general rejection by Nixon. He knew which one watched the Sunday pro football games with a good cigar in his mouth, even if he did not have a can of beer at hand.

Whether the life-style issues will become a basis for political coalitions remains doubtful. The free life can flourish only in a continually affluent society and this cannot be guaranteed. Recession and war in which all of the society is involved, as Kahn points out is the case in Israel, tend to dampen spontaneous expression by the upper classes. So, too, does an eventual adding up of costs by those who feel pushed around, especially when they have the votes. For the moment, swingers and straights draw the battle lines in the court room and in elections on constitutional amendments on abortion or pornography. Neither major political party is ready to identify with one side against the other.

Civil Liberties for the Bedroom?   The courts have always been full of such civil liberties conflicts, but since World War II when upper-middle-class judges began pushing their own more libertarian views for an affluent society which was ready to grab at it, the courts have been overflowing with cases. One old conflict that has had new life pumped into it, used to be rather indelicately described "keeping government out of the bedroom." The courts began to look at censorship, particularly on the grounds of indecency. Their ultimate stab was to permit complete freedom in publishing or presenting a work of artistic effort if some "socially redeeming" element could be found in it. For a while this encouraged a rash of exclusive showings of porno movies for judicial audiences, but in the end led to the conclusion that the judges should pay admission like everyone else. More recently, the Nixon Court, by a 5–4 vote, said that local standards should prevail. Hard-core pornography began running for cover, but more litigation was a certainty.

Exploitation or Human Right? The trend toward a freer, creative, and more open life can be characterized as the exploitation of one individual by another, depending on whose freer life is being discussed. Women's Lib claims that in pornography, females are sexually exploited by males as shamelessly as whites exploited blacks in the so-called hilarious minstrel show. At the same time, critics of Women's Lib call their stand on abortion, exploitation of the unborn child. Draft evaders frame the problem as society depriving them of freedom to live as their conscience dictates; their more traditional critics in the middle and lower-middle classes frame the issue as exploitation of their own sons who could not get draft deferments and had to fight and sometimes die in Vietnam.

Even the faculty gets into the act. A University of Michigan professor was ousted for showing 300 students in his three sections of Organic Chemistry 227, a thirty-minute slide presentation highly critical of the United States air war in Vietnam. The professor told reporters that the issue was one of "basic academic freedom." His administrative superior appeared to frame it as a matter of exploitation of a captive audience of students by "introducing totally irrelevant materials," and not what the University of Michigan catalog describes, "basic laboratory procedures for preparing alephatic (fatty) and aromatic compounds."[13]

The issue of all these cases of conflicting life-styles is first one of deciding how much of the claimed exploitation is genuine. These are the kinds of questions upper-middle-class civil libertarians relish. Are not Jews or atheists being deprived of rights freely to live their own life-style if their children attend public schools which hold Christmas programs? We suspect they are.

But equally significant are the questions of the short-run and long-term significance of such behavior. Are there immediate costs that should be taken off the backs of some and put on the backs of others? What externalities really do exist? Do the tiny tots who used to be entertained with stories of Uncle Wiggily and who now sit in silent awe of the dimly lighted TV screen on Saturday morning, watching one ignorant cowpoke kick another ignorant cowpoke in the head, grow up differently? No one really knows yet. To what degree should a faculty member or textbook writer be able to introduce his own irrelevant pet hobby horses to students? When does irrelevancy begin to degrade the learning process? When does it contribute positively by keeping students awake? These serious questions of externalities are the kind upper-middle-class social scientists and even judges are beginning to ask with more frequency since they have discovered that the electorate is not restricted only to the believers in upper-middle-class life-styles.

SUMMARY

We have left out many important civil liberties questions of today, including especially the degree to which society can accept the externalities of preaching revolution or, as the provision on treason states, "giving aid and comfort to the enemy" in time of war. These and many more issues we leave for another book, class discussion, or, as most scholarly articles conclude, further research.

Nor have we dealt with the horrors of McCarthyism in which government officials became witch hunters. This issue was the crucial one in a previous day. Now intimidation of dissent and the stamping out of diverse views are more commonly practiced by private individuals and groups than by government. The essential civil liberties conflicts, as we have portrayed them, deal with how far in an urban society one private individual or group may exploit another, or cause significant externalities for the rest of society, without government intervening.

What we have dealt with are three conflicts that give rise to such civil liberties friction in today's society: the conflict between law breaker and other citizen, between black and white, and between swinger and straight. In each case, we have argued action must be judged by consequences rather than by purity of motives. We have argued that costs are generally involved for someone and where they are not significant costs, the balance should be tilted for encouraging freedom of action. But judging what is a significant cost is not apple pie.

NOTES

1 Joseph S. Bishop, Jr., "Politics and the ACLU," *Commentary*, December 1971, p. 57.
2 Tom Wolfe, *Radical Chic and Mau-Mauing the Flak Catchers*, Farrar, Straus & Giroux, New York, 1970.
3 *Detroit News*, Apr. 6, 1972.
4 Criminal Law Revision Committee, *Report to Parliament*, 1972.
5 *Detroit News*, Apr. 22, 1972.
6 *Ibid.*, Apr. 15, 1972.
7 Charles Kadushin, "Who Are the Elite Intellectuals?" *The Public Interest*, Fall 1972, pp. 109–125.
8 Edward C. Banfield, *The Unheavenly City*, Little, Brown and Company, Boston, 1970.
9 *Detroit News*, Nov. 3, 1972.
10 Herman Kahn, a note in the *Intellectual Digest*, June 1972; interview, *Los Angeles Times*, Oct. 20, 1972.
11 Lee Benson, *The Concept of Jacksonian Democracy*, Princeton University Press, Princeton, N.J., 1961.
12 Alan Grimes, *The Puritan Ethic and Woman Suffrage*, Oxford University Press, New York, 1967.
13 *Lansing State Journal*, Oct. 11, 1972.

Chapter 10

Pentagon
and Foggy Bottom

The leaders of every nation have some choices in determining basic foreign policy and pattern of national defense, but as in the case with individuals, nations must act within the constraints imposed by their environment and their relationship to it. The story of American foreign policy since World War II is strongly shaped by the fact that the United States was forced, reluctantly and resentfully, to accept the role of the world's most powerful nation. This position is one that historically has required that nation to become involved in almost all major disputes around the world and many minor ones besides.

Even if a nation, as the number-one power, wishes to avoid becoming involved, it rarely can fend off the demands of nations on one side or another of a conflict to come to its support or to arbitrate the question. As a result, public policy thought in the world in the years since World War II has been strongly influenced by the U.S. Department of Defense (the "Pentagon") and the Department of State (located in Washington's "Foggy Bottom").

The great nations of history have almost constantly been involved in border disputes. The war in Southeast Asia is only another case of such frontier maneuvering, in this event a particularly extended and painful example. But the boundary problem has been with us as long as world powers have existed. Although we speak of the *Pax Romana*, readers of the comic "Asterix the Saul" know there was little peace along the borders of the Roman Empire. For a long time, there were continuing attempts to expand the boundaries of the state and, after they had reached their maximum, there were still skirmishes with the peoples of the Middle East, the German tribes, and others who sought to test the viability of those boundaries and eventually to push them back toward the capital city. A Gaulist, a Macedonian, or a German always stood ready to sink the dagger into the back of any careless Roman soldier. Similarly, the British Empire during its nineteenth-century apex was constantly fighting to secure or to reestablish its boundaries of influence.

The boundary problem is not limited to the most powerful nation, however. It is also one that must be faced by other nations that are great world powers and, by that very fact, often hope to displace the number-one power. ("We will bury you," Khrushchev once told us.) Thus, as the Soviet Union emerged upon the international scene as such a power, it swallowed up three independent Baltic states and a considerable portion of Finland and Poland. In order to maintain the boundaries of its sphere of influence, it also preempted the supposed sovereignty of both Czechoslovakia and Hungary, and considered doing so in Yugoslavia. The People's Republic of China which, like its antecedent Chinas, has the size and population that makes it a world contender, has sought to maintain and, if possible, extend its boundaries in Southeast Asia, Mongolia, and Bangladesh. In addition, it is confronted with the particular problem that it has an enormously long common boundary with another major power, the Soviet Union, with which it has engaged in a number of skirmishes and probably will become involved in additional conflict in the future.

The pressures, assumptions, uncertainties, as well as the ambitions, of major nations would thus seem to indicate that American involvement in Southeast Asia will not mark the end of the "brush fire" wars in which the nation became engaged in Korea, Vietnam, and more marginally in a number of other areas in the years following World War II. Until the nation outlives its role as world leader, as presumably it someday will as have all its predecessors, it seems only realistic to expect that some kinds of boundary conflicts will evoke tension, bloodshed, and disapproval from the citizens of other nations as well as of our own, in the future. But, of course, these tensions and conflicts need not involve the wrench and internal conflict that have characterized our involvement in Southeast Asia. There is a lesson to be learned from it. It is not that the number-one nation can voluntarily retreat into isolationism or that such conflicts can be completely avoided. Rather, it is that such situations can be recognized for what they are and their impact upon life and property can be minimized even though the pressures that create them probably cannot be completely avoided.

THE NAM

In order to understand American involvement in Southeast Asia, it is necessary to go back about one-quarter of a century and to keep in mind the boundary problem faced by world powers. In the late 1940s, the State Department accepted a theory for the "containment" of communism that had been advanced by George Kennan, one of the senior Foreign Service officers of the United States. In general, the theory was based on the assumption that peace could be maintained by the establishment of a boundary line for influence between the Communist nations and those neutral or oriented toward the United States. This boundary would describe a crescent around the Communist nations, beginning at the boundary between Norway and the U.S.S.R. and extending southeastward defining the line between the Communist satellites of East Germany and the Balkans, into the Middle East and then moving eastward and eventually northeastward, separating the Philippines, South Korea, and Japan from the areas of Communist influence and finally moving upward into the Arctic in the division between the United States and the Soviet Union itself. Minor redefinitions of this boundary were made on occasion, as in Korea in 1953, in 1954 when the demarcation line was established between North and South Vietnam, and later when the Soviet Union chose to side with the Arab nations against Israel.

This crescent boundary line served to help identify those nations that the United States was willing to support and those that it would give no help to under any circumstances. When Yugoslavia chose to follow an independent course from that of the other Communist nations (and got away with it), the United

States was quick to move the boundary line in order to provide aid to the government of Marshall Tito. The United States poured hundreds of millions of dollars during the 1950s and 1960s into what seemed to be a hopeless cause in supporting the government of Sukarno in Indonesia, because that country was within the American boundary zone. In this case, the United States government won against what for a time seemed to be hopeless odds. And the American government decided reluctantly at the end of the 1940s that the Communists had won the mainland of China and that support would have to be withdrawn from that area.

The theory of containment was thus firmly established as American policy when the question of drawing the boundary between American and Communist influence arose in Southeast Asia in the mid-1950s when the French decided that the contest there was beyond the capabilities of what had become at best a third-rate power.

How Defend the Boundary?   The logic of the crescent theory would call for certain areas where the line might be drawn through neutral nations, such as India and Pakistan, where there would be no expectation of a clear domination on the part of the United States. In areas where actual conflict might arise, the goal would logically be one not of attempting to win an undeclared war, but rather of pursuing a stalemate strategy. Such a strategy is not popular and particularly not so in democratic nations where the public has the opportunity to express its viewpoint. In general, the ordinary citizen will prefer either to avoid hostilities or end them promptly on the one hand, or to win the war on the other. Because this is the case, a stalemate strategy such as seemed to be indicated in Vietnam, if we were to maintain the crescent boundary, should involve conflict at the lowest possible level.

President Eisenhower, a five-star general, understood and accepted the logic of the situation. President Kennedy apparently was more restive under such a policy during his short administration. And he brought to Washington more than half a dozen liberal, academic intellectuals who in the early years of the war were superhawks. It was probably their advice, rather than that of the military, that prevailed in the Kennedy and Johnson administrations. (Eisenhower and MacArthur specifically warned against a wider war.)

In a manner that has not yet been made fully clear and may

not be possible to interpret for decades, if ever, Presidents Kennedy and—even more so—Johnson abandoned the policy of minimum conflict and began a series of escalations of the war, even though they must have realized that political considerations were always more important in Vietnam than were military ones. It was not possible to engage in an all-out war, or so it seemed, without bringing down the condemnation of the world upon the United States, a situation that would force us to back down if, indeed, it would not actually provoke World War III. The rapid escalation after the 1964 presidential election rather quickly led to public skepticism and then disillusionment.

The administration never did succeed in making clear the reasons why we were fighting in Vietnam. Possibly the President thought it "self-evident" that we should fight Communists whenever they challenged the boundaries of our sphere of influence, or that we should not "turn our backs" on Asia. Some critics complained that no serious explanatory effort was ever made. Yet it was important to justify such a war in a far-off land. As Douglas MacArthur, General of the Army, once said: "Men will not fight and die without knowing what they are fighting and dying for."

By the beginning of 1968, another election year, much of the public had ceased to support the war or to believe in possible American victory. Under the circumstances, people of all political persuasions, except only those on the far right, seemed increasingly resigned to a strategy of ending the conflict as rapidly as possible. President Johnson, unwilling to make the presidential campaign a referendum on the war, decided not to run for another term, even though the chances were that he would have squeaked through to a narrow victory. (Folk memory to the contrary notwithstanding, Johnson did not lose the 1968 New Hampshire primary. He won it; but he suffered a staggering psychological blow through the large number of votes that went to Eugene McCarthy.)

President Nixon pursued a policy of gradual withdrawal. During the 1968 campaign, he said he had a plan for ending the fighting. This was never publicly revealed, which led to attempts to ridicule him. But his plan almost certainly existed and it quite surely was to negotiate with the Soviet Union to get them to force North Vietnam to negotiate seriously. (Another American mistake was to assume that North Vietnam was more dominated by the Soviet Union and China than was actually the case.) Nixon was anxious to end the fighting, but he insisted on a "peace with honor," that is, no unilateral, unconditional withdrawal. The war still had not ended by the time of the 1972 election, although all American combat troops had been removed. It was clear that neither North nor South Vietnam was as anxious for peace as were Americans. A cease-fire was finally arranged in early 1973 under conditions that left little choice to South Vietnam and barely saved face for the United States.

Strategic Errors and the Credibility Gap In addition to the poor field position that the United States found itself in militarily in Vietnam, two bad decisions by the Johnson administration further eroded the public support that the President might have had. The first of these was a decision that the United States would fight a war of considerable size without calling for any restrictions on the production and sale of consumer goods at home. The call was for a policy of "guns *and* butter." President Johnson was under considerable pressure from organized labor to pursue this strategy and agreed to do so, even though there is an old political rule-of-thumb that says in the event a nation prosecutes a war, every citizen should be called upon to make some sacrifice in order for him to feel that he has a psychological stake in the contest. The "guns and butter" strategy undoubtedly served to weaken public support for the administration's policy and was particularly destructive of morale as it reenforced the frustration that was created as a result of an unintended but nevertheless de facto no-win strategy.

The second major error during the conflict was that of draft policy. This policy was the result, principally, of the position of the late Representative L. Mendel Rivers (Dem., S.C.), the chairman of the Armed Forces Committee in the House of Representatives. It was his view that college students should be eligible for draft deferment—another violation of the rule that everyone should make some contribution in war time. President Johnson might have been able, though only through extraordinary effort, to have overcome Rivers' position on this matter, but he made no effort to do so. The result, of course, was that the draft affected primarily lower-class and working-class persons and favored those young men of the middle classes who typically went to college. The second result, following quickly, was that these young men were affected by feelings of guilt and anxiety should they drop out of school and be drafted. Others of less fortunate family background were being called upon to fight and die in Vietnam for an obscure cause while they enjoyed the advantages of a college education and the privilege of taking part in the pleasurable activities of a college campus. They had a choice: either they could decide that the war was right but their situation was wrong and that they should therefore volunteer for military service, or that the war was wrong and so, therefore, was the draft and that they should call for an end to our involvement in Vietnam. The decision they would make was obvious. Some argued that their position was idealistic. Possibly it was. But what was much more incontrovertible was that the easier choice in the two-way option was the second one. As a result, instead of having strong support on the university campuses, as the administration and congressional leaders could easily have had, these places became centers of protest, sometimes of violent protest against the war. The policies of guns and butter and the deferment of the young men of the middle classes, neither of which was followed during the popularly supported World War II, resulted in a disastrous erosion of aid for the administration's foreign and military policies and a serious crisis of legitimacy for the government of the United States.

Just how the decisions were made that led us further into the nightmare of Vietnam is not yet known. What is known is that there are important lessons in foreign policy to be learned from it. Whether we have indeed learned cannot really be known until the next major crisis comes somewhere else along that long boundary that marks the furthest reaches of American dominance.

FOREIGN AID

Shortly after World War II General of the Army George C. Marshall, then the Secretary of State, proposed a plan for American economic aid for the rebuilding of Europe. (The occasion was one of the rarest of all academic phenomena—a commencement speech that is ever again referred to. It occurred at Harvard University in June, 1947.) What came to be known as the "Marshall Plan" was a set of assumptions that it was in our long-term interest to rebuild the industrial capacity of these nations. The purpose was no doubt conceived of by many as designed to build friends for our side against the expected onslaught of the Communist struggle to control the world. In other cases, however, support probably came from the traditional and very real American sense of mercy and generosity. We had destroyed these nations' productivity or they had been destroyed by the Germans, but the fault was that of governments and not of people. Therefore we had a responsibility for helping the nations get back on their industrial feet.

Both friends and former foes were to be given help, even those nations now within the Communist sphere of influence. (The leaders of the Soviet Union, being no political fools, of course prohibited these countries from participating.) A while later, the same principle of economic aid was extended to another former enemy, Japan.

In a third step, and in the face of the cold war which had now begun, the United States took the lead in establishing the North Atlantic Treaty Organization (NATO). This was frankly designed to be a military alliance to contain communism and, in effect, to establish the northwesterly anchor of the crescent boundary. Because all the nations of Europe were at this time impoverished, the early support for NATO came almost entirely from the United States. Established with the creation of NATO was an elaborate system of military aid to friendly and neutralist nations. Or perhaps we should say that the military aid program of World War II was reestablished.

The Marshall Plan, or Seed Money for Fertile Soil The Marshall Plan was an enormous success. It is unlikely that many of the early supporters of the plan had any notion of how effective it would prove to be. During the 1950s, the economy of Great Britain, and of many other wartime allies, was booming along again. They expanded even more during the 1960s, with few interruptions in the upward movement of national productivity. West Germany, which had ended the war in a state of almost total destruction and demoralization, was quickly rebuilt into an industrial giant, for which the ubiquitous Volkswagen became a symbol.

The plan was so enormously successful that something happened to it that is most unusual in American politics: The program was brought to an end in December 1951—a year ahead of schedule—on the grounds that it had accomplished what it had been intended to do. It had cost $11 billion. And, of course, the program was successful not only in Europe, but in Japan and Nationalist China as well. By the early 1970s, the productivity of Japan had risen to third highest in the world, exceeded only by the Soviet Union and the United States itself. West Germany was not far behind.

In the meantime, Communist expansion in Europe came to an end and the popular assumption was that NATO was at least partially responsible for this. A pattern of foreign economic and military aid had been established and, although it cost the American taxpayers $83 billion in economic aid and $40 billion in military aid between 1945 and 1970, it was widely viewed as being worth the cost. Americans believed that they were making important contributions to worldwide military and economic security.

What's Sauce for the Goose? In typical fashion, American decision makers, delighted with the outcome of the foreign-aid programs, assumed that if this approach had worked well up to this point, it should also work in other parts of the world. During the 1950s and 1960s, a large number of newly independent nations were created with the breaking up of the European colonial system. For these new nations, whether directly committed to alliance with the United States or neutralist, we pledged billions of dollars in economic aid. But it did not take long before it was obvious that the assumption that if billions had curative effects upon an economy in one set of cases, additional billions would not necessarily have the same effect in other circumstances. It became increasingly obvious that economic aid, with some exceptions in the case of agricultural aid, simply was not having the intended impact in the new nations. The reason for the difference was, of course, obvious to those who would pay attention. The United Kingdom, Denmark, West Germany, and Japan, among others, had long since demonstrated their competence at industrial organization and production. All they needed was seed money and machine tools. No such evidence had ever been presented by India, Dahomey, Haiti, or a host of other poor nations.

Foreign Aid: Who Benefits? Much of the money that was poured into the underdeveloped nations did not result in industrialization and employment together with increasing amounts of home-produced consumer goods. In many cases, aid hurt rather than helped the economy of a poor nation, as when labor-saving machinery was sent to lands having high unemployment levels or when free-trade policies were adopted that drained unindustrialized nations of raw materials but did nothing to permit them to compete effectively against the industry of established nations. Much of the aid money went to the ruling elite in the "benefited" nation, and served to broaden class differences without appreciably expanding the gross national product. In many cases, the funds were illegally siphoned off for Mercedes-Benz limousines for senior politicians, numbered Swiss bank accounts, or elaborate embassies in the major nations' capitals, in a manner that the American middle class would regard as an indication of "corruption," although this would have to be interpreted as another case of middle-class ethnocentrism. In the cultures where it happened, this is probably not the interpretation given to it and, in any case, the important damage it has done has been related to its failure to improve the economy of the new nation and hence could rightly be regarded as essentially wasted money.

Most Americans who pay any attention to politics and even those who have a fair degree of knowledge about it probably think of foreign aid as money that is spent for the most part in the nations who are supposed to be advantaged by it. Certainly, "foreign" aid seems to imply this. In fact, however, most of the money spent under the foreign economic-aid programs and even a larger portion of that devoted to military aid involve contracts to American firms and work to the economic advantage of American corporations and their employees. In other words, most of the money spent on so-called foreign aid never leaves the United States and has the effect of promoting the American economy and the welfare of American working men and corporate shareholders more than it does the people of the "undeveloped" countries that it is ostensibly designed to benefit.

Military aid has not only worked, in effect, most of all to benefit the American economy, but it has had little, if any, effect upon the political security of many of the nations it was designed most to benefit. As military aid was extended beyond the wealthier nations surrounding the Communist crescent line, the question became increasingly one of what was to be gained by such activity. Even along the line, as in Spain and Nationalist China, it became increasingly clear that billions of dollars were being committed with no knowledge beyond the basic assumption that these funds could help in the defense of the United States against possible Communist attack or even to protect a nation against possible internal disorders or attack from a neighboring hostile country.

Why Foreign Aid Today?   In the 1970s, the critical question had become whether or not foreign aid should be continued at all.

In both 1971 and 1972, the United States Senate had voted to kill foreign aid, although in each case it was continued on an interim basis. Each time, the vote against continuing a program that was by then approximately a quarter of a century old involved a coalition between conservatives and liberals, each voting against continuation, but for different reasons.

The conservatives saw additional funds for economic aid as being a waste, money that was poured down the drain with virtually no likelihood of it having a pronounced positive effect upon the local economy and producing the kinds of economic "miracles" that resulted from the Marshall Plan. Liberals, on the other hand, viewed economic-aid programs as being designed primarily to entice other nations into support for the American military position in its boundary maintenance objectives and many of them considered the policy as being designed to encourage American "imperialistic" incursions into the economies of such nations. Many such liberals viewed these activities as being designed to aid the profiteering of American corporations in their economic activities abroad. Liberals and conservatives, for entirely different reasons, had reached the conclusion that American foreign aid had extended itself to the end of its usefulness and that it was no longer working in the manner that had been originally intended and had seemingly been so enormously successful in its early years. And there could no longer be any serious question but that this was the case, even though one might argue about the reasoning behind those who supported the calling of a halt to the long years of the program and the enormous expenditure of funds from the taxpayers that had been involved. Many funds worked much as had been intended and had proved to further the goals of the American government; others that had been idealistic and well intended were based on assumptions that proved to be inadequate.

FOREIGN POLICY MAKING IN A DEMOCRACY

Alexis de Tocqueville, the nineteenth-century French observer of American customs, argued that democracies are less suited than other types of government for the successful carrying out of foreign policy. The national interest, he believed, would very often be placed second to the demands of local politics, the pressures of interest groups, the ambitions of politicians trying to "look good" at home, and the emotional impulses and demands of the electorate for quick and simple solutions. In foreign affairs, unlike in domestic politics, he argued, there was often no opportunity to correct mistakes. Therefore, he believed, popular participation in foreign policy decision making was a dangerous practice. During the years of World War II, the American commentator Walter Lippmann made a similar argument.[1]

Who Participates? In the United States, foreign policy making has always been open to all interests and individuals who have the desire and political resources to participate. Public disagreements based on differences in political ideologies have commonly spilled over into the foreign policy area, even though the President (whoever he may be) will typically attempt to argue that all Americans should unite behind his policy and not weaken the nation's hand in dealing with other countries. But great debates have centered in recent decades over the question of American involvement in both World Wars I and II, joining the League of Nations, policy toward the Soviet Union after World War II, and involvement in Korea. The conflict over Vietnam is scarcely a new situation in American history.

Like all nations, America has made blunders in foreign policy, and these, as well as other incidents that were not blunders, have been exploited in political campaigns and sometimes badly distorted. Sometimes, without doubt, these distortions for the sake of domestic electoral advantage may work to the detriment of the conduct of foreign policy. And even if they do not, it is often to the advantage of the incumbent party to claim that it will do so. Thus, in 1972, Sargent Shriver, the Democratic candidate for Vice President, claimed that the Nixon administration had missed a "golden opportunity" to achieve peace in Vietnam in late 1968. Spokesmen for the administration promptly responded that no such opportunity ever existed, that if it had it took place while the Democrats were still in power, and that if Shriver or Averill Harriman (our representative in 1968 at the Paris peace talks) knew of any such thing, he certainly did not brief the incoming Nixon administration. Besides, spokesmen said, this kind of "irresponsible talk" works only to the advantage of the North Vietnamese, with whom the administration was in delicate negotiations. At this point, neither the ordinary citizen nor a very well-informed one could be blamed for feeling confused.

Many Americans will not, however, concede that foreign

policy should be made differently from domestic policy. To make such a concession would be to suggest that there is consensus on the goals that foreign policy should pursue and the methods it should employ. Americans so far have preferred to risk disunity and some inefficiency to assure that a variety of views will be considered before action is taken and disliked policies criticized. Whatever its shortcomings, United States foreign policy fares well when compared by historians with that of less democratic nations. And in saying this, we have to keep in mind what was said earlier about the particular problems that the most powerful nations in the world encounter and the fact that the most powerful nation is viewed by most foreigners and even many of its own citizens as always being fair game. Despite some serious errors—and the chances are good that historians will count the Vietnam war as among them—the United States has had many foreign policy successes. Between 1940 and 1950, the nation accomplished a direct about-face in foreign policy—a revision of basic principles that had dated back 150 years to Washington's Farewell Address and his warnings about "entangling alliances." At that time, the nation moved with considerable boldness, making unusual sacrifices in money, materials, and men. The government that can so readily respond to the requirements of the moment perhaps deserves more credit than some of its critics have been willing to give it.

Emerging Trends in Foreign Policy In the early 1970s, President Richard Nixon appeared to be moving toward success in another dramatic and important modification of American foreign policy. New understandings were made with the Soviet Union and Red China became the People's Republic of China. The new approach seemed to offer the prospect of orienting American foreign policy more toward the realities of world situations than to questions of the morality of the governments ruling those nations. Similar changes were being considered in our relationships with our allies and with the nonallied nations. This did not signal a return to isolationism, but rather to something different from both it and the internationalism that had dominated our policy since about 1940. Congress, if not yet the President, was reconsidering foreign-aid policies that had seemed to outlive their time.

To be sure, one could argue that it should not have required a quarter of a century for the United States to acknowledge the

existence of a nation that now has three-quarters of a billion
people. But this merely demonstrates the complexities of foreign
policy making in a giant nation. It requires little cost and creates
almost no uncertainty for the People's Republic of China to be
recognized by Upper Volta, Peru, or Canada. But the United
States has an elaborate set of agreements with both allies and
neutralist nations. Some countries, even one as large and powerful as Japan, count upon the United States to defend it from
foreign aggression.

In its various mutual-defense and mutual-aid pacts, the
United States constantly exposes itself to credibility gaps. If it
does not keep its commitments to such a nation as Nationalist
China, other countries will immediately wonder what our commitments to them may be worth. And a major change in foreign
policy always runs the risk of becoming a political issue at home.
When President Nixon chose to visit Peking in 1972, he could do
so with only a minimum amount of static (from the far right
within his own party). Had any Democratic President attempted
to do this, he would have risked harsh and possibly devastating
criticism. (Richard Nixon himself, as a member of Congress,
would certainly have enthusiastically attacked any Democratic
President who had the temerity to propose a trip to Peking.) To be
sure, in order to come to an agreement with the Chinese, it was
thought necessary for President Nixon to bend some existing
agreements, to temporarily unnerve the Japanese (who for tacti-
cal reasons had been given no advance warning of the move), and
possibly to make some secret concessions to other countries in
order to soften the blow. All these activities require time and
great skill. They cannot be done overnight, as the simplistic
idealist often demands. But the important point is that they can be
done and they have been done. And the American leadership
continues the experiment of shaping foreign policy within the
framework of open democratic institutions. Yet we must also
keep in mind that foreign policy making is an extension of the
activities of the ruling elites. The function of a foreign policy is to
find ways to ensure the continued existence of the nation and to
protect its dominant values.

THE FOREIGN POLICY MAKERS

In its broad outline, the process of foreign policy making in the
United States is similar to domestic policy making: A policy

proposal is shaped in the executive branch and runs the gamut of criticism by Congress and interested publics. But foreign policy issues are more complex than domestic policy; there is often believed to be a need for secrecy and dispatch, and the stakes are too high to permit any avoidable errors.

In foreign policy matters, the executive branch, constitutionally and practically, has great power to shape policy, while Congress and the public have limited opportunity for review. The process of decision making is based on grants of constitutional power and on organizational structure. These define who the major decision makers will be.

The Formal Powers The major constitutional grants of power can be briefly summarized: The President is the Commander in Chief of the Armed Forces, but only Congress can declare war. The President may make treaties, but the Senate must ratify them by a two-thirds vote. The President may accept the credentials of foreign emissaries and appoint our diplomatic representatives, but the Senate must confirm the major appointments. In addition, the Constitution grants to Congress the power to make laws (over which the President has a veto) that affect such foreign policy matters as tariffs, foreign-aid appropriations and policy, and the organization of executive agencies for the carrying out of foreign policy.

The Practical Results The traditional American system of checks and balances applies in foreign policy making, but it is clear that the President is far more dominant here than he is in domestic matters. Alexander Hamilton observed long ago that the President would tend to gather to himself all powers in foreign affairs "which the Constitution does not vest elsewhere in clear terms." In practice, he has been able to extend his powers even further than that. The President can skirt the Senate's treaty-ratifying powers by making "executive agreements" which have all the practical effect of treaties, but do not require Senate consent. This power has been increasingly used since Jefferson and his advisers invented it in order to agree with the agents of Napoleon on the purchase of the Louisiana Territory. The power of Congress to declare war has been meaningful only in the case of the War of 1812—and Congress scarcely distinguished itself with its decision making during that period. In other cases, the effective commitment of American policy was made before

Congress was asked to make a formal declaration of war. Furthermore, in many cases both the United States and many other nations have engaged in wars without bothering with a formal declaration.

The President's power to accept the credentials of foreign diplomats has meant that he alone can grant United States recognition to a new foreign nation or regime and also to break off such recognition. Thus President Eisenhower decided, without action by Congress, to terminate diplomatic relations with Cuba, and President Nixon, without consulting Congress or even informing its leaders in advance, decided to reestablish a form of diplomatic relations with the People's Republic of China.

Congress has some formal as well as informal powers in relation to foreign policy making. Whenever the President and his advisers choose to make use of the treaty power, the Senate members can prevent ratification by securing only one-third plus one of the senators present and voting. The Senate also has the right to disapprove presidential appointments of ambassadors and other diplomats above the civil service level. Informally, during debates on treaties and appointments, senators have an opportunity to gain the attention of the mass media with their views and to influence public policy and public opinion thereby.

The House of Representatives also has some influence upon the process, particularly because of the formal rule that the House must initiate appropriation bills. If the House Committee on Appropriations refuses to act on particular foreign affairs bills, it can be bypassed only with great difficulty. This can have an especially important impact upon appropriations for foreign aid, but also for the prosecution of "brush-fire" wars and even for the size of a diplomatic legation in some other nation.

Still, when the record on foreign policy making is reviewed, the role of congressmen stands out as a frustrating one. The President and the executive departments are the major source of congressional information. If the President refuses to give information or indicates he must withhold it for security reasons, congressmen have little recourse but to accept his decision. Of course, information sometimes reaches congressmen by way of leaks and plants from foreign countries, but these encounter serious credibility problems which limit their effectiveness both in Congress and in relation to the general public. Sometimes bureaucrats who have access to classified information leak it to newsmen or to sympathetic members of Congress, but this seldom has any significant impact upon foreign policy or public opinion. The "Pentagon Papers," which were taken from government files by bureaucrats in 1971 and published by the *New York Times* and then other newspapers, created something of a sensation, but they revealed nothing important that was not already known and the public appeared to be little interested in them or in the well-publicized trial that followed.[2]

The Diplomats and Bureaucrats Beyond the President himself, the major forces affecting foreign policy are those of other members of the executive branch, including both political appointees and professional diplomats in the foreign service of the Department of State. Probably the most influential group in terms of incremental day-to-day decisions are the members of the Foreign Service. These professionally trained diplomats, many of them out of the upper-middle class and aristocracy and trained in Ivy League schools, tend to be highly conservative because one quickly learns in diplomatic work that only small incremental decisions can be risked with any degree of safety. Members of the corps also tend to think in terms of American diplomatic and economic interests in dealing with other nations. In other words, in a chancy business, they take no more chances than they must.

Thus, in regard to the Middle East, it has long been known that many members of the diplomatic group tend to believe that the United States should side with the Arab nations rather than with Israel, for the future of the Jewish nation remains in doubt, as it has since it was formed after World War II, while many of the Arab nations possess huge oil reserves which might well fall completely to the Soviet Union and other Communist nations if those countries are too much alienated by American aid to Israel. But these Foreign Service officers are severely limited in their impact by the realities of politics. The American policy toward Israel, under both Democrats and Republicans, has been favorable. This has been so not merely because many Americans believe this to be the morally correct attitude, but more importantly because most of the many American Jewish voters are pro-Israel, while there are relatively few Arabs or Muslims who can vote in the United States. In other situations, too, the Foreign Service officers tend to view American interests narrowly, conservatively, and outside the domestic political picture. This results in the minimization of their views in the policy-making process, though there are occasional exceptions when an unusual man like George Kennan comes along.

Traditionally, the most senior and prestigeful member of the

President's Cabinet has been the Secretary of State. In isolationist days, this position could be granted on the basis of being a political plum, for American policy was clear-cut, there were few decisions to be made, and few conflicts between the Secretary and the Foreign Service officers. After America shifted to a policy of internationalism, the traditional arrangement of a political appointee as Secretary of State guided by the professional members of the Foreign Service became increasingly unsatisfactory. President Franklin Roosevelt, who made internationalism the basis for American foreign policy, originally selected his Secretary of State, Cordell Hull, because of his high prestige in Congress, where he had served for many years. Roosevelt was later unwilling, however, to pay the political price of replacing the Secretary and equally unwilling to trust his judgment, except on reciprocal-trade policy. Under the circumstances, the President developed a number of techniques for bypassing his Secretary, such as working through his Under Secretary or special presidential aides, or by dealing directly with the heads of foreign nations himself. The problems that President Roosevelt experienced with the office of Secretary were not solved by him and became increasingly difficult in later administrations.

President Truman, after disastrous results in making use of James F. Byrnes as Secretary, tried to solve the problem by making use of the enormously prestigeful former Chief of Staff, General of the Army George C. Marshall, in that position. President Eisenhower, who had little interest in foreign policy, despite his own great diplomatic skills, turned the whole matter over to the Secretary of State, John Foster Dulles, who ran a one-man show and ignored the advice and entreaties of Foreign Service officers. President Kennedy sought to be his own Secretary of State—something that many other Presidents had sought to do before him—and appointed the drab, unimaginative Dean Rusk, who largely accepted the advice of the Foreign Service officers. President Johnson retained Rusk, but placed him in a new role, or rather a very old one, in essentially turning foreign policy making over to him.

Top Man in Foreign Policy: Administrator or Innovator?
When President Nixon took office, he recognized the problems recent Presidents had faced. That is, it seemed as if the President could be his own Secretary of State, or he could appoint a Secretary who would accept the inertia of the Foreign Service

officers, or he could turn the job over entirely to a strong-willed lone wolf, as James Monroe had done in the case of John Quincy Adams (who actually authored the "Monroe" Doctrine) or Dwight D. Eisenhower in the case of John Foster Dulles.

Nixon was a good student of American history and knew particularly well the problems of American Presidents in the twentieth century. He did not like any of the stopgap solutions that had been used by his immediate predecessors, and finally he came up with an ingenious solution that may well be imitated by Presidents in the next few years or decades: He appointed as Secretary of State, William Rogers, a likable person who was a good lawyer but had no professional diplomatic experience and who was expected only to preside over the routine administration of the Department of State; at the same time he named to his personal staff in the White House an experienced and already well-known professor of political science from Harvard University, Henry Kissinger, who was expected to be unconcerned with routine but to be innovative in policy development and skilled in the making of strategic moves. Whatever problems of morale this may have created in the State Department seem to have been offset by the fact that this approach resulted in a more vital and imaginative foreign policy than the United States had known since the Roosevelt administration moved to internationalism, and the Truman administration put forth the Marshall Plan (for foreign aid) and the Truman Doctrine and Kennan theory (both calling for the containment of communism).

There are many reasons for thinking that this arrangement may well represent the basic pattern of the future. In the first place, Cabinet members have been declining in importance for a long time, and particularly as the use of presidential staff has developed since Theodore Roosevelt's day at the beginning of the present century. More importantly, perhaps, the President needs imaginative yet highly responsible advisers who are not beholden either to the hide-bound Foreign Service or to the advocates of wild risks who hold no responsible government positions. In addition, the Department of State needs as its head someone who can handle the routine operations of an agency which has as its employees about 13,000 American citizens and some 10,000 foreign nationals. That person needs to be not only a skilled administrator and someone who understands the complex daily operational routine, but also someone who can be in that position long enough to make a real impact upon the Department. Secretaries of State, in the past, have had an average tenure of only between two and three years.

The State Department appears to have grown in importance since World War II, but its influence in foreign affairs, in both formulation and execution of policy, will probably never again be as great as it was during the period of isolationism when issues of foreign policy were not usually of central importance. Although the principal representative from the Department in each nation is designated as the chief of all United States personnel within that nation, he is not now and is likely never again to be the primary spokesman for the United States in cases where significant matters of policy are under discussion.

THE UNITED NATIONS

Since its formation as World War II ended, the United States has officially given strong support to the United Nations as an organization for dealing with problems in international relations. The aim of the UN has always ostensibly been to provide collective security against aggression. Shortly after it was formed, however, it became apparent that whenever major powers took opposite sides in a dispute, the UN would be less than effective—action might in fact end in destroying the organization. It was also recognized, however, that as a forum for expressing national viewpoints, the UN might serve a useful role as well as occasionally serving effectively as a mediator. But, like its predecessor, the League of Nations, the UN was not able to serve effectively in dealing with problems that one or more power formations considered to be of great importance to themselves. The United States suffered, in addition, from the fact that most of the Secretaries General of the UN, and particularly U Thant, were essentially anti-American. In the international organization, as has generally been the case, the most powerful nation was also viewed with the most distrust.

Why All Administrations Support the UN   Despite its limitations and inherent weaknesses, most American professional diplomats believe that the UN is of great value to the United States as a medium for propaganda designed to influence the neutral nations, a clearinghouse for technical information, an arena for settling conflicts between smaller powers, and a place in which the United States and the U.S.S.R. (and probably in the

1970s, the People's Republic of China) can meet without the elaborate formalities and the problems of who is to lose face that are involved in meetings of the heads of state or their foreign affairs representatives. It has also served effectively as an initiator of a number of international treaties. Some of these involve agreements concerning human rights, the abolishment of slavery, political rights for women, and the recovery and return of space explorers.

For whatever it may be worth in the future, the United States in the early 1970s was not prepared to abandon the United Nations and none of the principal candidates for the Presidency in the major parties would even hint at such a possibility. But on the other hand, the hopes and dreams of a generation earlier for the possibility of the UN acting as an instrument for bringing about world peace had largely evaporated. The UN had its effective uses and the United States was willing to continue to pay the bulk of the costs of operating it, but it was no longer viewed by either ordinary citizens or governmental leaders as the institution that could provide international stability and lasting peace.

CLOSING NOTE

In the early 1970s, a neoisolationism was developing in the United States and a new kind of foreign policy different from that of either isolationism or internationalism began to emerge in the Nixon administration. The view of many persons had come to be that America should pay less attention to the activities of other nations, Communist or non-Communist alike, in other parts of the world and that we should "mind our own business." On the left the argument was that communism was not a threat to us and its adoption should be a matter of self-determination. The left wanted to put an end to military foreign aid, on the logical assumption (given its basic premises) that there was no foreign enemy to defend against and that such aid was only an excuse for American economic interference with other independent nations. The right argued that we should end economic aid to foreign countries and let Communist sympathizers or those who naïvely drifted into the Communist orbit take the consequences of their unwise preferences.

Americans were beginning to face up to the frustrations of trying to be savers of the world. They had come to recognize that idealism and reality cannot be reconciled. Given the unlikely prospects for the ideal or utopia, they were increasingly choosing to accept reality and the safer goals of protecting what America had and was as against the far riskier goals of trying to impose American ideals upon other nations or to change their way of behaving through the bribery of American economic and military aid. What the future would bring, as usual, no one could knowledgeably predict.

NOTES

1 Walter Lippmann, *U.S. Foreign Policy: Shield of the Republic,* Little, Brown and Company, Boston, 1943.
2 John L. Greenfield et al. (eds.), *The Pentagon Papers,* Bantam Books, Inc., New York, 1971.

Chapter 11

Class, Real Class
—Middle Class

Perhaps the most salient characteristic of any democracy, including the American, is that it exists primarily to protect and defend the values, goals, and life-styles of the voting majority. Basically, this means that it acts on behalf of the various middle classes and those persons whom these classes are willing to tolerate, including the wealthy (who can, in any case, fend for themselves in nearly any political system) and the upper reaches of the working class.

Although some would like to make it such, democracy does not and, the authors believe, by its nature cannot serve as an instrument for radical social and economic change. It is fundamentally designed to work on behalf of little people with little minds and narrow vision. The British legal historian Henry Sumner Maine noted as long ago as 1886 that "There is no belief less warranted by actual experience, than that a democratic republic is . . . given to reforming legislation."

As we have already noted, this effective majority has little interest in giving the poor any more than a fighting chance, or in giving minorities more than is necessary to placate them. Certainly the overwhelming majority of those who feel that they have made a little something out of their lives and achieved a certain amount of material goods and personal security are never going to be in the mood to transfer the primary benefits of government from themselves to those whom they regard as the failures in society. Democracies can be developed and can pursue policies that benefit a very substantial proportion of the population, but they do not represent a panacea for all, particularly not for the confused, the weak, the personally incompetent decision makers, the seriously maladjusted, or those whose luck is chronically bad. Democracy is a more modest institution with more modest goals. As that old intellectual snob George Bernard Shaw once said: "Democracy substitutes election by the incompetent many for appointment by the corrupt few." (Shaw was both an intellectual snob and a socialist. For that combination, there is no way out within a democratic system. Yet it is not an uncommon combination. Similarly, the hopelessness of the dilemma when intellectual snobbery is coupled with a commitment to democracy, as is the case with many academic populists, is learned slowly and apparently must be relearned by each generation.)

HOUSING POLICY

The way in which democracy benefits the middle class could be demonstrated through hundreds of illustrations, but a particularly clear example is that of the Housing Act of 1937 and its

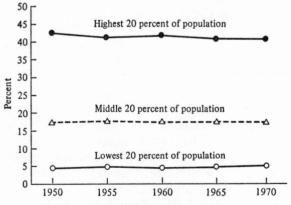

Note: Changing governmental policies do not importantly affect income distribution. These figures are before taxes, but the tax structure does not greatly modify the pattern.

Figure 11-1 The distribution of family income in the United States (percent of total). (*Source: U.S. Bureau of the Census.*)

subsequent amendments. President Roosevelt, in his 1936 inaugural address, had said that one-third of the nation was ill-housed. This act was designed to "do something" about that problem. Just what did it do? It did many things, of course, but the most important and enduring was to provide for Federal Housing Administration (FHA) guarantees of bank loans. It did not put government directly into the lending business, but encouraged banks and other financial institutions to grant home mortgage loans by guaranteeing the loans made to persons who qualified under the act. In the past, banks had been extremely reluctant to lend money for home loans and other consumer purposes, preferring to lend to potentially profitable productive enterprises. But this provision permitted banks to make loans with no risk as to whether the money would be repaid. (In fact, there were few defaults.) In other words, the banker was taking no chance and could set his interest rates low, because the home buyer was competing only against the opportunity costs that the banker had to consider in alternative uses of the money for lending purposes.

This part of the Housing Act was a fantastic success. It converted the nation, particularly in the years immediately following World War II, from one primarily of renters to one primarily of home owners (or at least home buyers). And who were the beneficiaries? Primarily, they were members of the middle classes and, in the prosperity after World War II, of the upper-working class, the "hard hats." The rich did not benefit because the homes that could qualify for FHA guarantees were limited as to their maximum value. This eliminated both the rich and most of the upper-middle class. Of course, this restriction had no limitation on their life-styles. They could afford to buy homes under conventional mortgages. But the provision benefited the poor nothing, for they could not qualify either as to income level or, in most cases, as to record of employment.

Housing for the Poor?   The Housing Act anticipated that a different kind of program would be required for the poor and hence it also established the Public Housing Administration. But the public housing program was a disaster from the beginning. Some have argued that this is because the American middle class is hostile to both government-owned housing and apartment-style dwelling units. This may be a small part of the reason, but there are many others much more important.[1]

The public housing units of the past were often badly

designed and badly administered. Very early in the history of their development, it became clear that living in such units classified a person in the lowest possible status position in society. As a result, persons in such housing moved out at the earliest possible moment and would never move into a housing project again if it could be avoided. Overwhelmingly, the units became the dwelling place of those chronically on welfare. This hard core was made up of the most inept, hopeless, helpless people in America, a group that had neither the ability nor the motivation to cooperate with housing administrators in an attempt to make the units minimally attractive as dwelling places. The large number of empty units in most tracts has been an eloquently silent testimonial to the fact that here was the bottom of the barrel. In some cases, as in St. Louis, huge high-rise projects had to be—in a final gesture of despair—torn down. The Housing Act of 1937 and its successors had done wonders for the middle class and the upper-working class. For the poor, it might not be an exaggeration to say that it had offered no improvement for their lot.

TRANSPORTATION POLICY

We could point to many other examples of middle-class benefit. As with housing, national transportation policy builds primarily to meet middle-class needs and convenience. Fundamentally, it calls for the moving of people either by airplane, or by automobiles over elaborate superhighway systems. This is true even within metropolitan areas, except for portions of the New York area, where this would be physically impossible. A transportation policy designed to benefit the lower classes, of course, would call for the movement of people within a city or a metropolitan area by public transit systems, preferably with no service charges for the individual trip and with the system paid for out of general taxation.

MIDDLE-CLASS WELFARE

The Office of Economic Opportunity and the organizations it has spawned in the antipoverty program have made virtually no impact upon the condition of the poor in America, but the OEO has supplied vast amounts of money that has benefited businessmen and the middle-class bureaucrats who receive their salaries from these public funds.

Even in such programs that are ostensibly designed to benefit the lowest classes, such as the school lunch and school milk programs, and the surplus commodities program of the U.S. Department of Agriculture, the benefit has been primarily to those in the upper-working class and the middle classes. This is so because the school lunch and school milk programs are not free. Although the charges are low and well below cost, many of the children of the poor have parents who cannot afford even this, or are unwilling to do so. And the surplus commodities program (not to be confused with the food stamp program), although of genuine benefit to the poor, was probably begun because of benefits to the middle-class commercial farmers who produce the food.[2] (Under this plan, foods that are produced in such excess supply as to make their sale on the open market unprofitable for farmers are bought up by the U.S. Department of Agriculture, thus artificially reducing the available supply on the open market. This "surplus" is then distributed among the poor who presumably are not in the market in any case because of lack of purchasing power.)

In some cases, governmental policies are such that they have been referred to as "middle-class welfare." Thus the federal government has a program for providing below-market-cost interest loans to the victims of earthquakes and on an ad hoc basis for other natural disasters, such as tornadoes, hurricanes, or floods. These programs, which often include some funds as outright gifts, of course, benefit property owners of the middle class. The middle class has the political clout to bring about such legislation and it will collectively band together to support its enactment, since no owner of a $35,000 home can anticipate at what moment his property may be leveled by an earthquake, exploded by a tornado, or floated away by a flood, leaving nothing intact but the mortgage. The poor who live in rental units, of course, have no such power and a natural disaster, a riot, or a serious fire may have no effect upon them other than to have their rent increased because housing for the poor in the community has become scarcer than ever.

The Lockheed Luck-out The advantage to the middle class in being able to insist upon the government bailing them out of difficulties is perhaps even more clearly demonstrated in the 1971 decision to provide a government loan to the Lockheed Aircraft Corporation. The corporation, as a result of a series of bad breaks and bad management, was near bankruptcy at that time. If the company were to go out of business, it would mean that a great collection of aircraft building talent would be disassembled and scattered all over the nation. It would also mean that, in the case of a national military emergency, one of the long-dependable producers of military aircraft would not be available to lend assistance. After hectic debate, Congress agreed, with the President's approval, to endorse a government-guaranteed loan to keep the company going. The effect of this, of course, was to continue employment for many engineers and other middle-class technicians who might have otherwise been out of work. It also made it possible for banks to make profitable loans to the company which they would otherwise have rejected as being in an unduly high-risk category. If the company had been hiring primarily unskilled workers, perhaps on a part-time basis, and had nothing to produce that was essential to the national defense, the case would probably have gone to the bankruptcy courts. But the national defense and middle-class jobs were at stake—the interests and life-styles of the middle class—and that made all the difference.

Waste and corruption can penetrate into programs of "middle-class welfare." For example, in February 1971, when a serious earthquake struck the Los Angeles area, persons whose homes were damaged found that the Small Business Administration allotted some $211 million for the repair of quake-damaged homes. Persons could borrow up to $3,000, but the first $2,500 was an outright gift, the balance to be repaid at a low rate of interest. The administration was swamped by some 50,000 loan applications. These were hurriedly processed. A subsequent investigation revealed all kinds of errors and cheating, including outright fraud. Homeowners and building contractors acted in collusion. Repair estimates were deliberately overstated in some cases, repairs were made that had not been caused by the earthquake, and some homeowners used the money to buy boats or automobiles, leaving the home unrepaired. And this type of white-collar crime was not uncovered by the Small Business Administration or the General Accounting Office (which is the federal government auditing agency) but by reporters of the *Los Angeles Times*.[3]

Another example of "middle-class welfare" is to be found in the $1 billion that the federal government has paid in subsidies since World War II to feeder lines that provide commercial air service to small-city airports. The $1 billion has not resulted in "the provision of efficient short-haul, low-density air service." It has only kept alive nine relatively weak feeder lines used mainly by a relatively few middle-class businessmen.

SOME EXAMPLES OF FUTILITY

Members of the middle classes and the upper-working class, generally speaking, claim to assume that only those programs that actually work should be continued in force. This is not their actual assumption, however, because it is clear that the majority of the middle masses actually support programs they believe *ought* to work and, like reformers, will continue to support programs even in the face of overwhelming evidence that they are of little or no avail. So we can picture this as the unarticulated assumption of the middle-masses majority: Those programs will work that ought to work.

The majority persists in believing that stiffer prison sentences serve to reduce crime, most adults on welfare are lazy people and do not want to work, and the drug problem in America could be solved by drying up the sources of supply. None of these assumptions are correct, but most citizens persist in acting as if they were. It is thus not just the far left and far right that assume that believing will make it so. It is a favorite weakness of a great many Americans, including many highly educated intellectuals. At least the latter should know better.

Outmoded Agencies Linger On The assumption that what ought to be true must be true leads to strong public support for anachronistic programs and agencies. When we consider that particular interest groups and the bureaucracies that profit from the existence of an agency also lend support, it is easy to understand why programs, once established, rarely are eliminated and why a government agency, even one that is extremely costly, may continue in existence even though it no longer performs any useful function, or, if it does, it does so less effectively or efficiently than could some other organization. We need only to offer two examples. One is the Subversive Activities Control Board. It was created during the peak of the cold war years of the early 1950s, when Senator Joseph McCarthy was pouring gasoline on the already burning fear of Communist infiltration into America. After the panic was over and the Supreme Court had sharply limited the authority of the Board, it really had nothing more to do. The members of the Board and its employees have, however, continued to draw their comfortable salaries. Congressional leaders, somewhat embarrassed by the situation, have tried to find useful activities for this organization, so far without success. The Board could probably be eliminated without much opposition from many Americans—the great majority of whom quite surely do not know that it even exists. But strong right-wing support from persons who assume that the Board can serve to keep individuals with Communist ties out of positions of influence in the United States has served to keep the agency alive. The American taxpayer, of course, pays for this kind of folly.

The National Guard offers another example. It was once an extremely necessary organization. In the years before World War II, the United States' standing army was always small and what there was of it was located along the frontiers, especially in Indian country. In the rest of the nation, however, there were all kinds of emergencies that required military troops. These included natural disasters and urban ghetto riots, which began to occur as early as the beginning of the 1830s. And in the event of war, some method was needed by which to recruit at least semitrained soldiers in a very short time. The militia, later called the National Guard, and since 1827 financed almost entirely out of federal funds, took care of these situations.

In more recent times, however, the establishment of a fairly large standing army with a great deal of physical mobility and with a substantially large reserve group has greatly lessened the earlier need for the National Guard. Furthermore, since World War I, at least, practically every use of the National Guard has encountered criticism.

In an age of specialization and professionalization, the Guard consists primarily of amateurs. The criticism has been particularly severe in those cases where the Guard has been called upon to deal with civil disturbances, as at Kent State. In such cases, its amateurism has been most evident. Another clear example that the Guard is outmoded for use in emergency situations was revealed during the Detroit riots of the summer of 1967. At that time, the Michigan National Guard was assigned to patrol the riot areas east of Woodward Avenue, a main street dividing the city, and the highly professional 82d Airborne Division of the United States Army was assigned to areas west of the street. The differences in the quality of performance, the number of lives lost, and the amount of property damage done were too obvious to be overlooked.[4] This strongly indicated that if experienced professional groups, such as the 82d Airborne, had been used in every case of ghetto riots during the 1960s, the amount of property damage, deaths, injuries, and bitterness caused would have been much less.

There would appear to be no rational reason to continue the existence of the expensive National Guard today (especially given the existence of armed forces reserve units), but of course it remains in existence and is likely to continue on for a long time to come. Many citizens believe the Guard continues to have an important social function in our society, and others support it by departing from the ideological assumption that it is desirable to keep government "as close to the people" as possible in all cases and therefore, whenever possible, to use state troops in preference to those of the federal government. Certainly governors, who are commanders in chief of their state's National Guard, would support this view as would the many persons who gain extra income by "moonlighting" as Guard training sessions. And the taxpayer, as usual not quite sure what the score is, pays the bill.

In addition to governmental waste that results from erroneous assumptions and rigid ideological beliefs, an enormous amount of squandering takes place as a result of experimentation in areas in which there is little possiblity of knowing what will or will not be effective in seeking to deal with a particular problem. In such cases, some proportion of middle-mass America will be outraged by what they regard as the waste of the taxpayers' money, but there will always be some who find the program to be justified. If there is anything that is easily rationalized, it is the use of the government's or someone else's money for one's personal benefit. Rich, middle-income, and poverty-stricken persons alike can easily think of reasons to justify this. Economists have an old proverb: "The marginal utility value of someone else's dollar is zero." In other words, it doesn't cost *us* anything to spend *your* money.

THE POVERTY ISSUE

One of the greatest wastes of taxpayers' money has come through the antipoverty program under the provision of the Economic Opportunity Act of 1964 and subsequent amendments. This act had its start in a Democratic party search for votes. When John F.

Kennedy survived the 1960 election by the narrowest of margins, he gave some time to thinking about the problem the Democratic party faced. It had not won an absolute majority of the popular vote since 1944. (By 1973, it had been able to do so only one more time, in the off-beat 1964 election.) Under the circumstances, the President asked his brother Robert to look into the question of finding new groups of voters. After all, throughout the history of democracy in the United States and Western Europe, the pattern has been one of the party in power seeking to find new groups to enfranchise or entice to the polls, hoping that they would give their votes in return. Thus democracy began after the Glorious Revolution in 1689 in Great Britain, as an upper-middle-class arrangement with fairly stiff property requirements for eligibility to vote. Gradually there and in the United States the requirements were lowered. Finally in the United States in the Jacksonian movement, they were eliminated altogether. Later blacks, first legally and much later in fact, and by constitutional amendments, women and all persons over the age of eighteen were also given the vote.

The Kennedys did not undertake the then-chancy task of lowering the voting age; instead, they noted that the nation had about 20 percent of its population in the "poverty" category, most of these in urban slums and in Appalachia, but with pockets of poverty in many other places in the country, such as the Upper Peninsula of Michigan and much of the rural South. At about the same time, a book by Michael Harrington, a socialist, had a sharp impact upon liberal Democrats.[5] (Harrington, ironically, pointed out that the qualitative makeup of the poor of the 1960s was very different from that of the 1930s, but he appears completely to have missed the fact that this might well imply vastly different public policies. Essentially, he advocated what amounted to a warmed-over New Deal program even though a substantial proportion of the poor of the 1930s were temporarily in that condition and more than anxious to move out of it, while the poverty-stricken in the 1960s consisted largely of the chronically poor. He did not address himself to the problem of the culture of poverty, but rather seemed to assume that today's poor were willing, able, and attitudinally prepared to help themselves, given some federal aid, as was the case with most of the temporarily poor of the 1930s.)

Generating an Issue   The Kennedys knew that the urban and rural poor alike tended to be apolitical, not looking for government assistance to work their way out of poverty and not expecting to have much influence upon the benefit structure of the welfare programs. Yet they were an important potential vote and the Kennedys were sympathetic to their plight. (They have always shown some guilt feelings over their vast wealth and some of the techniques their father used to gain it. The West Virginia primary of 1960 seems to have had a great impact on JFK.)[6] The political problem, then, was to get the poor interested in voting. The way to do it, while at the same time gaining credit for humanitarianism, was through a series of federally-financed spending programs. President Kennedy did not live long enough to bring these plans to full adoption as public policy (and probably did not have the congressional clout to do so), but the ideas were readily accepted by the populistic Lyndon Johnson and in his inaugural message of 1964, he declared a "war on poverty." The war was, in fact, already underway even though, as we noted in Chapter 1, the leaders knew neither the causes nor the cures for poverty.

Exploiting the Issue   Under the circumstances, it would have to be expected that the antipoverty program would be highly inefficient, but it is doubtful if many members of Congress who voted for the plan had any idea of how inefficient it would be or that it would engender as much political controversy as it did. One of the most controversial of all the programs was the so-called Community Action Program. This consisted of almost an endless variety of projects that would be approved if it could be assumed that in some way they might somehow help the poor. The programs became controversial for a number of reasons. In some cases they served to subsidize urban street gangs who apparently accepted the money with no intention of using it for rehabilitative purposes. The most notorious situation of this kind occurred in the case of the Blackstone Nation on Chicago's South Side.[7]

Programs also became controversial because attempts were made to use the provision for the "maximum feasible participation" of the poor in the decision process, as was required by the Economic Opportunity Act.[8] The origin of this phrase and the way it got into the act have not been determined with certainty, but we can be quite sure that congressmen who voted for the act, if they were aware of the phrase at all, certainly did not think of it as being any more than a pious homily. Yet some ghetto leaders, and particularly those with radical leanings, decided that this provision offered a great opportunity. Ghetto citizens, unaccustomed to making decisions that extended beyond their own immediate short-term interests and notoriously ineffective in problem solving, could surely be manipulated toward the political ends of the leaders and large amounts of federal monies, appropriated by liberal and moderate congressmen, could thus be used by radicals for their own purposes, a sort of legalized rip-off.

A third, but by no means final, objection to the Community Action Program was that it established, in effect, a second local government for certain purposes in competition with the ordinary city government and independently financed from Washington. The leaders of the local antipoverty program were thus in direct competition with local government officials, the mayor and members of the council—a situation that could scarcely be greeted with enthusiasm by the latter. The objections to this kind of situation were promptly made known in Washington, and the mayors, particularly those of the large cities, began to lobby for changes in the law, and particularly to give them a veto power over the proposed projects. The powerful Richard J. Daley of Chicago, after the Blackstone Nation fiasco hit the front pages, made it clear that there would be no more antipoverty programs in Chicago unless they met with his approval. A series of amendments to the antipoverty acts in the late 1960s and early 1970s eroded the independent position of local "economic opportunity" leaders. But the challenge to the political power of local politicians was not the only thing to engender opposition to the efforts of the Office of Economic Opportunity. It quickly became obvious that most of the programs, indeed perhaps all of them, were shockingly ineffective and—once again—more helpful to the middle-class businessmen and bureaucrats than they were to the poor.

The "Model Cities" Fiasco   Space does not permit an extensive examination of all the antipoverty programs, but a few examples should suffice.[9] Another of the programs was the so-called Model Cities projects. These had originally been called Demonstration Cities, but when the "demonstration" became a favorite form of political protest by antiestablishmentarians of the late 1960s, it was decided that such a title might give the ordinary citizen, with his casual interest in political affairs, the wrong impression. The original intention, of course, was that these cities or portions of cities could show how effective remedial programs really could be—more accurately, how effective their supporters hoped they could be. Again, because nobody knew quite what was going on, a great deal of leeway was allowed in the kind of modeling that might be undertaken in the various communities receiving grants under the program. It is instructive to examine what has happened and is likely to happen under the Model Cities projects in one county.

Model Cities programs were begun in the Los Angeles area in 1971 and were planned to cover a five-year period at a cost of at least $180 million in federal funds.[10] At the end of the first year, however, knowledgeable persons were in agreement that the program had had, at most, a negligible impact upon those living in the five "model neighborhoods." A handful of people had been given some meaningful assistance. Thus about 200 persons had received advice and assistance at a one-stop immigration service designed to aid Mexican-Americans. Another 400 had received legal services at no expense to themselves in a second center. A considerable amount of the money had been spent on such nonproductive enterprises as cleaning up of alleys and vacant lots. This effort, of course, would have no lasting effect, for the alleys and lots would very soon be as filthy as ever unless changes were made in behavior patterns and attitudes of area residents toward responsibility for the appearance of the neighborhood. The programs, however, were not directed toward that more basic problem. They were lacking in imagination and any hope among the more knowledgeable, who freely predicted that it would not last the projected five years and that it would have no important effect upon the impoverished sections of the city. As the liberal, black Los Angeles Councilman (later Mayor) Thomas Bradley noted, "The tragedy is that very few people will know what these programs were all about" after they have been completed.[11]

Practically none of the projects was designed to have any permanent effect upon the condition of the poor or to assist them toward finding routes that would lead to the escape from poverty. One program established portable swimming pools in ghetto areas. Another called for the establishment of a Greater Watts Administrative Center. In this case, inexperienced and incompetent decision makers chose to spend $293,000, all but $15,000 of it in federal funds, to buy land and put a portable office on it for a program that was designed to last for only four more years.

During the first year, $175,000 was spent on a weed-abatement program to clean up 1,000 vacant lots at a cost of $175 per lot. This would make them weed-free—until the next rain. In another program, an effort was made to assist the county Animal Control Officers by providing funds that helped in the impoundment of some 5,000 stray animals and the picking up of about 2,600 carcasses. Within the period of one year, of course, at least an equal number of stray animals and carcasses would be found within the same area unless effective efforts were made to change the life-styles and habit patterns of persons in the areas that had originally resulted in the existence of this condition.

Incompetent Administration   In addition to the shortsightedness and unimaginativeness of the programs, there was the general problem of the incompetence of those who were called upon to administer it. Nearly one-third of the money spent went for administrative purposes—in other words, primarily for the benefit not of the poor, but of middle-class bureaucrats. The problem was made more difficult by the fact that federal guidelines called for all employees at salaries up to $12,000 a year to come from the model neighborhoods—areas which by their very nature did not contain the administrators or technicians who were qualified for the jobs. In many cases administrators could not get through a projected program or spend the intended amount of money within a given fiscal year. Thus one of the Los Angeles area programs took fourteen months to complete what had been projected for twelve. (It turns out that this was not at all bad—Cleveland took two years to get through what was projected for its first Model Cities year.)

The poor administrative record no doubt stems in part from efforts to take literally the "maximum feasible participation" rule and because it is politically expedient to appoint persons to high administrative positions that extend beyond their experience and, sometimes, competence. The first of these problems results in attempts to recruit administrative personnel, except at the highest levels, from within the ghetto. But there are few qualified administrative or technical personnel living there—almost all such persons leave at the earliest possible moment, leaving only the unskilled and untrained. The result is incompetence. The second problem results from the fact that it is usually politically necessary to name blacks or browns to the top positions in antipoverty agencies. Some of these people show considerable potential for their jobs, but are simply not yet experienced enough to handle them competently. The result can be chaos and lack of accomplishment.

In Los Angeles, the antipoverty program, which spends about $36 million a year, was established with the Economic and Youth Opportunities Agency (EYOA) as the overall coordinating apparatus. From the beginning, the EYOA was criticized for poor administrative performance. One year it spent several hundred thousand dollars beyond its budget and on programs that were not authorized by the U.S. Office of Economic Opportunity. In 1971, it was ninety-three days late in submitting its application for renewal of Operation Headstart, one of the few antipoverty programs that seems to be working at least a little bit. Later that year thirty-three Chicano employees went on strike, complaining that the EYOA was dominated administratively by blacks and that a fair share of the annual budget was not being spent in Chicano areas.

In 1972, the Office of Economic Opportunity decided to abolish the EYOA and establish the city and county governments as the coordinating agencies for the program. Members of the EYOA board protested, arguing that this was action taken not because of agency failure, but because the Nixon administration does not favor the antipoverty program and believes that it will be weakened if it does not have a coordinating agency independent of the city and county governments. These charges are basically valid. Without doubt, the Nixon administration plans eventually to abolish the independent apparatus of the antipoverty programs at the local level, and to eliminate the Office of Economic Opportunity itself and redistribute its powers to the conventional agencies, where they will tend to be swallowed up. Nevertheless, the record of incompetence by EYOA could not be denied.

As to the overall quality of the programs, they can perhaps best be summarized by a Los Angeles city official who commented: "You can spend thousands of dollars on programs like this and they are forgotten the next day."[12] It was not just in Los Angeles, of course, that the program appeared to be an expensive exercise in futility. In 1972, 145 cities and counties were involved in Model Cities programs, and in all of them reports to the Department of Housing and Urban Development seemed to indicate similar troubles. Many of the problems seemed to stem from a lack of any notion of how an urban-area improvement program could be undertaken and it seems likely that one of the reasons for this is that there are no ways by which federal funds, without the assistance of those who are to be helped, can do any permanent good.

Exercises in Futility   Some of the programs were based upon middle-class notions of what behavior the poor and supposedly disadvantaged *should* demonstrate. Others showed a lack of any understanding of scientific laws, laws that could not be repealed simply through wishful thinking. Thus, in 1971, Detroit reserved something over $150,000 of federal Model Cities funds for a training program designed to "rehabilitate" prostitutes from Detroit's inner city. The idea was to make available, at no cost to the student, job counseling services and funds for learning new skills. After twelve months, the output of the program was exactly zero. Not a single prostitute had been located who wished to be rehabilitated. The assumptions of the middle-class designers of the program no doubt were that women in this occupation were there involuntarily and out of desperation and that they would surely accept any opportunity to escape their condition. But the inner city prostitutes were more realistic economic persons than were their well-meaning would-be rescuers. They apparently recognized that participation in any rehabilitation program involved highly uncertain prospects for improvement in their economic condition and that participating in such a program involves very high opportunity costs, namely, the abandonment of an established and predictable source of income.

The social and economic background of prostitutes is well known. Typically, they are persons of less than average intelligence with low educational levels. Their prospects for advancement in any social system based upon competitive achievement are very poor. By way of the grapevine, they probably know that retraining programs have not enjoyed very much success either in retraining or in the placement of those who have completed the courses. The human being, faced with uncertainty and a threat to his or her economic condition, tends to take a highly conservative approach. "A bird in the hand is worth two in the bush" is a cliché, but is nevertheless true.

As to the tendency to ignore the realities of scientific knowledge, one example will suffice. One of the most revolting evils that infest slums is the brown rat. The rat is a scavenger and a carrier of diseases. It bites small children while they sleep and these bites can become dangerously infected. It is understandable therefore that those attempting to improve slum living conditions would seek to eradicate the rat. Various methods for killing the rats have been undertaken in different cities, none of them doing any lasting good. When the program ran out of money and was ended in Los Angeles, a government official announced that the rats had not been eliminated, but that the program had done some good. He claimed the rat population had been greatly reduced. Bureaucrats are constantly being called upon to defend their programs, so perhaps he was being less than candid. If he literally meant what he said, he surely lacked even a high school knowledge of biology. A typical female brown rat first becomes pregnant when she is six months of age and she averages about thirty-six pups a year. If even a few rats live in a particular neighborhood, they will quickly breed to the limits of the food supply, and the rats killed in an "eradication" program—no matter how many—will be completely replaced within a matter of a few months. The decision makers could have learned this from any biologist, had they bothered to ask. Perhaps they did not want to know, of course. A rat "eradication" program at least *seems* to be doing something about slum conditions.

Rats can be eliminated from an area only by cutting off their food supply. This means the strict enforcement of hygienic conditions, particularly relative to the storage and disposal of garbage. Such conditions can be achieved only through the close cooperation of the residents of the area. Unfortunately, many slum residents are unable or unwilling to accomplish this.

CLOSING STATEMENT

Democracy, as a modern system of government, was devised by the British upper-middle class around the time of the Glorious Revolution (1688–1689), which established the principle of Parliamentary supremacy. Gradually, the power to participate was broadened and democracy became and has remained primarily a vehicle for the economic and social interests of the middle classes. This can be shown by examining any set of governmental policies, but is most obvious in the case of the antipoverty program which has provided lasting benefits for the middle classes but few, if any, for the poor.

NOTES

1   The literature on housing policy is vast. For a start, see Marshall
    Kaplan et al., *The Model Cities Program,* U.S. Department of
    Housing and Urban Development, Washington, 1969, and its cita-
    tions.
2   Various Associated Press dispatches, 1972 and 1973.
3   *Los Angeles Times,* Apr. 23, 1972.
4   Associated Press dispatches, Summer 1967, and later.
5   Michael Harrington, *The Other America: Poverty in the United
    States,* Penguin Books, Inc., Baltimore, 1963.
6   Richard J. Whalen, *The Founding Father: The Story of Joseph P.
    Kennedy,* Signet Books, New York, 1964.
7   Tom Wolfe, *Radical Chic and Mau-Mauing the Flak Catchers,*
    Farrar, Straus & Giroux, New York, 1970.
8   See any of the many books on the antipoverty programs.
9   See David J. Rothman (ed.), *Poverty USA: The Historical Record,*
    Arno, New York, 1971. See also Winifred Bell, *Aid to Dependent
    Children,* Columbia University Press, New York, 1965.
10 *Los Angeles Times,* July 16, 1972.
11 *Ibid.,* July 17, 1972.
12 *Ibid.,* July 18, 1972.

Chapter 12

The Unheavenly
Standard Metropolitan
Statistical Area

For most of the last fifty years, the United States has been a metropolitan, industrial nation with problems to fit this situation. These problems received a great deal of publicity in the 1960s and 1970s and are commonly lumped together under the somewhat hysterical term "the urban crisis." The fact that the city and its environs are far from perfect and, being the products of man, will surely not attain perfection, inspired Edward Banfield to write a highly controversial book about the subject, *The Unheavenly City*.[1] The most unimaginative bureaucrats of the Bureau of the Census call the regions where most Americans live, Standard Metropolitan Statistical Areas (SMSAs). It is in relation to those who live within them that most American domestic policy is developed.

According to the census of 1970, 65 percent of the American population lives within the SMSAs. Here live most of the rich and the poor, the able and the hapless, the white and the nonwhite. The SMSAs are rather arbitrarily defined, for the most part using the boundaries of contiguously urbanized counties, but even they do not describe fully the boundaries of our unheavenly metropolises. Empty beer cans and blackened acreage in the San

Bernardino National Forest are adequate testimony to the fact
that this is one of the recreational playgrounds of the Los Angeles
megalopolis. Polluted Lake Tahoe testifies that it serves the
people of the San Francisco Bay area and dozens of other
metropolises. The bucolic Pocono Mountains of Pennsylvania are
overrun by human beings every summer and their natural beauty
scarred by the residents of dozens of Eastern cities. Even the
great roadless natural preserve northeast of Duluth, Minnesota,
is, to hunters, fishermen, canoeists, and campers, a part of the
metropolitan areas of numerous Midwestern cities. And into all
of these recreation areas penetrates the merciless banality of
commercial television. The finest and the ugliest of modern
"civilization" is to be found in every nook and cranny of
America: from San Francisco to New York, from the deserts of
southern California to the rocky coast of Maine, from the great
pine forests of Washington to the endangered Everglades of
Florida. Affluence, mobility, and a seemingly endless questing of
the American people have made the unheavenly metropolis
ubiquitous. Even the commercial farmer is now more a middle-
class businessman than a quaint and naïve rustic.

Urban-Rural Proportions of United States Population, 1800 to 2000.

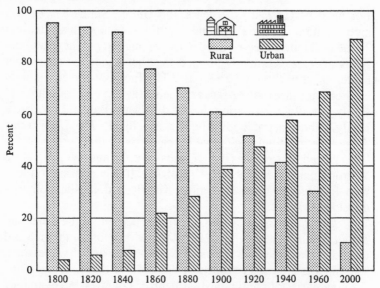

Figure 12-1   The American trend has been toward an urban nation.
(*Source: U.S. Bureau of the Census, U.S. Department of Commerce.*)

THE POLLUTION SOLUTION

One of the most dramatic developments in the late 1960s and early 1970s was the emergence of widespread publicity and even some public concern about the pollution of the land, water, and air of the nation and the area surrounding it. Interest in the protection and improvement of the environment became a major topic of conversation on college campuses and among various do-gooder groups. Ecology became a sacred, if often misused, word.

The concern seemed to have resulted from a number of factors. One was that pollution was becoming increasingly obvious to the casual observer. In some cases, as in the underground disposal of used crankcase oil, the damage done was not obvious. But in a great many other cases, it was. People became increasingly aware of litter along highways and in recreational areas. The increasing pollution of streams required more effective treatment of drinking water and taxpayers became more aware of the additional cost being assessed against them. Smog produced visual reminders of the huge amount of refuse that is dumped into the air each day. And there were many other kinds of warnings to the eye and the ear.

It was evident that part of the problem was being created by increases in the population. Biologists began to suggest that the human animal, like other animals, might well breed to the limits of the food supply with mass starvation in the most affected areas of the world and a deterioration of the environment even in the most fortunate areas. As a result, demands came to be made not only for a halt to population increase, but even for a mass cutback in the national population, an approach that was utterly alien to the traditional American belief that expansion is progress and that growth of any kind is good. In addition to this, college administrators and newspaper editors encouraged concern for the environment among middle-class young people as a constructive alternative to the riots, demonstrations, and disruptions caused by student activists in the late 1960s.

Whose Problem Is Pollution? You Cannot Scare Me

As usual, the actual extent of the damage to the environment and the threat in the future to the health and safety of Americans remained highly uncertain. What the future held, in the estimation of many more-or-less experts seemed to depend in large measure upon assumptions. Biologists, chemists, and physicists made various statements about the magnitude of the problem, but a credibility gap developed when it seemed as if for every doomsayer there was another person in the same field who disagreed with the conclusions.

Some of the forecasts were simply frightening, many of the proposed "solutions" were not believable. The biologist Paul Ehrlich thought that it would all be over with for mankind even before the doom year of 1984—by 1979, to be exact.[2] By then, he thought, we would run out of oxygen as a result of the pollution of the world's oceans.[3] A study by the Environmental Quality Laboratory of the California Institute of Technology recommended six policies that it believed could reduce air pollution in the Los Angeles area by 80 percent in 1975.[4] These included the conversion of commercial vehicles to natural or propane gas, the mandatory use and inspection of exhaust emission devices, compulsory reduction of the amount of driving by 20 percent, the cutting in half of industrial emissions, and a system by which industries would be required to shut down and vehicles would be banned from freeways under certain serious smog conditions. But the study seems to have gone largely unnoticed by both the general public and governmental decision makers. There was a good deal of doubt whether such stringent policies could be made politically acceptable within the foreseeable future and whether they would be effective, even if adopted.

Some persons are concerned about the threat to the environment, not just as an aesthetic matter, but as a threat to human life itself. Thus George Wald, a Nobel laureate, thinks that civilization may come to an end sometime between 1984 and the end of the century.[5] But scare tactics, so far at least, are not having much of an effect. For one thing, the superficial evidence easily available to the typical citizen—who thinks that ecology is a synonym for clean air and water—does not appear to be particularly frightening. For another, some people reading the latest prediction of doomsday will conclude that if that is what tomorrow brings, we might as well eat, drink, smoke, and make merry today. In addition, research indicates that an article that creates a strong sense of fear is easily counteracted by the placating words of counterpropaganda.[6] Perhaps above all, one wonders how valid predictions are and how accurate their assumptions. If the "experts" are correct, there is little hope for mankind. There is the widespread feeling that the individual, and very possibly any group of people, simply cannot do what is required to be effective against pollution.[7] There is some reason to think that public attitudes on the matter have changed somewhat toward governmental control of the environment, but the prospects for making much of an impact on major problems in the near future are poor. There are just too many reasons for information campaigns to fail.[8]

George Should Do Something about It The problem of controlling pollution is made even more complicated by what often happens when a person does come to recognize the reality of the problem and wishes to have something done about it. First he will suggest that someone else should do something about it. It is easy and popular to blame the automobile manufacturers or the producers of electricity and other industrial polluters. To be sure, they are somewhat to blame for they have over the years socialized much of the cost of production by using the atmosphere as a low-cost dumping area. But people use automobiles and electricity and the products produced by electrical power.

As in the case of highway deaths, we—not "they"—are to blame, and only we, acting collectively, can do much about the problem. The upper-middle-class lawyer or professor who makes a campus speech denouncing pollution probably owns at least two cars, one of which has an engine almost large enough to propel a Boeing 747 (and he probably himself arrived in town on a jet), his home is air-conditioned and supplied with electric blankets, electric mixers, power saws, and the like. He probably parks at least one car out-of-doors because space in the garage is used up by power lawn mowers, campers, snowmobiles, and other polluting devices. And of course the students listening to him also make use of these same items. Their notion of combating the problem is likely to be to haul newspapers, cans, and bottles to a recycling center. (The process of recycling also causes pollution, possibly almost as much as it eliminates, although detailed studies have not been completed.)

The frustrated citizen may conclude that government "should do something about it." Perhaps it should. Certainly it could. The problem with improving the environment is that the opportunity costs are enormously high. Just to start with, if we really wanted to become serious about the matter, it would be necessary to prohibit the manufacture and sale of gasoline-powered engines and to cut back severely on the consumption of electricity in our homes, by perhaps as much as two-thirds. In addition, if we were to stop industrial pollution of the air and water, the cost of doing so would no doubt for the most part be passed along to the consumer in higher prices. We would have to prohibit lower-income people from taking inexpensive vacations on public lands where they pollute the water sources of urban areas and burn valuable grass, shrubbery, and trees by careless use of matches. (Higher-income people do the same things, of course, but even under conditions of stringent environmental control, they could still afford to take comfortable vacations at private resorts and so forth.)

To put it bluntly, the restoration and maintenance of a high quality of environment, paradoxically, would mean a lower standard of living for everyone. The rich and members of the upper-middle classes could tolerate this with a fairly small amount of difficulty, but for all other citizens—and they consist of the large majority of voters—cost would cut deeply into their style of living. Some economists have predicted by 1977 at least 300 factories in the United States in 150 communities will have been shut down—at a cost of 125,000 jobs. Whose jobs? And what is the alternative for these workers and their families?[9] One simple illustration will indicate the complexity of the problem of opportunity costs. Until 1971, a chemical plant in Saltville, in the mountainous western part of Virginia, was dumping some 3,000 tons of waste salt into the river each day and the sun was dulled by blue smoke from the chimneys of the factory. Now the plant is closed. The river is coming to life again. The blue smoke is gone. So are 900 jobs.

Oliver Wendell Holmes once said that "Taxes buy civilization," and more recently some wag has suggested that he did not think we could afford this much civilization. Perhaps we cannot. Even the minor steps we are now proposing to take will have only a slight effect. Basically, a lower quality of environment than existed in a rural America is perhaps a necessary cost of what Americans have themselves chosen to define as their "civilization."

Some have suggested that if pollution controls result in widespread unemployment, the government should become the employer of last resort (presumably at nonpolluting jobs). But if this is the approach that is used, it will quite surely mean a lower standard of living both for those who are forced to that last resort and for the taxpayers who will have to support them.

EDUCATION: A DO-IT-YOURSELF PROJECT

There is no assumption about life-styles that is more characteristically American and more middle-class than the belief that economic, cultural, and social advancement requires a good education, usually a better education than that experienced by one's parents. This belief has led to a well-schooled nation, if not a well-educated one. It has also led to confusion and frustration. And in metropolitan America, the problem is more complex than ever.

We construct vast buildings in seeking to prove how important we believe education to be. We worry about the seeming inability of the poor to compete under what is pictured as a middle-class school system. At the national, state, and local levels, we spend about $40 billion each year on public education from kindergarten through the doctorate, more than for any other programs except welfare, which is first in cost, and national defense. And through much of our history we have assumed that if some part of the educational system does not seem to be doing its job properly, the answer is to spend still more on it. The values and goals of the middle classes dominate education as they do other activities within our democracy and their assumptions have been accepted by and incorporated into the values, standards, goals, and approved procedures of the teaching profession.

Middle-class assumptions include those that every child should be required to attend school until he reaches normal adolescent working age (in most states, sixteen) and that if he really wishes to achieve something outstanding in life, he should go on to college and very likely to graduate or professional school as well. But both of these assumptions have only limited validity and as a result both teachers and professors are pressured to go beyond their preferred role as guides for learning and become, in effect, baby-sitters.

It may well be questioned, and has been questioned, whether compulsory schooling makes any sense. Children with a negative attitude toward school and no interest in learning ("underachievers," educators call them) probably develop little other than frustration by being forced to remain in school.[10] One might well wonder whether it wouldn't be a more rational public policy to allow children to drop out at any time, provided that at the same time some kind of "lifelong learning" system is established to permit easy reentry for those who find that they have made a mistake. Every professor knows that a large portion of his students should not be in college. It is not that enrollees are necessarily stupid, but rather that they lack interest in learning, have no respect for intellectual processes, and have no goals that would require a college education. It seems likely that in many an upper-middle-class family, the one and only thing that the parents ever insist upon is that their children go to college. In the 1970s, many college enrollees were dropping out after a year or two in order to try some other life-style experimentally, with the notion of deciding later whether they really want college degrees. This is probably a healthy development, even though it is unnerving to public college and university administrators, who equate warm bodies with budget dollars.

The Myth of the Teaching Role   Despite   the   problem caused by the need to perform a dual role, dealing alike with the eager learner and the unwilling captive, schools manage to do a good job overall. Despite the great amount of criticism constantly aimed at them by self-appointed experts, the high schools, for example, are without question doing a vastly better job of educating people than they did a generation ago. The criticism probably stems in considerable part from a false assumption made by many people and especially by would-be reformers. This assumption is that the quality of education and hence the amount that the students learn depend upon the quality of the school, its teachers, and equipment. (And by simple-minded, but not illogical extension, the assumption is made that the quality will depend also upon the amount of money spent.) But these assumptions are not correct.

Recent research indicates that the amount of money spent by a school district, the quality of the teachers (however that may be measured), the elaborateness of school equipment, or teaching techniques used all have very little to do with how much a student learns.[11] The incorrect, unarticulated assumption seems to have been that a person's brain is an empty vessel that can be filled with a small or large amount of information, depending upon the teaching techniques used. The truth, however, is that one can lead a person toward knowledge, but he cannot make him learn. The person has to decide for himself that he wishes to learn. And failure in school is not related to teachers' attitudes or what they do, but rather is learned at a very early age, perhaps three or four years, and not in the school, but in the home and from one's peer group.[12]

Yet, in education as in many other areas of public policy, the methods used depend not upon data, but upon the assumptions that are made. Recent research, for example, has disproved one of the most sacred assumptions of elementary school teachers, an assumption firmly backed by middle-class parents: Students learn more in small classes than they do in large classes. This is simply not so. There is no significant difference in the test scores when one measures for difference in class size.[13] The assumption to the contrary probably stems from a firm belief that size *ought* to make a difference, combined with the fact that, very simply, teachers prefer small classes to large classes, for they are easier to manage. In similar fashion, most college professors piously deplore the lecture system (they know that most of their students will applaud this outlook) and they argue that students learn more in small groups with informal contact with the instructor. In point of fact, however, there is no evidence to support these assumptions, and, indeed, they are probably not so. What a college student learns depends upon what *he* or *she* does, not what the professor does. No matter how arrogantly the college professor may insist that he is the key to learning, such is not the case. Irrespective of teaching techniques, all that a university or college campus is, ultimately, is a place where knowledge can be made potentially available for those who wish to use it.

Putting Aside Conventional Wisdom   Here are some points about American public education that are often overlooked by the ordinary citizen and by the newspaper editor:

1. Probably the most important reason for the erosion of authority in America is to be found in the educational system. Our schools teach students to be skeptical of authority, and a general questioning of all values that are accepted on faith in the absence of empirical evidence. This questioning of authority, of course, applies in all instances, resulting in the undermining of an orderly system which has traditionally been dominated by parents, employers, and governmental leaders.

2. In recent years, a great deal of attention has been paid to the regretfully inadequate records of schools in serving the poor. Various inaccurate and incorrect explanations have been offered, including the notion that the teachers of poor students expect them to have poor performance records and that the schools in impoverished areas are poorly financed. Neither of these accusations appears to be correct, however. The fact is that the children of the poor, with the exception of a small percentage of students, have historically tended to have bad performance records in school. We do not know why this is the case, but the best guess is that it stems from parental attitudes toward the value and importance of education.[14]

3. Special programs designed to aid the "slow" (more accurately, unwilling) learner do not work. There is ample evidence that this is so. In one case, for example, a study of a special learning project in the Ocean Hill–Brownsville area of New York found that students who were two years behind the average of children of their own age in 1967 were three years behind in 1971, despite expensive special programs designed to benefit them.[15] In other cases, money designed to aid the poor could not be evaluated as to its effectiveness because it did not even reach the poor.[16] Much of it was mismanaged and it was discovered in 1971 that thirty-seven states were violating rules established by the national government for aid to schools. Much of the money, amounting to more than $1 billion, apparently was being used for the supplementing of regular school programs. This is another example of the way in which governmental appropriations tend to be directed toward the needs of the middle class, but it seems likely that such expenditures, even if directed toward only those schools in poverty areas, would not change the pattern of performance. A federally funded study in 1972 concluded that apparently it is "how the money is spent rather than how much money is spent, that determines the benefits children derive from" such programs.[17]

4. Particular efforts have been made in recent years to politicize the public schools at all levels. This, of course, is to be expected in a public policy area that is so important to so many persons in the voting population. The New Left has particularly been interested in finding and influencing the thought of teachers at the elementary level (the most impressionistic age for students) as well as in the colleges, where the effort has been made to convert the educational system into one that propagandizes for the goals of the leftists and against the values supported by the Establishment. Quite in contrast to this has been the effort of some federal government agencies and particularly the Department of Health, Education, and Welfare, to establish quotas in the educational system for various minority persons. The conflict between the goals of offering opportunity and those of seeking the most qualified person for a particular job had not been resolved in the early 1970s.

5. The bussing of students from the area in which they live to another one where educational performance by conventional measuring methods is greater is probably based upon the assumption that schools in ghetto areas are of "lower quality" and manned by less qualified teachers. As we have indicated earlier, these assumptions, even if true, probably are irrelevant in relation to the problem. Students learn what they wish to learn.

The question of whether it is desirable to bus children in order to improve educational standards is much older than most people realize. As Thomas Jefferson noted, "It is better to tolerate the rare instance of the parent refusing to let his child be educated than to shock the common feelings and ideas by the forcible asportation [transportation] of the infant against the will of the father." Jefferson, probably more wisely than many of those leaders of following generations, opposed making education compulsory, for he viewed policy in this area as being another matter of individual liberty and choice.

6. In the early 1970s, an approach to providing the best possible education for the individual student in terms of what he was most interested in achieving seemed to be emerging in the so-called voucher system. This was a plan under which parents of school-age children would be provided with a voucher that would indicate the amount of money the parents could use from the tax revenues of their district toward the education of their children in any school in which they preferred to place them. The great advantage of this plan was that it recognized the reality of the fact that although most children in minority areas, irrespective of race or creed, would not perform effectively in school, the exceptional ones who wished to compete at a higher level and who would probably become successful leaders in society could move into a more highly motivated school system where they were likely to learn more and be prepared to enter schools of higher education at a level more appropriate to their abilities and motivation.

This type of approach continued to be unusual in the 1970s, and a violation of the traditional American assumption of equality of ability and motivation, but it was more likely to be found politically acceptable than was the case with many proposed innovations in public policy. This was probably the case because large numbers of persons in the middle classes believed in the pattern of competition for grades and honors that had traditionally existed in the public schools and also because the voucher system would probably have little effect upon most members of the middle classes who would typically send their children to neighborhood schools. (Not because of political power, but only incidentally, the plan might also be acceptable to most lower-class persons simply because they would give no thought to sending their children to other than neighborhood schools.)

Colleges Besieged—and Rightly So? Higher education has come under particular criticism in recent years, probably both because the 1960s represented the peak postwar enrollment and hence the highest expenditures for higher education and also because of student riots and various other manifestations of "unrest." These in turn stemmed both from behavior resulting from guilt feelings over being deferred from the armed forces while the country was at war and also from the dissatisfactions of large numbers of students who had no real intellectual interests. There were probably other reasons, too, including the unwillingness of most faculty members to attempt to accommodate to the new type of student.

Colleges and universities are primarily responsible for three areas: (1) the transmittal of existing knowledge and culture; (2) the expansion of the boundaries of human knowledge; and (3) criticism of society. It is the third of these roles, together with the student demonstrations of the 1960s, that caused universities and their professors and students to fall into public disfavor. University faculty have often, in recent years, been accused of being all too willing to say what they think to be wrong with the economy, the social system, race relations, foreign policy, or whatever, while at the same time vigorously resisting efforts by legislators, citizens groups, or anyone else from evaluating them. Of course, this is characteristic of all professions (newspaper editiors, for example, do the same thing and piously stand on the First Amendment when criticism is attempted), but perhaps professors—highly conservative in their academic, if not always their political, orientation—have been even more hidebound than most.

Two examples will suffice. After the Soviet Union in 1957 put a space vehicle into orbit ahead of the United States, both national and state governments began to place huge amounts of additional money into the higher education system. The primary goal, of course, was to develop better programs and more scientists in physics, engineering, and other areas that would allow us to catch up with the Russians and beat them to the moon, as we successfully did. Because faculty members have always effectively applied pressure to prevent very much discrepancy in pay from one department to another, professors in fields that are essential to the national welfare, say, biology and economics today, are little better paid than are persons in less central areas, say, art history and—would you believe?—political science. The result was that in order to win the space race it was also thought necessary to provide additional equipment and, in particular, better salaries in all academic fields.

When the sense of urgency passed (and professors had become accustomed to their new affluence), legislators and others began to call for greater efficiency in the higher education system. In particular, educational budgets became very tight during the recession of the late 1960s and early 1970s, and demands were made for increasing the productivity of higher education in return for salary increases. These demands were strenuously resisted. Many faculty members argued (and probably many actually believed) that productivity could not be increased without lowering academic standards. Businessmen, who have always expected increases in productivity in return for increased salaries and wages, found this very hard to believe. But the problem is not unique in education. It exists wherever it is very difficult or impossible to measure productivity in such simple and convenient terms as profits and earnings per manhour. As a result of the efforts of powerful trade unions, for example, the costs of operating New York City have increased enormously since 1960 while the quality of service rendered has actually declined by virtually any standard of measurement. The same thing is happening in the nation's secondary and elementary schools as the teachers organize and strike, or threaten to do so.

Another arena in which university and college faculties receive a good deal of criticism is that relative to permanent tenure, that is, the right of a faculty member to a lifetime job after he reaches a certain level (frequently promotion to associate professor), except only for flagrant violation of what is expected of him, such as proof of moral turpitude or failure to perform one's duties. In practice, however, a professor on tenure can rarely be removed from his job. When the basic permanent tenure rules were worked out in the 1920s by a committee of the American Association of University Professors, the idea was to protect the *institution* from ignorant legislators and governors who did not understand the purposes of higher education. Through time, however, the original notion of protecting centers of learning from ignoramuses has been lost and today tenure is almost exclusively thought of as protecting the *individual*.

The large majority of experienced professors would no doubt agree that tenure has, in practice, served vastly more to keep incompetent faculty members in their jobs than it has to protect the institution from assaults upon its integrity or efforts to subvert its purposes. Yet a large number of faculty members, perhaps the great majority, would argue for preserving the tenure system "just in case." Still, there is no or certainly very little doubt but that the quality of faculties would increase if the system of permanent tenure were abandoned and bad appointment mistakes could be corrected. In the 1970s, with a decline in college attendance, it is possible that young assistant professors, fearful that no jobs will be available for them because of the tenure rule and lack of new positions, will begin to demand changes in the practice, or its elimination. If they do, they will gain a good deal of support from legislators, but also they will encourage the tenured faculty to organize and resist these efforts. Many alternatives to tenure exist: a variant of the military system, with mandatory retirement at partial pay if satisfactory progress is not continuous, or a five-year contract system, for example.

Particular efforts have been made in recent years to politicize the universities more than ever. The New Left, in particular, has sought to convert the universities into launching pads for drastic social reform or, if necessary, revolution. Its members have attempted to justify this by use of the half-truths that knowledge and social action cannot be separated from one another and that learning in the social sciences cannot be neutral. Attacks upon the fundamental functions of a college or university, listed above, have come not only from radicals however. Even such a basically conservative source as the Nixon administration has placed pressure upon institutions of higher education that could lead to "reverse discrimination," that is, to establish some kind of a quota system for the hiring of minority persons in order to qualify for all-important federal aid, particularly to hire blacks, browns, and women. Although the administration denied any such intent, this approach, known euphemistically as the "affirmative action" program, could be used in attempts to pressure universities to violate an ancient rule, that is, to hire only the apparently best-qualified person for any position that is open.

The vast majority of faculty members, no doubt, favor opening up routes to university faculty positions for persons of minorities (and, perhaps somewhat less enthusiastically, for more women on faculties), but most professors are still opposed to any hiring of ill-prepared or lesser-ability persons who would lower faculty quality merely for the sake of achieving a different ethnic or sexual balance. The issue promised to become a major one of the 1970s and, indeed, in 1972 the Anti-Defamation League of B'nai B'rith began a vigorous protest against the quota system. To be sure, the organization was concerned primarily about the interests of Jews, who represent a disproportionate percentage of outstanding faculty members. But their concern was also that of faculty members who wish to preserve institutions of higher learning as places where ability is the only criterion for hiring.

Perhaps the greatest issue for the 1970s in elementary and secondary education will be that of bussing students in order to desegregate schools. The idea of bussing was presented in the early 1960s, when liberal reformers assumed that integration was the only practical way to find an end to the deprivations experienced by black and brown Americans. This assumption was never accepted by many whites and has since been rejected by a large number of blacks. By the early 1970s, it was clear that a large majority of both whites and blacks were opposed to bussing and for a number of reasons. The approach was contrary to the idea of the neighborhood school and the potential for local domination of it, an idea that was supported by large numbers of both blacks and whites. Bussing also involved young children in the dangers of highway travel, particularly a threat in bad weather. The time factor was also important, for bussing often required parents and children to get up earlier in the morning than they otherwise would and it involved the dreary business of waiting for a bus on a strange and often unprotected corner. In the meanwhile, the benefits to be gained from bussing remained unclear. Quite obviously, it did not make much of a difference on matters of social interaction and it was not at all clear that black ghetto children being bussed into "better" schools were learning more as a result of the extra effort.

Today, the assumption that education should be compulsory until about the age of sixteen is so nearly universal among Americans—even those who complain the most vigorously about skyrocketing school taxes—that it may be a long time before a cool-headed reexamination of the assumption is made. As for bussing, it would undoubtedly be worth the cost, inconvenience, and risk if it would result in improved race relations and a better education for the children of the poor. However, at the present time, there is no reason to believe that it is, in fact, accomplishing either of these goals.

PUBLIC WELFARE

In the early 1970s, around 14 million Americans were dependent for survival upon the public welfare system. This represented an increase of more than 70 percent in a five-year period. Nearly 7 percent of the national population had become unable to support itself for one reason or another and therefore had to live off of the earnings of other Americans. The total cost of welfare in 1972 was about $15 billion annually, half of which was paid by the federal government and most of the rest by the states, with some paid by various local governments. The actual proportion on welfare differed to some extent from one part of the country to another and depended somewhat upon local attitudes toward the proper use of the welfare rolls and to a lesser extent upon local economic conditions. Thus, in the core cities of metropolitan areas, one in five was on welfare in Boston in 1971, one in seven in Baltimore, New York, St. Louis, and Washington. In contrast, only one in twenty-three was on welfare in Dallas, one in thirteen in Cleveland, one in twenty-five in Miami, and one in fourteen in Pittsburgh. In most cases, an even greater proportion was below the Department of Labor's definition of poverty. Thus in New York, one in five was officially rated as being poor.

Society's Rejects   The issues and high costs of welfare in the 1970s stem from a number of factors. One is the dramatic pattern of the movement of people off of the land in rural areas into cities hoping for something better in another environment but having no skills that could help them to move upward economically. Another is the declining need for unskilled labor in today's industrial system, one that is based increasingly upon the use of the computer and complex machines. In addition, persons with the lowest skills have had the highest birthrates in the years after World War II and these have been the same persons who have had the greatest increase in life expectancy. The result has been an enlarging number and an increasingly discontented collection of poor people with no apparent prospects for improving their situation.

The American public welfare system is based primarily upon the Elizabethan Poor Law of 1601, the principles of which were adopted in colonial America. The basic approach taken in the days of the first Elizabeth in England remained unchanged in the American states until it became clear that this approach was inappropriate during the Great Depression, when millions of persons who ordinarily would not need public assistance were forced to accept public welfare for a period of several years. The Social Security Act of 1935 represented the first major modification of the old welfare system. From that time on public welfare has largely replaced the private assistance through churches and upper-middle-class do-gooder organizations that prevailed before the Depression years. The act of 1935 left ordinary welfare payments and such things as the supervision of child-care agencies and of adoption services to state and local governments. It established, however, along with subsequent amendments, a number of categories of persons who were thought to deserve special aid without the full stigma of "welfare," even though that was in fact what was involved, since none of these programs involved any notion of prepayment insurance, as is the case with "social security" (old age and survivors' insurance) itself.

The federal government furnishes today grants-in-aid to the state for old-age assistance, aid to the blind, aid to dependent children (now, somewhat euphemistically, called "aid to families with dependent children"), aid to the permanently and totally disabled (since 1950), aid for hospital care for anyone eligible under these four programs (since 1956), and medical aid for the aged (since 1966).

By far the largest and most controversial of the so-called categorical aids is that for dependent children. The act of 1935, however, was based upon most unusual conditions and certainly far different from those of the 1970s. A large proportion of those on welfare were then middle-class or upper-working-class persons unaccustomed to being dependent upon the government or anyone else and eager to take any available job. In the 1970s, most welfare recipients were lower-class persons, relatively few of whom are on welfare because they are unwilling to work, as is still the popular image and one that is being reinforced because of the burgeoning welfare rolls and the huge increases in costs for welfare in recent years.

Actually welfare clients are a motley group: persons suffering from an extensive period of bad luck; alcoholics and those hopelessly ensnared drug addicts; persons physically or psychologically unable to work; hippies and mentally retarded persons not requiring institutionalization; persons who marry young, have several children, but still have low seniority in their factory jobs and are thus often laid off; above all others, women with young children who have been divorced or abandoned by the fathers of the children; and many other types. In other words, most of the people on welfare are not realistically members of the working force because they are children, aged, or are physically or mentally disabled. Thus, in California in 1970 about 8.5 percent of the population was on welfare, but only about 0.9 percent were persons who ought to be in the labor force. To be sure, this represented about 195,000 people, but it is likely that a small minority of them were *voluntarily* unemployed.[18] The point is this: The problem is vastly more complicated than persons who describe the poor as "lazy" would like to believe. The chances are that the solution, if there is one, is also more complicated than many people would like to believe. It is quite clear, however, that the most important immediate step would be to reduce drastically the number of children being produced by persons who are economically nonproductive. But to accomplish this will require an enormous amount of education within the segment of the population that is most resistant to being educated. (It is probably not irrelevant to note that when the United States Postal Service issued an 8-cent stamp in 1972 promoting family planning, it was described as "the slowest-moving commemorative we've ever had.")

The Poor Are People—So Why Be Sentimental?   The realities about the poor on welfare are often misunderstood. Here are a few important points that help to clarify the situation:

1. Although some 25 million Americans fall below the official line defining poverty, this makes up only about 13 percent of the total population. What is handed out to the poor therefore depends upon what the majority of Americans are willing to give them, for they are not sufficient in numbers to win elections. Furthermore, the vast majority of Americans who are not poor cannot be expected to be very sympathetic to those on welfare. Indeed, the vast majority of Americans probably believe that welfare programs are unduly generous and do nothing toward moving persons on welfare toward becoming self-sufficient.

2. Unlike the poor of two or more generations ago, when the impoverished had no access to mass communications media (they did not even read newspapers), television today appears to

be increasing the level of discontent among the poor. This is so because television tends to picture situations in middle-class homes and to pitch its commercial messages toward the relatively affluent. The aspirations of the poor therefore, and unlike in times past, center on the achievement of middle-class consumption goods. This, together with the agitation of self-appointed leaders for the poor, has increased the level of dissatisfaction without contributing toward an improvement in the conditions of the poor.

3. Welfare matters are common as issues in political campaigns and the welfare budget is often highly sensitive to the election schedule. In New York City, welfare expenditures increased by 400 percent during the first six years after Mayor John V. Lindsay took office (1966). In 1971, they amounted to $1.2 billion. When Lindsay's term began, recipients were being added to the welfare rolls at the rate of about 2,700 each month. Admissions rose rapidly, reaching a peak of 17,700 in early 1968. Then they shrank again in 1969, when the mayor was up for reelection, and were down to only 6,300 monthly just before election. Six months after he was reinaugurated, the figure was up to 15,800 again. It seems likely that he was allowing decisions about welfare policy to be established by professional social workers between elections, but was able during the reelection campaign to point with pride to his reduction in the huge welfare expenditures.

4. Perhaps for the first time in history, in recent years some welfare workers have encouraged people to refuse work and remain on public assistance. This takes place in part because under some circumstances a family can make more from welfare payments than if the head of the family is employed full time. This is especially the case when the mother is the head of the family and the father is away from home. But probably nothing could be more demoralizing or less likely to offer any hope for improvement to welfare parents or their children than encouraging them to accept handouts rather than jobs, for the effect of this is to say that they can achieve more by doing nothing than by attempting to become socially productive. There is little more frustrating than to imply that about another human being.

5. Almost every knowledgeable person agrees that the traditional welfare program with the major modifications made under the conditions of the Great Depression are no longer appropriate for today. Various proposals have been made to modify the system.[19] Many of these call for making a distinction between persons who are able to make decisions for themselves, and those who are incompetent (the senile, the alcoholic, the serious drug addict, the very young, the mentally retarded). The former would be given some kind of guaranteed annual wage which they could spend as they preferred, that is, they would be allowed to make decisions for themselves and presumably would no longer be intimidated by the matriarchal caseworker and would at the same time be encouraged to seek employment that would allow them to expand their budgets. Most plans also include some kind of method whereby an individual could move gradually from welfare to self-sustenance, that is, he or she would be able to accept a paying job without necessarily losing all welfare benefits.

The lack of incentive to move off of welfare because of the possibility of no additional gain in income or even a loss by accepting a job has long been one of the greatest weaknesses in the present welfare system. In 1971, President Nixon proposed to Congress a Family Assistance Plan that was devised by Daniel Patrick Moynihan. It called for more rigid work requirements, better incentives, and a job training program. It also proposed a guaranteed minimum income of about $1,600 for a family of four and called for supplemental benefits to families where the parent or parents were working but still fell within the poor category. The plan also had the effect of calling for the federal government to assume basic responsibility for direct welfare benefits, something it has never done except under emergency conditions during the Great Depression. The Nixon proposal got little encouragement in Congress and in 1973, the President did not call again for its adoption.

Many variations of this kind of a plan have been introduced by others. George McGovern, the 1972 Democratic Presidential candidate, first introduced into the Senate a proposal on behalf of the National Welfare Rights Organization which provided for a preposterously impractical plan calling for a guaranteed income of at least $5,500 for every family of four. Later, McGovern introduced his own plan which called for a guarantee of $1,000 for each person annually. When both of these plans were shown to be disastrously expensive for the middle class, McGovern retreated, but no one doubted that some kind of guaranteed annual income, with its imposed necessity for effective budgeting and an incentive system that will move all possible persons into the work force, was necessary.

PAYING THE PIPER

This is not the place to examine the federal budget in any detail. There is a good deal of information available that can provide a breakdown both on expenditures and on revenue sources. We can, however, pay some attention to the major characteristics of the American government fiscal pattern. We also need to recognize the large number of misconceptions that exist concerning revenue income and its uses for public purposes. In general, in a democracy, two basic budgetary rules apply. One holds that taxes should be imposed in such a manner that they produce the wanted revenue with the minimum amount of protest. The other says that funds should be expended in such a manner that everyone who is of any political importance at all receives some benefit but not all that he would like to have. In other words, it is much more important to give many people some portion of what they would like to receive than it is to give a relatively few people all that they want.

The federal government's budget is so complex that no brief volume could begin to explain how it works. State and local budgets, although smaller, are hardly less complex because it is difficult to distinguish between the expenditure outlays at one level from those at another and it is particularly difficult to make comparisons between the parts of the complex pattern of intergovernmental financing between the two levels of government. There are, fortunately, publications to assist both the laymen and the experts on the subject.[20]

Budgets: Something Intended for Everyone   Many misunderstandings and much folklore centers around the budgets of governments at all levels. The main points to be made, perhaps, are two. One is that budgets tend to be large because virtually every government program aids some group, or is intended to aid some group. Secondly, all governmental programs are extremely difficult to evaluate because profit-and-loss statements can rarely be generated by accountants. In the absence of firm data, assumptions, folklore, and wishful thinking tend to take their places. For example, many liberals seem to assume that increased governmental expenditures imply increased service levels for the needy. In fact, however, most of this money appears to be going to middle-class and upper-working-class persons in the form of higher wages and salaries, even though actual productivity per man-hour remains the same or is actually declining and this is especially the case where the governmental service is handled by union labor, as is increasingly the case.[21]

There is also the impression that most of the increases in the federal budget are for military spending. In fact, however, in the twenty years before 1972, this part of the budget increased by two-thirds, rising to $77 billion, a great deal of money, but considerably less than the rise of $85 billion that occurred during the same time for health, education, and welfare expenditures. In these fields, the increase amounted to 1,246 percent. Contrary to the impression held by many politically active persons in the 1970s, the largest governmental outlays were not in the area of military spending, but rather in the area of welfare and retirement benefits as broadly defined.

Of course, with a little practice anyone can lie with statistics, so that one could show that various additional costs should be added to the military budget, such as veterans' benefits, the Veterans' Hospital program, subsidies to defense-related industries, or anything that could be described as being residual costs from World Wars I and II as well as those of Korea and Vietnam, together with various expenditures designed to prevent World War III. At the same time, welfare could be narrowed by eliminating such things as grants to college students, and retirement plans that are at least partially financed by withholding income from the intended beneficiary. There is probably no way to determine which synthetic category receives the most in the way of governmental appropriation. The principal point is that they are complex expenditures and are used to benefit a broad spectrum of the American public, mainly persons of the middle classes and the wealthy.

Who Benefits?   The federal budget is indeed an enormous document, about the size of a Sears-Roebuck catalog in its unabridged version. And it involves sums that boggle the mind. It ·is impossible for most people to grasp how much is involved and this helps keep calls for economy in government meaningless to the average citizen.

For the fiscal year 1973, President Nixon—a man who had made economy in government at least one of his lesser campaign demands—called for a budget of about $246 billion. This was to be allocated in an extremely complex fashion to a huge number of different programs. Most immediately, of course, it was designed to pay the salaries of about 2.8 million government civilian workers as well as more than 2.3 million military personnel. While these people receive their salaries directly from the federal government, large numbers of other persons benefited less directly, but their numbers made their expenditures even more important. In the area of welfare, for example, more than 16.1 million persons received direct welfare aid of one kind or another, another 23.5 million were assisted by Medicaid, and some 13.2 million received food stamps at drastically reduced cost in comparison with the value of the materials received. Beyond this there were huge numbers of persons who benefited from various kinds of governmental insurance programs that were partially paid for by the individual or his employer, but were also subsidized in varying amounts by the government. These included people receiving old age and survivors' insurance (social security), some 28.3 million people, nearly 1 million persons on military retirement benefits, another million who had retired from railroad jobs, no less than 11.3 million receiving Medicare benefits, nearly 5 million persons who were veterans or their survivors who collected pensions or various kinds of compensation, more than 1.1 million Civil Service retirees on pension, as well as 875,000 veterans receiving hospital care in Veterans' Administration hospitals.

In addition to all this there were many educational programs that were to some degree designed to benefit the individuals in a subsidized manner and could hence be regarded as at least in part a welfare program. Some 3.3 million adults were subsidized in vocational education programs, more than 4 million college students (not counting veterans) received grants or low-interest loans, and more than 2 million veterans received various types of educational aid. And these represent, of course, only a scattering of the categories through which various persons were subsidized or benefited beyond what they would receive without governmental assistance. In addition, there were huge subsidies to the railroads, the airlines, defense industries, commercial farmers, education at all levels, and a host of industries that were viewed as being for one reason or another important to the national defense or welfare. There were also the programs designed for the benefit of the poor but, as we have noted, of principal importance in their impact upon the middle classes. Almost anyone with any important political clout was benefited to some degree, though by no means necessarily in proportion to his need, by some federal expenditure program.

Paying Those Endless Bills How is all this huge budget paid for? At the local level it has primarily been financed by general property taxes from colonial times, although it is increasingly today the product of grants-in-aid from state and national government. Starting in 1972, the federal government began supplying block grants to local governments through a "revenue sharing" plan. State governments also depended primarily upon the property tax until the Great Depression of the 1930s, when this no longer remained possible because so many persons were forced to default upon their tax bills. Subsequently most of the states turned toward the sales tax, leaving the property tax to their local units of government. Eventually, a majority and probably almost all of the states will levy both general sales and income taxes in order to finance their increasing levies.[22]

The national government depended upon revenues gained from tariffs upon imports throughout most of the history of the nation, but these became inadequate in the twentieth century, and shortly before World War I the national government transferred its primary reliance to the personal and corporate income taxes, taxes that are levied at a much higher rate than are similar taxes at the state level. In addition, and particularly since the time of the Great Depression in the 1930s, the federal government, which controls its own credits through control of the monetary system, has increasingly depended upon the financing of part of the annual expenditures through deliberate deficit financing, that is, by borrowing money from the public or from financial institutions and actually raising less revenue in a given year than is required to meet the expenditure budget. This has become so common, in fact, that in only a very few years since 1930 have federal revenues exceeded expenditures. Indeed, it is expected that any attempt to systematically pay off the national debt—and no such attempt has been made during this time—would have highly unfavorable effects upon the economy and would tend to plunge the nation into serious recession. Even such cautious and conservative Presidents as Eisenhower and Nixon have not fought for such policies. The problem has thus become one of *managing* rather than *retiring* the national debt and has become a complex economic matter that has long since ceased to be a matter of concern for most of the public.[23]

The public assumption has come to be that governments can somehow raise whatever amounts of money they may need, so the typical citizen does not worry very much about how this may be done, except in those cases where he can clearly determine the general impact of the tax upon himself, and this is particularly the case with the general property tax at the local level. (He could probably also make some approximation of this impact in regard to the income tax, except for the development of the practice of withholding the tax, in which case it becomes noticeable only when it is first imposed or changed, for the typical citizen counts only his "take-home" or net income, rather than his gross income.) Somewhat ironically, the least unpopular tax seems to be that of the sales tax, which affects the lower-income persons more than others because they spend a greater proportion of their income upon what is regarded as necessities, but because the tax is paid only a few cents at a time, the overall impact upon one's income is scarcely noticed. (In other words, in taxes as in almost everything else about governmental activities, one's assumptions and perceptions about reality tend to dominate one's attitudes towards what is acceptable public policy.)

Who Gets to Pay in the Future? In the 1970s, the issues on governmental finance seemed likely to center around two primary proposals. The one, which went into effect on an experimental basis in 1972, called for block grants from the national government to state and local governments for the general support of their programs and to reduce the need both for chronically large amounts of borrowing and for dependence upon the highly unpopular property tax. This plan, which came to be called "revenue sharing," was passed just before election time with the support of both the Democratic Congress and the Republican President, both anxious to impress upon taxpayers that they were seemingly concerned about their tax burdens. (Federal taxes have a much less obvious impact upon the average taxpayer than do those imposed by state and local governments.)

The 1972 act provided for $5.1 million to be distributed by a complex formula to state and local governments during the following fiscal year and the funds were gradually to increase over a five-year period, after which the effects of the plan and its desirability were to be reevaluated by Congress. Of course, by that time the funds will have become so basically a part of state and local revenues as to make it almost impossible for Congress to reduce them substantially. President Nixon favored the plan, arguing that it was a first step toward property tax relief and that it would return basic decision making to the local level where decisions could most knowledgeably be made—an assumption that was certainly highly doubtful given the parochial views of many local decision makers. Many others questioned the likely effectiveness of federal "revenue sharing" because of the doubtfulness of the capabilities of local officials in many areas and even many state officials to make use of the money in other than traditional "pork-barrel" ways.

On the federal level, the issue of the 1970s seemed to be one of whether additional revenues should be sought by a highly productive but very well hidden tax known as the turnover, or value-added, tax, one which would tax the amount of value added to a product each time title to it changed, a tax commonly used in Europe.

CLOSING STATEMENT

Governmental expenditures today are concentrated in metropolitan areas—which is where most of the people are. The money is spent, however, not on the basis of some overall plan by some (probably nonexistent) wise man, but rather on the basis of the amount of political power various groups possess, and their assumptions about what will ameliorate the problems they perceive. The American metropolitan area, even outside of its festering slums, is not particularly pleasing aesthetically. But then most cities throughout history have been ugly, except for only a few spectacular areas. (Ancient Athens was not typified by the magnificent Acropolis. Most Athenians lived in hovels at the foot of the hill.)

There is little planning that is effective, little coordination among the millions of activities that take place within a metropolitan area. Probably in an American-style democracy, effective planning is a forever elusive gossamer. We are condemned to "muddling through."[24] There is to be no heavenly utopia in our metropolises. Still, they house the highest standard of living and the greatest number of creature comforts the world has ever known. Few of their residents ask for more.

NOTES

1 Edward C. Banfield, *The Unheavenly City,* Little, Brown and Company, Boston, 1970.
2 Paul R. Ehrlich, *The Population Bomb,* Sierra Club, San Francisco, 1969.

3 Paul R. Ehrlich (ed.), *Man and the Ecosphere,* W. H. Freeman and Company, San Francisco, 1971.
4 *Los Angeles Times,* Oct. 13, 1972.
5 George Wald, *ibid.,* July 16, 1972.
6 *Los Angeles Times,* Sept. 7, 1972.
7 *Los Angeles Times,* Dec. 3, 1972.
8 Unpublished research by R. O. Loveridge.
9 *Los Angeles Times,* Nov. 22, 1972.
10 See Banfield, *op. cit.,* chap. 3.
11 Associated Press dispatches, Fall 1972.
12 See Chap. 1, note 8.
13 Associated Press dispatch, Nov. 21, 1972.
14 Race is not a significant factor. See *ibid.*
15 *Ibid.*
16 President's Special Message to Congress, February 1973.
17 Office of Education news release, Dec. 6, 1972.
18 Data from California Department of Human Resources Development, 1970.
19 See, among others, Daniel P. Moynihan, *The Politics of a Guaranteed Income,* Random House, Inc., New York, 1973; President's Commission on Income Maintenance Programs, *Poverty amid Plenty,* 1969.
20 See Charles R. Adrian and Charles Press, *American Political Process,* 2d ed., McGraw-Hill Book Company, New York, 1969, chap. 7.
21 *Ibid.,* chap. 19.
22 See Charles R. Adrian, *State and Local Governments,* 3d ed., McGraw-Hill Book Company, New York, 1972, chap. 17.
23 Adrian and Press, *op. cit.,* chap. 19.
24 Charles E. Lindblom, *The Intelligence of Democracy,* The Free Press, New York, 1965.

WRAP-UP

Camelot

Ask ev' - ry per - son if he's heard the sto - ry;—

—— And tell it strong and clear if he has not:

That once there was a fleet-ing wisp of glo - ry—

—— called Cam-e-lot. Don't let it be for-

got That once there was a spot For one brief shin-ing

mo-ment that was known As Cam - e - lot.

Chapter 13

We Have Met the Enemy
and They Is Us

By the time we start the last chapter, it is likely that the reader has
discovered (if he did not already know) what Walt Kelly's Pogo
had to learn the hard way, that man is not only the most
dangerous enemy of other animals, but also of himself. His own
frailties, his uncertainties, his shortsightedness, his insecurity,
and his fear of the unknown (and we have emphasized that there
is much that is unknown) tend to make him what he is.

In looking at political matters, we have not tried to make
him out as either a monster or a potentially perfectable creature.
As an animal who is the product of evolution, man is not much
better than he has to be in order to survive. At his worst, man is
more depraved and cruel than any other animal. (In their natural
habitat, most other animals do not kill unnecessarily or for the
thrill of it and they do not unnecessarily despoil the environment.) At his best, man seeks an ideal society in which all men
live in security and happiness. (Unfortunately, millions of people
have died in wars resulting from disputes as to whether such
allegedly ideal societies are, in fact, that.)

RECAPITULATION

In this short book, we have concentrated upon eight central points that we consider significant in shaping both the institutional processes through which government operates and the policies that result from the system. These are as follows:

1. Uncertainty   Man is not absolutely sure why he exists on the earth or, for that matter, why the earth or the universe itself exists. He invented the concept of "progress," that is, the notion that change can be desirable because it leads to some kind of improvement, but he cannot be certain as to just what "improvement" is or whether mankind is advancing toward something higher and better. Above all, man is uncertain as to the results a change in policy or adoption of a new policy would have.

We have noted that in such a case as the "poverty problem," he is unsure about the causes or cures for poverty, however that term may be defined. (Poverty itself is, of course, a cultural concept, and one that can never be eliminated because as the overall standard of living increases, the concept itself is raised to a higher level.) Often, a policy has totally unintended and sometimes disastrous results. The development of universal public education in the United States had the intended effect of making people wiser and happier; instead it made some people no wiser, but more discontented. Stringent laws and penalties against the sale or use of heroin, designed to price the goods out of the market by greatly restricting the supply, primarily had the result of forcing large numbers of users into a career of crime in order to raise funds to meet the price. Minimum wage laws, designed to improve the income of unskilled workers and to give them a "fair" return for their labors, had the effect of making it economically feasible to convert many activities from hard labor to the use of machines, thus providing fewer jobs and in many cases adding more persons to the poverty level and the humiliation of welfare.

2. Assumptions   In the face of uncertainty, public policy is made largely on the basis of what people assume to be reality. Some persons derive their assumptions from religious faiths, others turn to ideologies such as secular humanism, or hedonism, or place their faith in scientism or a political creed they believe to have unraveled the secret of history or of man's existence.

Data are used whenever they are available by one side or the other, but there are so many possible factors (variables) that can influence a decision or its outcome that what causes what can seldom be known in the social sciences.

There are, of course, a few exceptions to this. We have a great deal of engineering knowledge or applied science, for example, which can help us with many decisions, such as in bridge building or the planning of fire-resistant skyscrapers, but even in these cases we are generally talking in probability terms rather than anything precise. We say that a highway built according to certain specifications "should" last "about" a certain number of years. We know that certain kinds of drugs will tend (again an expression of probability) to control the *symptoms* of mental illnesses, but we know very little about their causes, or of cures for those in our mental hospitals. Much of the time we have even less information than this. We simply *assume* that action A will lead to result B. And because Americans tend to be both moralists and optimists, we often assume that if A *ought* to cause B, then it will do so. The argument that it may do no such thing and, indeed, may only worsen the situation, is frequently thought to come from some cranky old killjoy or worse. Thus conventional liberals have argued that the serious problems that result when black fathers desert their families could be overcome or at least reduced considerably by more generous welfare payments, allowing the family to live in dignity and comfort. However, when the sociologist Daniel Patrick Moynihan pointed out that it would likely do no such thing and, indeed, would probably increase the rate of desertion by lowering further the father's sense of essentiality and self-esteem, he was villified and even charged with being a "racist."[1]

Most of us believe what we *want* to belive. We make assumptions that are compatible with comforting beliefs and if alternative theories or even convincing data confront us, rather than reexamining our position, we find it easier and more satisfying to attack the theory or the data.

3. Opportunity Costs The economist, who specializes in the analysis of the allocation of scarce goods and services, understands that it is often necessary to give up one thing in order to gain another. He calls the choices involved "opportunity costs." In a world in which there are virtually no free goods, that is, those available to all at no cost, it is necessary to develop public policies that in some way or another determine how to allocate those goods and services for which there is not enough to go around to everyone. Every citizen intuitively recognizes the nature of opportunity costs, no doubt. The housewife recognizes that if the family vacation is extended by one week, she may have to give up a new coat for next fall. The student knows that if he goes all out for an A in Statistics, he may have to settle for a C in Medieval French Literature, simply because of the pressures of time.

But politicians rarely express programs in terms of opportunity costs. It is to their advantage to make it seem as if individuals can keep all that they have while at the same time gaining some other desired thing. The voters, in turn, tend to think the same way because they think, or at least hope, that someone else will have to pay the cost, or that through some mysterious rearrangement of the economic laws, no additional costs will be involved. Thus increases in social security benefits are often used as a political gesture toward the elderly (who certainly often need the additional income), but much less is made of the fact that such an increase reduces (however slightly) the standard of living of those currently employed and not eligible for benefit payments. The proposals for the cleaning up of polluted streams and lakes are almost universally greeted with enthusiasm, but there is little discussion of the fact that the net result will be a lowering of the standard of living through the building of expensive sewage or industrial-waste treatment plants (which will ordinarily have the effect of raising the cost of that manufacturing plant's product), or that it will have the effect of making recreation more expensive at a particularly high cost to lower-middle-class and working-class people (through reducing the available number of hunting areas and campsites in the watershed supplying a lake or stream). Because Americans have not been taught to associate taxes with governmental benefits, there is a tendency of both the politician and the hopeful beneficiary of government programs to ignore opportunity costs. Governmental goods and services are free goods, or at least someone else has to pay for them, is often the unrealistic hope.

Perhaps even more of an obstacle to effective public policy is a view that, oddly enough, seems to be more common among well-educated political activists than among typical citizens. It assumes that persons active in politics should be judged according to their good intentions. But such intentions are rarely the basis for historical evaluation. Social evils and political disasters often flow from noble motives and social good from self-serving positions. The only valid basis upon which to judge political acts, we conclude, is their results. This was the view of the Founding Fathers as expressed in *The Federalist.* It remains valid today. In more recent times, the political scientist Harold Lasswell has effectively explained why good intentions are not enough.[2] He has pointed out that personal motivation explains one's entrance into politics. The individual's private motive becomes displaced upon a public object—an office or policy—and this, in turn, is rationalized into being the "public interest." No matter how much the individual claims to be concerned for the "good of mankind," we are justified in remaining skeptical and judging only upon actual results (which are difficult enough to determine).

Yet another assumption (often unarticulated) made by those with an amateur's interest in politics is that, even if we should consider opportunity costs and the fact that intentions may not equal results, political policy decisions are made in isolation, having no effect upon other activities or decisions of the real world. In fact, however, almost any political decision or the policy that flows from it has a spillover effect upon other human activities. In relation to these, we have used the economist's term of "externalities" or "external costs." Whenever greater latitude of speech is given to those who prefer to express themselves in vulgarities or what used to be called "obscenities," innocent bystanders pay the (often unintended) costs in embarrassment or other discomforts. Whenever a known felon is released on some technical procedural point (often beyond the ability of the prosecutor to anticipate), law-abiding citizens are unknowingly placed in jeopardy regarding the criminal's next act.

4. Solutions It is a fond American belief, a part of our chronic optimism, that all problems have solutions. Mathematicians long ago learned that this is not true in their area of knowledge, but the political world is so complex that it is not known and probably cannot be known whether there is some possible approach that would actually help alleviate a particular social or economic condition. The likelihood is that for many culturally defined problems, there are no "solutions," at least under our system of government. For example, democracy, and particularly the highly decentralized form found in this country (as compared with the United Kingdom and the Scandinavian nations), does not lend itself to effective planning. In a decentralized decision system, planning tends to be made on the basis of economics rather than social imperatives. Similarly, if one way to minimize social tension would be to greatly redistribute the wealth, it probably cannot be done in American democracy because the dominant middle classes and the upper-working class are opposed to it. And it is probably impossible to help persons who are not willing or able to attempt to help themselves, whether this involves a portion of the American poor or persons in some of the world's poor nations.

Closely associated with the notion that all problems have solutions is the belief that a proposed policy *will* work because it *ought* to work. Americans have always been a moralizing people and whether we look at the ideas of Jefferson, the populism of the Jacksonians, the tendency of Woodrow Wilson to see all Presidential problems as moral issues, or the demands of the New Left for instant social reform, we see a tendency to equate political problems with moral problems. This, in turn, leads us back to the ideal of the inevitability of solutions. Obviously, if a political issue is also a moral problem, it *must* have a moral solution. To the colder, less romantic eye of the political scientist, however, social issues do not have "solutions"; rather they represent areas of dissatisfaction that must be controlled, managed, compromised, or otherwise placed within tolerable limits of pressure. But they rarely are literally "solved" in the sense that a final answer is found and the problem is forever done away with.

5. The Elite We have emphasized that every political system has an elite and that "the people" nowhere ever literally rule themselves. This is probably true even of the hunting party in the most primitive tribe, for in such circumstances natural leaders emerge who make the major decisions about when and how to go about the job of killing enough game for the group to live on.

We have emphasized that the American elite is not a monolithic whole that conspires to run the country purely on behalf of its own membership, but rather that it is a complex pattern of leadership with a great deal of competition within various components of the Establishment. Competition within the dominant elite leads to counterelites with anti-Establishment views. These, too, have to be taken into consideration in the governmental decision process. These may be would-be revolutionary leaders or radical reformers who wish to displace the prevailing elite. Hence we have the revolutionaries as a remnant of the disintegrated Students for a Democratic Society (SDS), who talk about "power to the people," but whose dream is to tell the people what they must do, in other words, to make themselves an elite to displace the existing one. And we have Ralph Nader with his followers, who would seemingly replace the current leaders with an elite consisting largely of young lawyers who would act not in their own interests, but on behalf of Nader's version of the "public interest."

The point we make is simple: All social systems are dominated by elites that make the principal decisions. Even in a "hippie" commune, there is a leadership elite. If there were not, the group would soon starve to death. The only serious question is whether the existing elite or the Establishment should rule and is deserving of its position of power, a question of ideology that has to be considered in light of the question of whether a better alternative is available. And it must be decided in the face of the enormous uncertainties that confront any nation during and after a revolution. Thus, for a good reason, elites are rarely displaced: Most people would rather accept the known in the present circumstances than risk the unknown under someone else's different set of rules.

6. Imperfect Man and Woman: Dissatisfaction and Competition There is always dissatisfaction and competition for scarce goods, services, and status symbols in every social system. This results, in part, from the fact that there are no final solutions to social and economic issues. Enough goods, services, and statuses are never available to go around. If the third of these were to approximate a solution by making everyone's status symbols equal—an almost inconceivable accomplishment, given the iron law of elite leadership—competition for goods and services and dissatisfactions about the distribution system would remain. The problem, then, is one of "who gets what, when, how."[3]

Governmental systems deal with the problem of who should be the most rewarded and who should receive lesser awards, as well as who should be punished and by how much. What all governmental systems, democratic or otherwise, seek to do is to channel competition within acceptable limits as determined by human nature and cultural factors. The objective is to achieve a reasonably acceptable level of domestic tranquility, but there is no known way of achieving perfect harmony, or even anything approximating it, at least in modern, complex society. Governments also seek to contain dissatisfactions within acceptable bounds. No way is known by which it would be possible to make all persons satisfied, whether this is done by offering the common people "bread and circuses" or by seeking to seduce them by promising "power to the people," or by any of thousands of techniques. The goal is an orderly society in which the rules of the game are reasonably well understood and the behavior of other human beings is reasonably predictable most of the time.

It is true that anthropologists have found some very primitive societies in which virtually no dissatisfactions are expressed and no competition, at least of the sort that we recognize, takes place.[4] But such circumstances exist only where political and economic structures are simple and where, so far as the individual member of the society knows, economic and social conditions are changeless, always having apparently been as they are today and presumably always to be the same forevermore. Above all, the Western idea that there is such a thing as "progress" has served to aid and abet dissatisfaction and to create competition within a social system.[5] Of course, competition, sometimes a fierce variety, also is to be found in some very primitive societies, even where the idea of "progress" or of change does not exist. And some students of ethology, the study of animal behavior, believe that the human animal is inherently aggressive, and therefore dissatisfied and competitive.[6] Even if the ethologists are wrong, as some scientists and most idealists believe, there can be no question but what in modern, complex, industrial societies such as that of the United States, there is no known way by which to do more than manage the levels of dissatisfaction and the patterns of competition.

7. An Imperfect System   We have emphasized, but scarcely need to develop further here, the fact that the American (and any other) political system is imperfect. One could scarcely expect anything else from imperfect human beings. We have therefore placed emphasis upon the fact that political systems of any kind do not move toward "utopia" (the Greek word for "no place"). We have emphasized that there are few, if any, "solutions" to human economic and social problems and that the decision process, particularly in a democracy, is a slow and inefficient one. This is so for many reasons, including the need for time for bargaining, the uncertainty of the effect of any new or basically revised program, the apparently necessary preoccupation of the individual with his own concerns, and a host of other factors.

Perhaps the ultimate test of political competence in a democracy such as ours is not one of sufficient idealism, but rather of the ability to tolerate ambiguity and uncertainty. In an imperfect system with imperfect information, one cannot become politically sophisticated unless, within a reasonable degree of comfort, he can accept and live with the notion that governmental policies may often seem to contradict one another. However, offsetting activities are designed to accommodate the interests and concerns of different groups. Thus few citizens are ever completely satisfied, and much of the time our leaders, *regardless of who they may be,* have at best only a hazy notion of what the consequences of their decisions may be. Indeed, often the system is simply moving along under the force of inertia and without anyone actually being "in charge." And when difficult problems arise that threaten the social order, the best that *any* political leader can seek to do is to cope with them—in the original meaning of that word, to strike out at them and seek to contain them.

8. A Bias for American Democracy   Finally, we have emphasized that this imperfect system of government, with all its weaknesses and all the inequities that are attributed to it by dissatisfied citizens, is for most people, most of the time, a system worth keeping when we take into consideration the opportunity costs, the uncertainties, and the risks that would have to be taken in order to establish some other and only hopefully better system of government. Winston Churchill suggested that democracy is "the worst system of government ever invented except for any other." We have argued not that it is the best system of government, but only that it is the least bad of those that are known and that, furthermore, some kind of government is absolutely essential to the existence of mankind.

Government has existed from the earliest times of preman, when our ancestors left the forest and became carnivores on the plains. Man, competing against other, more efficient carnivores, had to use his brain in order to overcome his muscular deficiencies. He formed the hunting party and the nomadic village. From that primeval moment, government and elite leadership existed. In the score of millennia that have followed, he, like other animals, has adjusted to his environment.

With the beginnings of the industrial revolution in the late seventeenth century, man began moving toward the circumstances under which he has had to exist in modern times. That is, the city became his most common dwelling place and, with the expansion of the middle class in an industrial and commercial society, he developed democracy as a means by which a government could accommodate to the broadly dispersed power of an industrial system in contrast to the much more tightly held system of power under the landed aristocracy of feudal times. And so, being transported to America, the British system of democracy that emerged after the Glorious Revolution of 1688–1689 gradually became the American system of democracy. Institutions, like animals, have a way of developing to a level of efficiency that is good enough to get by on, but they tend not to evolve toward perfection or utopia. That has seemingly been the pattern of American democracy. It is what we have to live with. Whether it is good enough over the long run is another question. In the past, no government has lasted for more than a handful of centuries. Ours is, together with those of England, Switzerland, and Iceland, among the oldest in existence, so it appears to have been satisfactory to many individuals through a considerable period of time. Governmental systems, like plants and animals, cannot always evolve fast enough to adjust to their changing environments. Probably the best ours can do is to give it a try.

We remain committed to democracy despite the doubts raised by the events of the scandal-ridden Nixon administration. The Watergate affair and the resignation of Vice President Spiro T. Agnew in 1973, after he pleaded "no contest" to income-tax evasion charges, together do not mean that democracy has failed. Such events do raise questions about the adequacy of our screening methods for high elective and appointive offices. These need improvement.

POSTLOGUE

One may well wonder in what direction America and the human race will move in the future. It is easy to be pessimistic. The threat of thermonuclear war hangs over the world. As each new nation gains nuclear capability, the risk of a decision to use the weapons becomes disproportionately greater. Famine and starvation face much of the world before the end of the twentieth century, particularly in Bangladesh, Egypt, Pakistan, parts of India, and several parts of Africa. (In the 1970s, even China and the Soviet Union needed foodstuffs from us.) The prospects for finding a sufficient food supply seem poor in the extreme and many of the people who will starve are already born.[7] The pressures that will be placed upon an increasingly isolationistic America to share our wealth will be great. But we could impover- ish ourselves without giving any lasting help to these countries.

At home, the gap between the affluent and the poor will continue to widen, even though the floor of poverty will continue to rise. So will that between the intelligent and the unintelligent. (Intelligent men tend to marry intelligent women and raise intelligent children; unintelligent men to marry unintelligent women and raise even more children.)[8] The environment will continue to deteriorate—apparently it will have to get much worse before we will be prepared to pay the opportunity costs to make it better.

The 1960s marked a high point in the cheerful optimistic, naïve view of man as perfectable, one who could transcend his heritage and his environment. It was a period of antiintellectual- ism, when college students were often led to believe that there were "instant solutions" to complex social issues if only "they" of the Establishment would permit them to take place. Herbert Marcuse talked (foolishly, we believe) of a leap to faith in knowledge—belief, really—that lies beyond scientific examina- tion.[9]

After passage of the Economic Opportunity Act of 1964, some people talked euphorically of turning much policy making over to persons who had neither the experience nor even the interest to make complex decisions about their lives. The liberal notion that one can spend one's way out of any social problem foundered on the reality that this is simply not true. What worked for the New Deal in the 1930s (and it did not work all that well in any case) did not work at all for the poor of the 1960s because the population involved was vastly different, with a different culture and set of attitudes toward themselves, among other contrasts.

In the 1970s, the notion that "progress" could not be counted upon simply through good will, a faith in the equality of men, the spending of government money in an effort to redis- tribute the wealth (it must go back to the middle classes), or a faith in the perfectibility of man, led to an overdue reappraisal, in a hard-nosed way, of the condition of America and its prospects. The social sciences, which had been supplying uncritical and unexamined assumptions about human behavior to liberal government decision makers for forty years, were placed on the defensive and came under great pressure to reexamine their assumptions and their roles in public policy making.

Disappointment in the behavior of man when living only under the constraints of environment, and the haunting possibility that he is innately aggressive, territorial, and interested primarily only in his own community and reference group, rather than in the welfare of his entire species—in other words, that he is much more like other carnivorous animals[10]—has led some psychologists to suggest that the hope of survival and a "life worth living" lies in artificially modifying man's behavior. The idea is not new. It goes back at least to Plato and his *Republic*.[11] The hard question, though, is who is to play God?

A few years ago, in the presidential address to the American Psychological Association, Kenneth B. Clark suggested that it might be necessary to develop mind-controlling drugs "to contain" human cruelty and destructiveness if we were to eliminate war, "racism," and the abuse of power by public officials.[12] He thought this might be the only alternative to the "ultimate destruction of the human species." He suggested that such drugs might be pretested on criminals, hopefully volunteers. Of course, he thought these drugs should not, at the same time, turn people into robots lacking "the creative, evaluative and selective capacities of human beings." (Opportunity costs, once again, ought to be zero!) Clark did make one concession to political reality: He suggested that widespread use of such drugs should not take place until the adoption of an international agreement for their use in all countries.

Another psychologist, B. F. Skinner, in a book appropriately titled *Beyond Freedom and Dignity*,[13] argues that we use man's intelligence to develop a "technology of behavior." Unlike Herbert Marcuse, he suggests that "We play from strength and our strength is Science and Technology." (The fact that Skinner relies specifically on what Marcuse has specifically rejected shows again the pervasiveness of uncertainty concerning what would be effective public policy.) Skinner thinks that "freedom and dignity" are laudable, but inadequate. We must apply the "methods of science . . . to human behavior." Man is not autonomous, as he likes to believe; rather he is *conditioned* by his environment. So we should examine the relationship between behavior and the environment, forgetting about "states of mind." And the environment can be manipulated. But who can agree, by whom? Skinner faces this problem honestly, but not from a very helpful angle politically: "This conflict is itself a problem in human behavior and may be approached as such." Skinner remains the optimistic believer in the powers of science, pointing out that even the basic idea of the role of natural selection in evolution was unknown until just over a century ago.

Yet even if man's behavior can be manipulated for "good" irrespective of possible innate tendencies and the personal desires of the "autonomous" human being with free will, is there likely to be found a way by which to make this feasible even if we gain consensus that it is desirable? The political scientist would have to conclude that the odds against it are fantastically long. And this would be true under any form of government that is now known or conceived of as being a practical possibility.

The foreseeable future for American politics probably lies somewhere within a vast territory of possible choices. The belief systems from which men will derive the assumptions to guide them are bounded on the one side by such nonsense as that of Herbert Marcuse or the optimistic scientism of B. F. Skinner and on the other by stoicism or a confident religious faith. Man is a flawed creature. He must work within the resources available to him. These are limited and he has never used them particularly efficiently. But use them he must. We believe he can "muddle through." Speaking in probability terms and viewing the currently known alternatives, we have little choice but to believe in his ability to endure. Even that would be no small accomplishment.

The United States offers to the individual as much freedom of choice as is to be found almost anywhere today in the nations of the world. Ours is the richest nation on earth and everyone, although not equally or easily, is entitled to a chance at a share of that wealth. The greatest prospect, as well as the greatest threat to failure, is still to be found in the word "opportunity." For the restless person, questing for the elusive thing known as "meaning" in life, no nation, even today and even if this nation may have passed its peak in social and economic development, can rightfully claim to offer more.

Cheers!

NOTES

1   Daniel P. Moynihan et al., *The Negro Family in America: The Case for National Action*, 1965.

2   Harold D. Lasswell, *Psychopathology and Politics*, University of

Chicago Press, Chicago, 1930; *Power and Personality,* W. W. Norton & Company, Inc., New York, 1948.

3   Harold D. Lasswell, *Politics: Who Gets What, When, How,* Meridian Books, Inc., New York, reissued with postscript, 1958.
4   See any introductory textbook in anthropology and its citations.
5   Georges Sorel, *The Illusions of Progress,* John Stanley and Charlotte Stanley (trans.), University of California Press, Berkeley, 1969.
6   See Peter A. Corning, "The Biological Bases of Behavior," *World Politics,* 23:321–370, April 1971.
7   Paul R. Ehrlich, *The Population Bomb,* Sierra Club, San Francisco, 1969.
8   *Los Angeles Times,* Dec. 16, 1972.
9   Herbert Marcuse, *One-dimensional Man,* Beacon Press, Boston, 1964.
10 See note 6, above.
11 Plato, *The Republic,* many editions.
12 *Los Angeles Times,* Sept. 16, 1971.
13 B. F. Skinner, *Beyond Freedom and Dignity,* Bantam Books, New York, 1971.

Glossary

Alienation A psychological state in which the individual feels estranged from society. He believes that he is not performing a role at a status level for which he is qualified or to which he is entitled. The concept was first presented by Karl Marx. Its validity remains unproved and uncertain today. Many college students of the 1960s considered it fashionable to be alienated.

Amnesty A general pardon to a class of law violators. The satirist Ambrose Bierce put it nicely: "The State's magnanimity to those offenders whom it would be too expensive to punish." See his classic, *The Devil's Dictionary,* World Publishing Company, Cleveland, 1911.

Anarchist One who believes that human beings are fundamentally good-intentioned so that each can thus pursue his or her own goals without having to be restrained lest he or she trample on the rights of others, i.e., one who has not been involved in heavy traffic either as a driver of a motor vehicle or as a pedestrian.

Anxiety A vague, unfocused, and highly persistent fear. It produces a compulsion toward some type of behavior, which may involve political action. The level of anxiety quickly returns to near its former level after an effort is made to assuage it. Much in politics consists of the exploitation of anxieties. For example, those who fear a nuclear attack on America want us to build more nuclear weapons, but they do not feel safer when we have 5,000 such devices than they did when we had 2,000. For a contrasting concept of human behavior also meaningful in politics, *see* Marginal Utility, Diminishing.

Apartheid A discrimination on the basis of race that holds that all contacts between races must be eliminated. It is the official policy of South Africa, the Ku Klux Klan, and some black nationalist organizations.

Attitude A predisposition to act in a given way, e.g., when we hear the words Spiro T. Agnew, Angela Davis, peace with honor, the profit motive, X-rated movies, class-action suits—well, we all know what every "right-thinking" individual thinks about those things.

Authority The power accorded someone to control the actions of others because he is recognized as acting by legitimate right. Authority is seriously under attack in all areas of present society, even in professional football. That such a situation is not new may be deduced from the fact that Moses' fifth commandment to his followers (right before the ones on murder and adultery) was that one must at all costs respect the authority of one's father and mother. He added as bait the promise of a long life (Exodus 20).

Bentham, Jeremy (1748–1832) An English philosopher and reformer who popularized the principle of "the greatest good for the greatest number" as the goal of all government. The principle proved to be less simple in application than it would at first appear.

Blackstone Nation A federation of black street gangs on Chicago's South Side. They were originally called the Blackstone Rangers. An auxiliary of younger members was called the Black Princes. Later the combined groups were called the Black P. Stone Nation. For a more sympathetic treatment of them than we offer, see John R. Fry, *Locked-out Americans,* Harper & Row, New York, 1973.

Bureaucracy In political science, any large organization characterized by specialization of work assignments, essentially impersonal relationships with external clientele groups, and a formal hierarchical structure. To the layman, a bureaucracy conjures up a host of unpleasant images. Many specialists share this view.

Chamberlain, Neville (1869–1940) The British Prime Minister who struck a bargain with Adolf Hitler at Munich in 1938 to exchange a part of somebody else's country (Czechoslovakia) for "peace in our time." This was called "appeasement" and was a disaster. Any politician following this policy today must give it another name.

Charisma A term borrowed by the sociologist Max Weber from a religious context and applied to political leadership. Jesus was described by his followers as speaking with authority and obedience was freely accorded him because of his nature. In the political realm, an example may be found among one of Theodore Roosevelt's most fervent supporters (William Allen White), who described this leader's irresistable attractiveness with the phrase "He bit me and I went mad!"

Checks and balances Separate branches of American government are given legal powers by which they can check one another and thereby maintain a balance in which no branch can consistently override the others.

Class, social In some social models, a self-conscious group whose members occupy similar social positions and who share a similar life-style, set of values, and behavior pattern. In practical terms, members of a class are commonly identified by certain quantitative indicators, in particular, wealth, income, education, and occupation.

Coalition A temporary alliance of several diverse individual factions or parties, presumably for their common good. Its virtues and drawbacks are similar to those of a leaky lifeboat when the main vessel is slowly sinking down to the bottom—indispensable, but with a tendency to be unstable.

Communism A political system followers imagine is based upon the ideas of Karl Marx (1818–1883) and his intellectual successors. Legitimate rule rests exclusively with the working class (proletariat). It is characterized by a small leadership elite, a single political party, and complete control by the elite over social and economic institutions. Many people think communism is a permanent enemy of the American Way of Life. Communists agree.

Confederation An association of independent states in which legal power resides with the states with little power in the central body, e.g., the United Nations, which might better be called "the World Confederacy."

Conservative One who believes that we should keep (conserve) whatever we have that is good. He accepts change, but believes that the burden of proof rests with the advocates of change. He recognizes that rapid changes are more likely to have bad than good results. As Bierce, *op. cit.,* put it, a conservative is "A statesman who is enamored of existing evils, as distinguished from the Liberal, who wishes to replace them with others." *See* Liberal.

Constitution The rules about rule making. A constitution need not be written and all of them are at least partially unwritten. The typical citizen reveres the Constitution, but does not read it.

Containment A principle of American foreign policy since 1947. It states that a primary aim of American policy is to contain communism within existing boundaries. It was at first applied only to Europe, but later, some argue inappropriately, was extended to Asia as well.

Conventional wisdom Popular beliefs that are unproved and may be contrary to empirical evidence. Such "wisdom" includes, for example, the belief that prisoners can be rehabilitated by the earnest efforts of "friends outside" or trained psychologists, or the belief that the death penalty is a deterrent to murder.

Counterelite The elite that opposes the dominant elite. The upper-middle-class persons who are members of the New Left are examples.

Cross pressure Political pressures on the same person or group coming from opposite directions—generally results in paralysis of the will as occurred to some voters when faced with the choice between a Nixon and a McGovern.

Cultural values (*See* Values.)

Culture All the learned behavior of a society, including the patterns of use of material goods as well as decision-making patterns. In this, the social scientist's sense, one does not have to be a Picasso connoisseur in order to possess culture.

Democracy (liberal) Democracy in a complex society is a political system that affords frequent opportunities for changing the governing officials and a social mechanism that permits nearly all the adult population to influence major public policy decisions by choosing from among genuine competitors for public office and through other procedures viewed by most citizens as legitimate.

Disraeli, Benjamin (1804–1881) Prime Minister of Great Britain in the nineteenth century. A favorite of Queen Victoria, the British Conservative party, and President Richard Nixon.

Elite A ruling class or group. Every social system has one as well as a counterelite of those who wish to rule. The size may vary from one system to another, but it is always a small percentage of the total population. For a good review of elite theory, see Kenneth Prewitt and Alan Stone, *The Ruling Elites*, Harper & Row, New York, 1973.

Establishment All of the mass and elite who support the legitimacy of the ruling elite and its system. It originated in England, where it referred to the leadership of the Established Church—the Church of England.

Ethnic group Any subcultural group not based on class. A collection of persons who think of themselves as a minority group, often based on nationality background, but also on race, religion, and other factors.

Ethnocentrism The practice of judging other persons or cultures in terms of one's own values. For example, many middle-class Americans have accused the government of South Vietnam of being corrupt. This is an ethnocentric view. To the Vietnamese, "corruption" is traditional, and hence normal and accepted, behavior. By Vietnam's standards, American governments—even the cronyism of Massachusetts or Mayor Daley's Chicago—are viewed as puritanical.

Executive budget A budget, or statement of proposed revenues and expenditures, prepared at the direction of the chief executive and subject to his control. The budget is a statement of policy recommendations made to the legislative body.

Externalities, or side effects The costs imposed upon innocent others by one's actions. A factory with chimneys that emit foul fumes imposes costs upon residents downwind from it. A policy relative to narcotics that increases their cost creates external costs for those who are mugged and robbed by addicts seeking the funds needed to satisfy their craving. In medicine, this phenomenon is referred to as "side effects"—as consumers of pills well know.

Fascism A system that rejects the notions of liberty of the individual and equality of opportunity and strives instead to give all power to a single group of what are claimed to be inspired and wise leaders, and slot everyone else somewhere down the line to do their duty for the state. Mussolini and Hitler appropriated this term for their movements and so it can no longer believably be applied to any of the governments in existence today, despite its clear resemblance to a number of them.

Federal system A union of states in which some powers are exercised by the states and others by the government of the whole body. The distinguishing feature is the state's and central government's power to act directly on the individual rather than one being completely dependent on the other in this respect, as in a confederation or unitary government.

Fiduciary One who acts on behalf of someone else, or holds something in trust for him. Every politician acts as fiduciary for the political rights of his constituents. As in the business world, some political fiduciaries are more able and honest than are others.

Folkways A sociological term referring to customs that may be broken without incurring serious sanctions. Being a nonconformist, or accepting the Academy Award if you happen to win it are examples of folkway violations.

Frontier individualism An American ideology that was dominant from the beginning of the nineteenth century until the Civil War. It emphasized the values of the frontier yeoman farmer. In general, it held that government should perform functions that could benefit the common man. It was, hence, intensely empirical. The ideology was individualistic, not for doctrinaire reasons, but because most of the problems of the frontier farmer or merchant could be met only by himself, sometimes working in concert with his neighbors.

Glorious Revolution The bloodless revolution of 1688–1689 in England that established the principle of parliamentary supremacy—the right of Parliament to make the laws, interpret the Constitution, and choose the sovereign. It established the first modern democracy, though quite different from today's because only the aristocracy and upper-middle class could vote. It was called "glorious" because winners name revolutions and they portray themselves as "the good guys" when writing up their own history.

Government (as an institution) The machinery that administers the state.

Grant-in-aid Funds granted by one government unit to another. Stipulations ("strings") are generally made on procedures to be followed in spending the funds. Most specific grants-in-aid require contributions by the recipient unit. Broader, or bloc, grants are popularly termed "revenue sharing." (*See* Revenue Sharing.)

Gross national product As calculated by the U.S. Department of Commerce, this figure is equal to the total amount paid for the production of goods and services, plus indirect business taxes paid, plus allowances for the depreciation of capital investments.

Gumperson's law The law, briefly stated, is that whatever can go wrong will go wrong. Gumperson discovered the law on the basis of his experience with life. Just as he was going to publish a book on it and make a fortune, he was tragically killed. He was walking along a highway in South Carolina, in the left lane against the traffic, when he was hit from behind by an English driver.

Habeas corpus A writ or order directing a jailer to produce a prisoner in his custody in court so the judge may determine if the person is legally detained. The basic purpose of habeas corpus is to prevent arbitrary arrests and detention in secret.

Hoi polloi The Greek term for the ordinary citizenry.

Ideology Ideology may be described as "folk philosophy" concerning the good life. It is not as systematic or as sophisticated as philosophy; it evolves gradually, not as the product of any single thinker. In this case, it resembles folk songs more than works of serious composers. Ideology consists of a network of interrelated normative values that emerge from a particular life-style and environment. It serves a double role: It helps to direct action toward the satisfaction of existing wants and to establish new goals for an individual or group.

Image The way in which an event, institution, group, or person is perceived. The image does not necessarily reflect reality and is not perceived in the same way by all persons.

Industrial individualism An American ideology dominant between the Civil War and the Great Depression. It was characterized by the belief that business was the most important component of the social system and that government should perform only traditional services—services that politically significant businessmen desired.

Influence (political) The control of one person by another that is accorded without command. Influence may be based on such intangible factors as respect, love, friendship, or such tangible rewards as money or sex.

Information costs Information is not free. It must be paid for in one way or another, so all of us look for short-cuts. Symbols are an example of something that drastically lowers information costs. But the symbol must be understood in context. The clenched fist has been used by such diverse groups as Women's Lib, student strikers at

Harvard, Black Power, the Italian Fascists, and diverse communistic societies.

Institution A formal component of a system which presumably has a role in carrying out the system's purposes. The function of such governmental institutions as the New Hampshire primary or the CIA remains a puzzle even for some scholars. A few have formed conclusions similar to those reached by the medical profession in respect to a ruptured appendix.

Interest group A collection of individuals who, on the basis of one or more shared attitudes or common habits of response, make certain claims upon other groups in the society for the establishment, maintenance, or enhancement of forms of behavior that are implied in the shared attitudes. Groups become *political* interest groups by making their claims directly upon government or indirectly upon other groups through government. *Interests* exist independently of *interest groups.* Interest groups differ from political parties chiefly in that they do not seek to capture public offices for members, but rather attempt to influence public policy. (*Pressure group* has the same meaning.)

Keynes, John Maynard (1883–1946) British economist whose ideas have strongly influenced American public policy since the 1930s. The most important aspect of his theories was the idea that governments can partially level out swings in the business cycle by spending more than they receive in revenue during downswings in the cycle and less in the upswings. Both aspects of the theory were feasible economically, but the latter was less so politically. Once while explaining the short-run implications of his ideas, Keynes was asked about the long-run effect. His answer: "In the long run, we are all dead."

Leadership The ability to unite people in pursuit of a goal.

Left, New Typifies the politics of conscience and, like those who would save sinners, members may be more concerned with their own individual psychic satisfactions than with the effect of their policy recommendations on the plight of the object of their concerns. In contrast, the Old Left was more concerned with intellectual hair-splitting than social action.

Left (political) The portion of the political continuum that includes liberal and radical positions. An individual's position on the continuum may differ by issue.

Legitimacy, political A condition that exists when people believe in their government's (or ruler's) right to rule and in the rightness or propriety of the principal institutions, procedures, and policies of the political system of which they are a part.

Liberal One who is optimistic concerning the results of change. He advocates that change be made through legal means. *See* Conservative.

Life-style A concept (with impressionistic connotations) that refers to the kind of life lived by people in different situations. It covers the ways of living that accompany life cycles, statuses, career stages, changes through time resulting from technological developments, and other stages of development of individuals or groups of individuals.

Lobbyist The agent or representative of an interest group, who seeks to influence public policy. Lobbying consists of seeking to influence legislative and administrative officials in a variety of ways so that their actions will be favorable to the group doing the lobbying. Lobbyists may also be in charge of the dissemination of propaganda to the general public.

Log rolling A basic strategy in legislative bodies in which support on one bill is traded for support on another.

Marginal cost The cost incurred by adding the last unit of a good or service.

Marginal utility, diminishing A principle of demand theory in economics. It holds that each additional unit of a good is less valuable than the previous one. A person with two Jaguars has a diminished need for a third. But the characteristics of an anxiety neurosis are more important to politics than is this principle. *See* Anxiety.

Mass The great bulk of the population that is not included in the elite. The elite and counterelite constantly battle for the loyalty of at least part of this constituency. *See* Elite. A characteristic of the American masses is that they do not know they are masses—but the elite knows.

Mobility, social The degree to which an individual can move upward or downward in social status. In the United States, it is *relatively* easy to move upward or downward. The child of middle-class parents may become a self-made millionaire, or a lower-class "hippie." Most will stay middle-class.

Mores Customs in a society which, when broken, bring serious formal and informal punishment. (The authors find it difficult to think of any example from today's political life.)

Nader, Ralph (1934–   ) The "consumer advocate" who earned the gratitude of many by attacking some of the shoddier products of American industry. He has the quaint point of view that professional lawyers know more about economics than do professional economists.

Nazism A form of fascism practiced by Adolf Hitler and his followers. The legitimacy of power was based on a doctrine of "Aryan" racial superiority.

New Deal A political program that occurred in a period (the 1930s) later made famous by revelations of the Roosevelt children. The program was aimed at some redistribution of social, political, and economic benefits through a greater amount of government planning and regulation. It was denounced as too audacious by the critics of his day and as too timid by later Monday morning political quarterbacks.

Noblesse oblige The "obligation of the nobility." The traditional expectation that those of the higher classes look after the concerns of members of the lower classes.

Norms Standards of behavior or shared common understandings that define common expectations in a culture or society.

Oligarchy Government by the few, as distinguished from government by the many. *See* Elite.

One great cause theory It holds that all important social events can be traced to a single event or phenomenon that is the exclusive or overwhelmingly dominant cause of other events or phenomena. Most social scientists are now convinced that there are usually many casual factors in social events, no one of which is ordinarily predominant.

Opinion leaders Individuals who act as agents for conveying political information and sentiments to less informed or passive audiences.

Opportunity costs The costs involved in giving up one thing in order to gain something even more desired. One may stop trying for an A in mathematics in order to keep from losing a girl friend, or vice versa.

Parkinson's law Actually, there are two. The first, the *law of work,* holds that work within a bureaucracy expands to fill the amount of time available. The second, or *law of triviality,* says that the amount of time spent on any bureaucratic problem varies inversely with the importance or cost of the problem. The former is based on the fact that every project can involve greater or lesser amounts of time, depending on its availability. The latter is based on the fact that the simpler the issue, the more people there will be who have an opinion about it. Everyone has an opinion about whether coffee should be served at the next committee meeting, but few will know whether a new quaffindorf is worth $1,007,250.44. See C. Northcote Parkinson, *Parkinson's Law and Other Essays in Administration,* Houghton Mifflin, Boston, 1957.

Peter principle One continues to rise in his job assignments until he reaches one step beyond his capabilities. This is his "level of incompetence." The rule was first discovered by Laurence Peter. It applies in all cases not covered by the seniority rule (which see). Lyndon B. Johnson, a superb Senate majority leader, may have reached his level of incompetence as Commander in Chief. See Laurence Peter and Raymond Hull, *The Peter Principle,* William Morrow and Company, Inc., New York, 1969.

Philistine One more interested in seeing the same movie free on television than paying to see it at an expensive art theater. Reserved for those regarded as prosaic and crude as compared with the more polished types who pursue "higher" intellectual and artistic goals. The readers of this book will have little difficulty in fitting themselves into the appropriate category.

Pluralistic society A community composed of groups holding a variety of ideological positions, each possessing political power through its ability to share in decisions regarding public policy.

Plurality More votes than anyone else. A plurality may be less than a majority, which is at least one-half of the votes plus one.

Political party A group of people banded together for the purpose of winning elective public offices. As such, a political party differs from an interest group, which is a collection of people banded together for the purpose of promoting or protecting social, economic, or ideological interests. American parties are loose confederations of persons who may hold conflicting ideologies. The political party, like the golden eagle, the whooping crane, and the hump-backed whale, is today on the endangered-species list.

Political science The study of the strategies by which allocations of benefits, rewards, deprivations, and punishments for members of a society take place through government. The name of the field is misleading, for only a small part of political science involves the scientific method. Political scientists are plagued by the fact that almost everyone interested in politics considers himself to be an expert on the subject.

Politician Anyone who seeks elective public office. To many, a "politician" is anyone they disagree with; those with whom they agree are "statesmen." To the farmer, a politician is the fellow who meddles with the system by applying price controls; to the surburban housewife, that man is a statesman!

Politics Defined by Bierce, *op. cit.*, as "A strife of interests masquerading as a contest of principles." We cannot improve on that.

Polity The political arrangements of a state as compared to the society (its social arrangements) or the economy (its economic arrangements). A state orders the rewards of each area—power, honor, and material benefits—in a way that may be judged as just or unjust. The idea is Aristotle's derived from Plato and Socrates.

Pork barrel Public works projects undertaken by the government mainly because of their political value to local congressmen and not primarily for engineering or economic reasons. Each year Congress passes a bill containing a long list of such projects—often they are to deepen river channels or harbors. The source of the term, but not its frequent occurrence, is uncertain.

Poverty, culture of A view of life that emphasizes a concern for the present to the exclusion of planning for the future. It is essentially hedonistic and dooms the individual to continued poverty. It is, technically, a subculture rather than a culture.

Power Being able to say "yes" or "no" about others' actions (C. P. Snow), through force or the threat of force. A necessary ingredient in all social interaction involving men, women, children, or lesser animals.

Pressure group *See* Interest Group.

Projection The process of ascribing to other persons one's own values and beliefs. Thus, by projection, the voter may assume that a politician whom he admires shares his views on public policy.

Projection of trends Predicting the future, using assumptions. In *Life on the Mississippi* (1883), Mark Twain noted that in the previous 176 years, cutoffs had shortened the Mississippi River between Cairo, Illinois, and New Orleans by 242 miles. He calculated that in 742 years (by 2625) the two cities would be less than two miles apart. See Chapter 12 for a discussion of ecological projections.

Propaganda A technique of social control. "As a technique, it is the manipulation of collective attitudes by the use of significant symbols (words, pictures, tunes), rather than violence, bribery, or boycott." (Harold Lasswell et al., *Propaganda and Promotional Activities: An Annotated Bibliography,* University of Minnesota Press, Minneapolis, 1935, p. 3.)

Pseudoevent A contrived event intended for the propaganda benefit of the planner of the "event." A press conference to announce concern over the plight of the people of Bangladesh is a pseudo-event. So is a speech inserted in the *Congressional Record* but never actually delivered.

Public interest A working hypothesis, not an analytical concept, that is used by elected officials and public administrators in their decision making and that operates to remind them that the survival of the groups they represent hinges on their consideration of the legitimate interests of others. To politicians, editors, and many lay persons, the "public interest" is often to be found in policies they personally prefer: it is a propaganda term. Its great value to a political system lies in its mystical importance: It is a goal that every citizen and official of goodwill should strive for.

Radical An advocate of rapid and extensive change toward new social and economic policies, even if such change would destroy or greatly alter existing legitimatized institutions. *See* Left.

Radical right A popular term for the extreme right portion of the political continuum. Technically, a person who fits in this portion of the continuum is a *reactionary.* As terms are used in this book, this one is self-contradictory.

Rationalization A justification offered for one's wants, beliefs, or behavior. The individual often convinces himself that his invented reasons are the real ones. A common political use of this is to convince oneself that his private interests coincide with the public interest. "What's good for General Motors [Ralph Nader, Lawrence Welk, Abbie Hoffman, Adrian and Press, etc.] is good for the country."

Reactionary An advocate of return to a real, romanticized, or imaginary earlier ideology, political process, or set of social, economic, or political institutions.

Red tape Strict adherence to the rules and routine of office and to the resulting forms, procedures, and delays. The name comes from the earlier practice of bureaucrats in tying their correspondence in bundles using red-colored tape.

Reference group Individuals or groups (real or imagined) whose values as standards an individual takes into consideration in the making of his self-evaluation and in forming attitudes. One eminent authority has said, "The main problem with people is that they respect too damn many reference groups."

Revenue sharing The Nixon administration's term for bloc grants-in-aid from the federal government to state and local governments. These grants may be spent for a variety of purposes rather than only for a specific purpose as in most grants-in-aid. There are thus fewer strings attached.

Revolution A change in the constitution made illegally. It need not involve bloodshed, but always results in the coming to dominance of a new elite, together with a new distribution of resources, i.e., political power, economic resources, and social status. See Aristotle, *Politics.*

Right (political) The portion of the political continuum that includes conservative or reactionary attitudes. An individual's position on the continuum may differ by issue.

Rising expectations A behavior discovered in modern man that may be described as "the more he gets, the more he expects to get." Implied is the notion that modern man feels such rewards are his due and right. The wonders achieved by science and technology have helped encourage this attitude and the related cliché, "If we can land a man on the moon, why then can't we. . . ?"

Role The manner in which society expects a particular status position to be filled. The role of the President, for example, calls for him to be dignified, firm but fair, confident but not cocky, and decisive. Some Presidents have trouble fitting this image.

Sanction That which includes compliance, including rewards and punishments.

Seniority rule A means of deciding rewards on the basis of the improbable assumption that there is a one-to-one correlation between age and wisdom. Seniority is used to select congressional leaders, kindergarteners, and occasionally for promotion in bureaucracies such as the army and universities.

Social capital Goodwill credits earned by one individual in relation to another. A President, for example, who has given patronage to a state politician has earned social capital. He may hesitate to expend it for a trivial purpose because he may later need the politician's support on an important matter. The folkways of politicians require that claims against accumulated social capital be honored.

Social science The systematic study of human beings and human behavior as people interact with one another. Social science includes social anthropology, economics, political science, social psychology, sociology, and some fields of geography.

Social service state An elaborate set of federal-state-local relationships that have developed to meet heavy demands for government service. In the social service state, government is one of the first rather than one of the last, social institutions people turn to for help with personal and social problems (as they define them individually).

Socialism A type of economic system. The term is variously used to describe an economic system in which the principal means of production and distribution are owned and controlled by the government; in Marxist-Leninist theory, the transitional stage between capitalism and communism; or the program of any Social Democratic or other party that seeks a greater sharing of wealth and security through the activities of democratic government. In the last case, the term refers to both an economic and a political system.

Socialization The process of learning to know and be guided by the values of the culture in which one lives.

Society A group of people sharing a common culture. Forget about the popular usage, which refers to the social affairs of high-status groups.

Sovereignty The supreme power of the state; the locus of ultimate decision making from which there is no appeal. It is a legal concept introduced by Jean Bodin in 1576. In modern political science, the term is generally not used, except in international relations theory. When applied to political relationships within a nation, the concept is often vague and ambiguous.

State An organized political community possessing sovereignty, independence, and territory. *See* Government.

Statesman A politician whose views I like. *See* Politician.

Status An individual's position in relation to other positions held by other individuals in a social group or grouping.

Statute law Ordinary written legislation, normally enacted by a legislative body. These are the rules rather than the rules about rule making.

Stereotype A simple, generalized concept or image, especially of a social group. Stereotypes tend to be widely shared by members of a given society. The term comes from a mold used in newspaper production.

Stewardship theory This theory holds that the President has something akin to inherent powers of office that permit or even require him to do anything necessary to protect the nation, so long as his acts are not unconstitutional. It is a theory also closely associated with the idea that the President has an obligation to provide leadership in policy development. Twentieth-century Presidents since Taft have generally risen to this obligation without being pushed. *See* Whig Theory.

Subculture A part of the total culture that is distinctive in its values, life-styles, and background (e.g., a nationality, racial, or regional group). The current vogue is to refer to a subcultural group as a "community," e.g., "the black community."

Symbol A term or visual sign that is used to represent something else. The elephant is a symbol of the Republican party; so is G.O.P. The donkey is the symbol for the Democratic party. It was selected by Thomas Nast, a Republican.

TANSTAAFL Some amateur etymologists believe this term to be derived from the German, *tanzteufel,* "dance devil." Actually, it is an acronym for "there ain't no such thing as a free lunch." This is the first law of economics and politics. *See* Opportunity Costs.

Theory Throughout this book, the term refers not to models of an idea as seen by some individual, but to an explanation for the functions performed by the various parts of an interrelated system and to the way in which these parts relate to one another. In this sense, "theory" does not differ from "practice"; rather, the former explains the latter.

Totalitarian democracy Government by opinion of those doing the governing presumably for the benefit of those who are being governed. Plato first had the inspired notion that if these governors would be like himself, that is, philosophers, they would be good and wise and rule with impartial justice for everyone else. His idea of the benevolent despot has been picked up by such assorted types as Southern racists, Communists, B. F. Skinner, ecclesiastics, and, of course, monarchs who viewed themselves as especially selected by the Divine Power.

Values Beliefs about what is "good" or "bad." Values reflect the culture of a society and are widely shared by its members. These values become guideposts for policy making in both individual lives and public affairs.

Voluntary group An association of people organized to pursue a particular activity or objective. The purpose of the voluntary group is often limited to a particular interest that is not necessarily valued by society as a whole. Voluntary groups are formed without government coercion and gain their membership from persons who join of their own volition.

Whig theory This theory holds that the President can do only those things clearly authorized by the Constitution or Congress and should leave policy development to Congress. *See* Stewardship Theory.

Index